Cultures in Conflict

Cultures in Conflict

The Seven Years' War in North America

Edited by Warren R. Hofstra

ROWMAN & LITTLEFIELD PUBLISHERS, INC.
Lanham • Boulder • New York • Toronto • Plymouth, UK

ROWMAN & LITTLEFIELD PUBLISHERS, INC.

Published in the United States of America
by Rowman & Littlefield Publishers, Inc.
A wholly owned subsidiary of The Rowman & Littlefield Publishing Group, Inc.
4501 Forbes Boulevard, Suite 200, Lanham, Maryland 20706
www.rowmanlittlefield.com

Estover Road
Plymouth PL6 7PY
United Kingdom

British Library Cataloguing in Publication Information Available

Library of Congress Cataloging-in-Publication Data

Cultures in conflict : the Seven Years' War in North America / edited by
Warren R. Hofstra.
    p. cm.
  Includes bibliographical references and index.
  ISBN-13: 978-0-7425-5129-9 (cloth : alk. paper)
  ISBN-10: 0-7425-5129-6 (cloth : alk. paper)
  ISBN-13: 978-0-7425-5130-5 (pbk. : alk. paper)
  ISBN-10: 0-7425-5130-X (pbk. : alk. paper)
  1. United States—History—French and Indian War, 1755–1763. 2. United States—
History—French and Indian War, 1755–1763—Social aspects. 3. Culture conflict—
North America—History—18th century. 4. North America—Ethnic relations—
History—18th century. 5. United States—History—French and Indian War,
1755–1763—Influence. I. Hofstra, Warren R., 1947–

E199.C96 2007
973.2'6—dc22   2007001921

Printed in the United States of America

⊗™ The paper used in this publication meets the minimum requirements of
American National Standard for Information Sciences—Permanence of Paper
for Printed Library Materials, ANSI/NISO Z39.48-1992.

~

Contents

~

Preface

The North American phases of the Seven Years' War have long been a subject of historical study and popular interest. The conflict figured heavily in romantically inspired, nineteenth-century histories of early America, especially those of Francis Parkman. For Parkman and contemporaries, woodland warfare and heroic struggle with a noble but savage and doomed adversary shaped the character of a chosen people and the destiny of a providential nation. The imperial school of twentieth-century American history likewise invested significantly in studies of the war. In the words of one of its most expansive chroniclers, Lawrence Henry Gipson, the epic struggle was the eighteenth century's "great war for empire." More recently Fred Anderson's masterful narrative of the war years has revived concern for a conflict that had grown "forgotten." Its 250th anniversary commemoration has transformed the rhetoric of the "war for empire" into "the war that made America." To Anderson it was a more significant turning point in American history than the Revolution.

Throughout this century and a half of writing and scholarship, the Seven Years' War has been portrayed consistently as a military and imperial conflict. Yet, from 1754 to 1765, it touched—if not engrossed—the lives of practically every man and woman in eastern North America. These were the varied peoples of the British and French empires or Native American nations. Despite a generation of excellent social history scholarship, these lives have rarely been the subject of historical inquiry with the exception of several outstanding studies of colonial soldiers.

It is in this context, therefore, that *Cultures in Conflict: The Seven Years' War in North America* addresses the broad pattern of events that framed the causes of this struggle, the intercultural dynamics of its conduct, and its consequences for subsequent events, most notably the American Revolution and a protracted Anglo-Indian contention for the North American continent. Contemporary scholarship on the war, on ethno- and social history, and on cultural history provides the means to view it anew from the perspectives of all its major participants. Needless to say attitudes on the war varied considerably from different cultural vantage points provided by northern and western Indian groups and the varying experiences of European imperial authorities versus those of their colonial counterparts. In many instances the progress of the conflict was charted by cultural differences and the implications participants drew from cultural encounters. These encounters, their meaning in the context of the Seven Years' War, and their impact on its unfolding are the subjects of this book.

Certainly the national cultures of Great Britain and France shared a common European identity throughout the eighteenth century. Yet enmity between these two imperial powers was rooted deeply in cultural intolerance—British loathing for the extravagance of French court life or French disgust at the brash swagger of British militarism. Similarly the peoples of neither nation can be regarded as culturally homogeneous. Centuries of physical and political separation often set off colonial peoples from their imperial authorities. It is well known that the term "American" came into usage among British colonials around the time of the Seven Years' War. Many colonists, moreover, condemned the imperial purpose of the conflict. Virginia militiamen, for instance, refused to muster in their own defense as a popular protest against imperial authority more harmful than helpful to their interests.

Ethnohistorical scholarship over two decades has moved academic as well as popular understanding of Native American peoples far beyond assumptions that Indians were only allies of the true combatants during the Seven Years' War. The culture of Covenant Chain diplomacy allowed the Iroquois, for instance, to distance themselves from the war by a determined, if imperfect, neutrality. What were the consequences of Iroquois autonomy? Did knowing that the basic fabric of Iroquois life mediated against involvement in imperial conflicts affect the strategy of the French, the British, and the Ohio Indians?

The Ohio Indians must also be regarded autonomously. Their role in the Seven Years' War was not reactive but proactive in defense of homelands across the Appalachian Divide. But why did they attack British settler families living along this divide so violently? The brutal murder of noncombatants, especially children, had never been an objective in the culture of Indian warfare. If terrorism is organized violence against civilian populations for political purposes, did the Indians intend woodland warfare to be terrorism designed to reverse British policies on colonial expansion? Or was it the unintended consequence of ethnic diversity and the absence in the Ohio Valley of the cultural coherence that had allowed the Iroquois to maintain a long peace during most of the eighteenth century through the rituals and practices of the Covenant Chain while at the same time maintaining highly disciplined mourning wars for the sake of cultural revitalization?

These are the kinds of questions this book is intended to address. This collection—this particular assemblage of authors and topics—began, like so many others, as a conference. In the open and fluid setting of a conference, new ideas can be forged and the interconnections identified that can render a collection of essays something more than a proceedings—something more than the sum of independent parts. With these intentions the authors of this collection assembled at Shenandoah University, in Winchester, Virginia, on October 21–23, 2004, for give and take on the Seven Years' War with a large public and professional audience.

The concept, organization, and program for the conference had emerged in conversations with conference cochair, Joseph W. A. Whitehorne, of Lord Fairfax Community College, and our project advisor, Fred Anderson. Perpetuating the traditional perspective on Anglo-American conquest in the "French and Indian War" was not, we decided, a possibility. Thus we proposed that each presenter view the conflict as it was perceived separately by its major participants: British, Native American, and French. We further divided these fields asking Paul Mapp to explore British imperial perspectives on the Seven Years' War. British colonial attitudes fell to Woody Holton. Timothy Shannon agreed to examine the responses of Iroquois Indians to a conflict exploding all around them. The world of Ohio Indians became Eric Hinderaker's purview. Jonathan Dull took on the

French imperial perspective, a field to which he has been making important contributions. The views and viewpoints of French colonists came under the domain of Catherine Desbarats and Allan Greer.

What attracted us to cutting these six facets on the prism of the Seven Years' War is reflected in the old adage that a giraffe is but a horse created by a committee. The horse, of course, is the war itself. Our hope—quite rightly fulfilled—was that we could all learn something new, say something original, and better inform our listeners and readers by rendering the beast as interesting and unusual as a giraffe. Or, in the familiar language of historians, to "complicate" it. This approach comports well with multiperspective histories that do indeed portray the past as complex, variegated, and more accurately reflective of the diverse viewpoints of all active agents.

As the project developed, however, from conference to book, it also subtly, but significantly, changed. Instead of asking how different peoples and groups viewed the war or the issues that caused and shaped it, the question became: How was the war a conflict of cultures? Thus almost imperceptibly cultural theory and cultural studies entered the discussion. Historians, like it or not, have rounded the corner of the cultural turn. Culture, at worst, does little more than insert a layer of needless abstraction into a process of historical explanation based traditionally on common sense and reason. If history is the search for the springs—both as source and force— of human action, then historians, at least until the cultural turn, assumed that people and their institutions have always acted out of overt—if not always rational—self-interest. Nations, out of national interest.

Such an approach, however, runs the risk of producing little that is original about an old conflict, widely understood as a French and Indian war against Anglo-American expansion. All parties, in this view, acted to protect their own interests. Enough said. But a cultural approach poses some interesting alternatives.

Clearly the cultural turn is a later response to historiographical tendencies unleashed by the social movements and political forces of the 1960s. The lesson that a generation of graduate students—one of the largest in American academic history—learned from the Civil Rights, antiwar, and counterculture movements was that ordinary people make and change history. New methodologies emerged in the endeavor to understand how. The computer-assisted reconstruction of ordinary lives in the otherwise overlooked communities of early America demonstrated how voiceless people lived and invested meaning in their lives. Anthropological and ethno-historical theories of culture also helped explain the behavior of people who did not account for their actions in their own terms. From fresh ideas about agency driven by new methodologies and innovative theories, un-named peoples emerged as instrumental in shaping their own lives.

The problem by the late 1980s and 1990s became how to incorporate or-dinary people as agents in the master narrative of American history. How, in other words, to revolutionize the canon of textbook history. Here cul-tural theory helped. It holds that people act not only from evident interest but more deeply from all-encompassing complexes of attitudes, ideas, and assumptions functioning below the horizon of reason. In this formulation, followers influence leaders because all share sets of learned behaviors, both social and psychological. The great shape history only insofar as they share and understand the mind of the masses. They act less than they are acted upon. Thus great decisions and heroic actions appear meaningless without understanding the culture that gives them context. Culture thereby pos-sesses interpretive power, and historians fixed on race, gender, class, and ethnicity as those cultural attributes with the greatest power to influence behavior. Not eternal verities, but constructions fixed in time and place by historical circumstances, these attributes allow for an inclusive past and for fundamentally new ways of writing about American history.

The authors in this book plot their own ways through the oft-confused currents of contemporary historiography. In the final analysis this book is a blend of the new and the old. That individuals, institutions, and states act out of self-interest is an idea that retains its power in the essays that follow. The efficacy of culture to explain human action in history is also evident throughout. Thus, from the balance that each author strikes, arises a set of perspectives casting the Seven Years' War not as a conflict of cultures but as cultures in conflict. In the former configuration, culture functions as an abstract, static surrogate for authentic people acting in real circumstances. Instead, the war emerges from these pages as cultures in a conflict in which a horse for one is a giraffe for another.

Acknowledgments

The process of explaining why and how has obligated the time and services of many generous friends and colleagues. Collaborating with Joe Whitehorne on the conference program was a great privilege and an illuminating experience for which I am very grateful. As volume editor it has been my opportunity and reward to work with a superbly talented and unduly tolerant set of authors, namely, Fred Anderson, Catherine Desbarats, Jon Dull, Allan Greer, Eric Hinderaker, Woody Holton, Paul Mapp, and Tim Shannon. The efforts of a host of people made possible their conference presentations and the hard work toward publication that followed. Many are associated with the Shenandoah University History Center. The idea of contributing to the 250th commemoration of the Seven Years' War with a major conference in a state like Virginia so profoundly affected by the conflict but outside the major theaters of combat belonged to Patricia Zontine, program coordinator for the History Center. The unflagging efforts of other staff members at the History Center, most notably Sandy Snyder, administrative assistant, and its program director, William Austin, made the conference possible. A large supporting cast—including Joel Achenbach, René Chartrand, Alison Games, Donald Graves, Dean Jacobs, Gregory Nobles, and John Sygielski—chaired sessions, commented on papers, read additional papers. Greg Nobles went several extra miles in evaluating and improving the manuscript as a peer reviewer for publication.

Editors and staff at Rowman & Littlefield made light the burdens of preparing this book for publication. Laura Gottlieb, Andrew Boney, Michael McGandy, Asa Johnson, Melissa McNitt, and Lee Miao skillfully shepherded the manuscript through the acquisition, review, copyediting, and production processes. The excellent index is the work of Becky Hornyak. A number of other people lent a very welcome helping hand in launching this project and bringing it to fruition. Laura Fisher, director of the French & Indian War, 250 Inc., not only made a conference presentation on the work of this organization in raising public awareness of the historical significance of the war, but she also helped direct publication efforts to a happy home with Rowman & Littlefield. A grant from the United States Small Business Administration (award #SBAHQ-02-1-0012) to Shenandoah University made the conference possible. Faculty, staff, and administration at Shenandoah University—especially James A. Davis, president; Tracy Fitzsimmons, vice president for academic affairs; and Calvin A. Allen, dean of the College of Arts and Sciences—helped create the kind of academic environment in which projects such as this one can flourish. And finally thanks and acknowledgments go to all the students, colleagues, and Seven Years' War enthusiasts who in two conference days created the charged atmosphere out of which this book could be born.

Warren R. Hofstra
September 2006

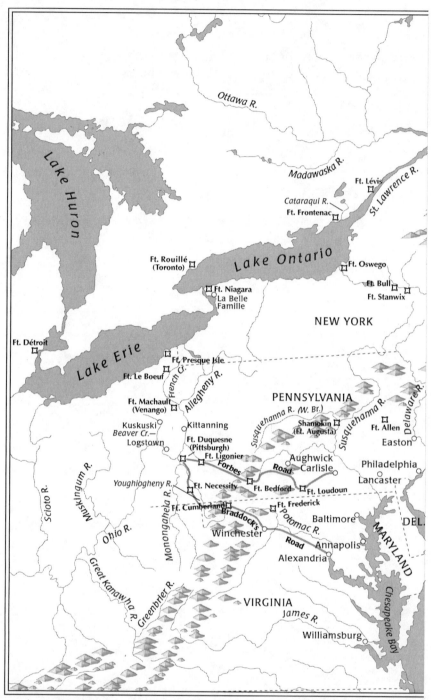

North America during the Seven Years' War. (Maps by Dick Gilbreath at the University of Kentucky Cartography Lab)

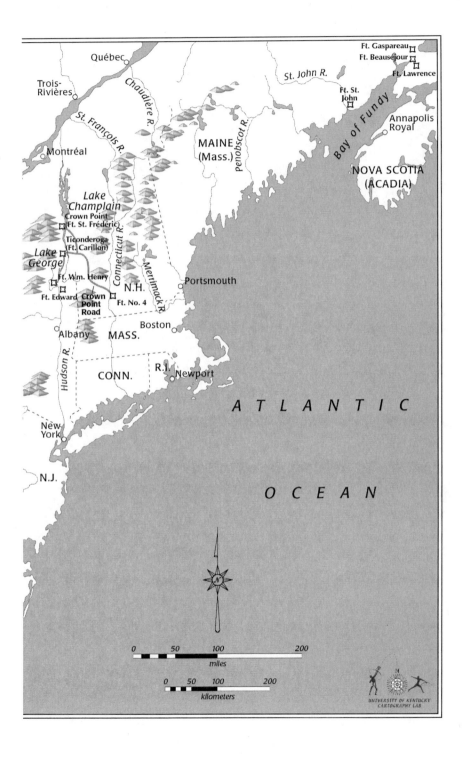

Ft. Gaspareau
Ft. Beauséjour
Ft. Lawrence

Québec

St. John R.

Trois-
Rivières

Ft. St.
John

Chaudière R.

St. François R.

Bay of Fundy

Annapolis
Royal

Montréal

MAINE
(Mass.)

Penobscot R.

NOVA SCOTIA
(ACADIA)

Lake
Champlain
Crown Point
(Ft. St. Frédéric)

Ticonderoga
(Ft. Carillon)

Lake
George

Ft. Wm. Henry

Connecticut R.

Merrimack R.

Ft. Edward   Crown
Point
Road

N.H.

Ft. No. 4

Portsmouth

Albany

MASS.

Boston

Hudson R.

CONN.

R.I.

Newport

A T L A N T I C

New
York

N.J.

O C E A N

N

0   50   100   200
miles

0   50   100   200
kilometers

UNIVERSITY OF KENTUCKY
CARTOGRAPHY LAB

CHAPTER ONE

~

Introduction: Old Forts, New Perspectives—Thoughts on the Seven Years' War and Its Significance

Fred Anderson

Just north of the pedestrian mall in Winchester, Virginia—a charming street of shops and restaurants in the oldest part of town—the ground rises sharply in a hillside, at the top of which stands a neighborhood of brick and frame homes, lining handsomely shaded avenues. Most people strolling along Loudoun Street today would have no reason to suspect that 250 years ago this hilltop, shorn of trees, was home to a stout square fort that covered per-haps a half acre of ground; or that the twenty-four cannon mounted on its walls dominated the countryside for a thousand yards in every direction. That post, Fort Loudoun, was the most important military installation on the Virginia frontier during the Seven Years' War. The headquarters of George Washington's Virginia Regiment, it anchored a long, delicate chain of forts, sixty-eight in all, that lay along the valleys of the Shenandoah, the Potomac, and their tributary waters. Mostly small affairs, no more than farmhouses and outbuildings enclosed in stockades, these offered what protection they could to the Anglo-American settlers who had been unwilling or unable to flee east of the Blue Ridge when Indian raiders first devastated the frontier in the summer of 1755. For four years, Fort Loudoun and its tiny fragile sisters were all that stood between life and death for thousands of frontier settlers. Today you need a guidebook to find them.[1]

Students have to search with almost equal diligence to locate the Seven Years' War in their American history textbooks, where the conflict usually goes by its nineteenth-century name, the French and Indian War. This is not because the authors of textbooks are unaware that it was the largest and most consequential military conflict of the eighteenth century, and certainly not because the war has escaped the attention of historians and historical novelists.[2] Rather it is because textbook accounts reflect a received national narrative that centers on the American Revolution and the creation of the United States, and that narrative is hard to square with a story of Anglo-American colonists standing shoulder-to-shoulder with redcoat soldiers to expand the power and scope of the British Empire. Thus to search out the meaning of the Seven Years' War in American history is a task not dissimilar to hunting up the sites of vanished forts; indeed, the two enterprises are enough alike that each may help us understand the other, and together illuminate dimensions of the American historical landscape that have escaped our attention because we have been so familiar with the surrounding terrain that we never had reason to wonder what their significance might be.

There is no better way to understand the shape and power of what historians would call "the grand narrative" of American history—the overarching story that we share as a kind of common cultural property, which deeply informs our notions of who we are, as a people and a nation—than to visit the Mall in Washington, D.C.[3] The three great monuments that define the Mall's long axis—the Washington Monument, the Lincoln Memorial, and the new World War II Memorial—draw our attention to three great American wars. They commemorate the birth of political liberty in the Revolution, the expansion of that liberty and citizenship to all Americans irrespective of race in the Civil War, and the defense of freedom against fascist and militarist tyrannies around the globe in the Second World War. But the Mall tells us little about America's other conflicts. No monuments commemorate, much less explain the significance of, a dozen major colonial wars, the forty Indian wars that took place during the century after the establishment of the Republic, the War of 1812, the Mexican-American War, the Spanish-American War, or the twenty-odd interventions in the Caribbean basin during the last century.

Why not? The Vietnam Veterans Memorial gives us a hint. Sitting in the semiseclusion of Constitution Gardens on the north side of the Mall, it differs from the three great monuments in more than just its location. Low in profile and made of black granite, it neither obtrudes itself on our attention nor offers instruction on the meaning or purpose of the war it commemorates. Thus it is precisely the opposite of the Lincoln Memorial, an imposing Greek temple that houses not only an immense statue of Lincoln but the immensely powerful words by which Lincoln gave meaning to the most sanguinary war of American history. The Vietnam monument has no stirring words, only fifty-eight thousand names: it is the human *cost* of the war, not the power of any ideal, that gives the memorial its meaning and power. Indeed, the monument's twin walls, joining at an angle of 125°, point like black arrows toward the Washington and Lincoln memorials, triangulating Vietnam with wars whose significance is less subject to debate or doubt.

The great wars commemorated on the Mall's central axis speak to a national narrative with three climactic moments. The story of the colonial period rises from the founding of Jamestown and Plymouth in an upward curve of population growth and institutional maturation that climaxes in the Revolution; then the storyline curves down as internal tensions recede in the early national period, only to rise again as the irrepressible conflict over slavery intensifies. The second climax, the Civil War, settles the issues of equality and liberty that the Revolution had left unresolved. Internal tensions again diminish in the relative calm of the late nineteenth century before the plot sweeps upward once more in the twentieth, with inescapable demands for the defense of liberty abroad and a reluctant acceptance of world leadership. From the great modern climax of World War II to the present, tensions again diminish through the long twilight struggle of the Cold War, leaving the United States the most supremely powerful, as well as the freest, nation on earth.

While the three great wars lend dramatic form to the narrative, however, they punctuate more than shape the underlying pattern of American development. In most citizens' consciousness that story remains the essentially peaceful one that Frederick Jackson Turner described more than a century ago as the expansion of a democratizing, liberating frontier: the tale of a continent settled, not conquered.[4] Our three great wars for liberty remain exceptions that prove the rule of peaceful development, for all three were forced on the United States by those who despised America's commitment to liberty, equal rights, and the rule of law.

The Seven Years' War, like other conflicts that have no monuments in Washington, fits awkwardly with this narrative and hence remains marginal to it. Because the Seven Years' War took place in the late colonial period, it generally appears as part of the back-story of the Revolution and not a particularly significant one at that. Yet there are other ways to narrate America's history. Another tale, which implies a different set of meanings, takes shape if we construe the geographical and chronological limits of American history more broadly. If we think not in terms of a *national* story beginning in 1607 and 1620, but rather of a *continental* narrative beginning around 1500 with contact between Europeans and Native Americans, the picture looks strikingly different. For one thing, it is five hundred years long; and that in turn means that more than half of it takes place before the founding of the United States in 1776.

What the grand narrative treats as the "colonial period" and reduces to a protracted prelude to American nationhood appears, in this broader scheme, as two different eras. First is an Age of Contact that lasts the whole of the sixteenth century, when Spain alone had permanent colonies in the Americas and Indian people retained virtually unchallenged control of the territory from the Atlantic to the Pacific, north of the Gulf of Mexico and the Rio Grande. Indian needs and desires, far more than those of Europeans, shaped the continent during this hundred-year period.

A second phase begins with the establishment of permanent European colonies in the early seventeenth century and lasts until the middle of the eighteenth century—a hundred and fifty years. This is an Age of Colonization and Conflict, when permanent European settlements to the north of Mexico and the Caribbean altered the disease environment there and radically increased the volume of trade goods that flowed, along with pathogens, into native communities. The results of this transformation were manifold, powerful, and enduring.

First, epidemic diseases dealt a series of body blows to native populations. The Indians in closest contact with the Europeans were of course hit first and hardest by disease. They responded to demographic collapse by raiding other groups for captives to be adopted as replacements for the dead. These so-called mourning wars supported population levels that would otherwise have plummeted uncontrollably. Because the Indians who lived nearest the European settlements not only suffered the most from epidemics but enjoyed privileged access to trade goods and weapons, they could also (ironically) gain unprecedented military advantage over other native groups. As Indian warriors acquired not only captives but beaver pelts, furs, and skins to exchange for gunpowder and arms, native warfare became both commercialized and far more destructive, and led to the extinction of whole nations and the depopulation of vast stretches of the trans-Appalachian west.[5]

In this context the Five Nations of the Iroquois League grew powerful by exploiting connections with the Dutch traders of Albany in the mid-seventeenth century. The adoption by the Iroquois of a policy of neutrality early in the eighteenth century enabled them to cope with changing circumstances and the erosion of their military advantages by playing the contending French and British empires off against one another and acting as a kind of balance wheel in the interactions among European groups in northeastern North America. By the 1730s several major Indian groups east of the Mississippi—Cherokees, Creeks, Choctaws, Abenakis, and various Algonquians—were engaging in similar balancing acts, rendering the maneuverings of French, British, and Spanish empires against one another indecisive. While it lasted, this fragile balance enabled Indian and European groups to develop along parallel paths. When the period of balanced competition ended, the calculus of cultural interaction in North America changed forever and ultimately brought the whole edifice of native power crashing down.[6]

The great shift came with the Seven Years' War, which ended the Age of Colonization and Conflict and began another 150-year-long era, the Age of Empires and Revolutions. The transition was not immediately perceptible, for every stage of the Seven Years' War reflected the importance of native power. The conflict originated in Iroquois miscalculations concerning the Ohio Valley and its peoples, which allowed agents of the French and British empires to confront each other over control of the Forks of the Ohio—the site of modern Pittsburgh and the strategic key to the trans-Appalachian west. The fortunes of war in North America ebbed and flowed according to the engagement and withdrawal of Indian allies who acted according to their own calculations of advantage. The decision of French-allied Indians on the Ohio to make a separate peace in 1758 enabled Anglo-American forces to seize the Forks, bringing peace to the Virginia-Pennsylvania frontier after four brutalizing years of war. The following year the Iroquois League shifted from neutrality to alliance with the British, permitting the Anglo-Americans to take Fort Niagara and with it, effective control of the Great Lakes. In 1760, Iroquois diplomats preceding Jeffery Amherst's invading army persuaded the last Indian allies of New France to make peace, facilitating the bloodless surrender of French forces at Montreal.

Recognizing the central role of Indians in the war does not deny the importance of French and British interventions in America or diminish the critical part played by large-scale mobilization of colonial populations. Britain's war leader, William Pitt, knew that the British army was too small to confront the forces of France (much less those of Russia and Austria) on the battlefields of Europe. He therefore used the navy and army together to attack France's coasts and its most vulnerable colonies, while subsidizing Prussia and smaller German states to do most of the fighting against France and its allies in Europe. Similarly, from late 1757 Pitt promised to reimburse North America's colonial governments for raising troops to help attack Canada and the French West Indies, treating the colonies less as subordinates than allies. This policy, so well-calculated to appeal to the colonists, stimulated a tremendous surge of patriotism among America's Britons. From 1758 through 1760, the numbers of Anglo-Americans voluntarily participating in the war effort as soldiers, sailors, privateers, camp followers, and civilian contractors approximately equaled the population of New France.

Their enthusiasm for war lasted beyond the conquest of Canada. Britain's colonists continued to enlist in 1761 and 1762 in numbers that suggest they had come to believe they were full partners in the creation of a new British Empire—the greatest since Rome. When Spain belatedly entered the war as France's ally in 1762, American provincial troops and seamen joined with redcoats and tars in attacking Cuba, with an intensity and a success that convinced the Spanish crown its New World empire was at risk and brought it quickly to the peace table. These extraordinary exertions made for a decisive outcome, but one that came at a fantastic cost. And that in turn had an impact that extended far beyond the Peace of Paris.

Over the next decade and a half it would become clear that while the effects of the war had been dramatic for all its participants, the long-term damage it did to the vanquished was considerably less severe than what it inflicted on the victor. Despite military humiliation, the loss of its North American possessions, and the destruction of most of its navy, France survived defeat and rather rapidly recovered. Because the Peace of Paris allowed it to keep its most profitable West Indian sugar islands and deprived it of those parts of the empire that had never produced enough revenue to cover the costs of administering and defending them, the war inflicted no unsustainable blow to the French economy. In 1763 French import/export levels picked up more or less where they had left off in 1756, and the economy resumed its growth at more or less the prewar rate. The crown had funded the war by borrowing; rather than impose crushing burdens on taxpayers to repay those war debts, it merely continued to borrow the money it needed for a great postwar rearmament program. Hence there was no taxpayers' revolt in France, but rather a serious effort to reform the military and the state in a variety of areas. The fleet, largely destroyed during the war, was rebuilt according to the most advanced designs of the day. The army underwent reforms it desperately needed in recruitment, training, discipline, housing, officers' education, health care, and administration. The senior generals who might otherwise have been expected to resist could not do so effectively because they had performed so ineptly during the war. Meanwhile the crown's ministers attempted, albeit with less success, to reform the administration of the state by attacking aristocratic privilege in government and the law. These military and civil reforms had one great goal: to turn the tables on Britain in the next war, and that of course was precisely what happened between 1778 and 1783. Only the expense of this revenge, and the desperate need for new revenues, tempered its sweetness. Even so, it was not until 1789 that it became clear exactly how severe the reckoning would be.[7]

In the case of Spain, the traumatic losses of Havana and Manila to British expeditions in 1762 suggested an alarming degree of weakness in Europe's oldest Atlantic empire. Spain's response was a remarkably effective program of reform aimed at boosting the colonial trading economy (an initiative that eventually produced free trade within the empire), and also at attacking bastions of privilege like the Church and the merchant guilds, which had long inhibited metropolitan authorities from exerting decisive influence in the colonies. These so-called Bourbon reforms built up new, direct connections between Creole elites and the crown through the creation of new military and administrative institutions and fostered both greater colonial loyalty to the Spanish state and economic expansion. An empire tottering toward ruin in 1762 regained a surprising vitality between 1763 and 1810. Populations in the American colonies doubled, while their standard of living rose to the highest levels seen since the conquest. The imperial renaissance lasted until the Napoleonic Wars devastated Spain, creating a new crisis of empire in the 1820s.[8]

For Britain the consequences of the war were equally remarkable and more seemingly paradoxical.[9] The essential problems of its epoch-making victory centered on finance and control. The virtual doubling of the national debt between 1756 and 1763, a direct result of the way William Pitt fought the war by subsidizing allies and colonists alike with no thought to the debts he ran up in the process, produced irresistible demands for retrenchment in the postwar period. Simultaneously the extension of the imperial domain to include the eastern half of North America created an intensely felt need to impose coherence and efficiency on a disorderly, haphazard imperial administration. The goal was not only to control the three hundred thousand or so Canadians and Indians whom the war had ushered into the empire, but also to make the old North American colonies cooperate with one another, take direction from the metropolis, and pay at least some of the costs of imperial defense. But unprecedented victory had done more than create unforeseen problems; it had also persuaded Britain's leaders that their nation was militarily unassailable. Given the extraordinary string of battlefield triumphs Britain had experienced between 1758 and 1763, this was not an unreasonable inference to draw. Neither was it a safe one, especially insofar as it contributed to the peremptory tone imperial officials used in addressing Britain's American colonists in the postwar years.

Even before the Seven Years' War, a popular understanding of the colonists' place in the British Empire had been emerging around the notion,

Colonist Thought Equalled to England

best articulated by Benjamin Franklin, that the empire was in fact a trans-Atlantic (partnership) composed of Britons who shared a common identity, heritage, language, interests, and rights, irrespective of which side of the ocean they lived on. This was not a view favored by British imperial administrators like the Earl of Halifax, who before the war began had been pursuing reforms that would have subjected colonial polities to the control of a sovereign king-in-Parliament and made it clear that the colonists were anything *but* the legal and constitutional equals of subjects who lived in England. The problem was that Pitt's expensive win-the-war strategies had granted the colonists exactly the sort of autonomy that encouraged them to imagine that the empire was in fact a voluntary union of British patriots, a vast partnership united rather than divided by the waters of the Atlantic.

When Halifax and other metropolitan administrators reasserted their hierarchical conception of empire in the postwar period, colonists were shocked to find that the reforms being proposed were ones that seemingly recognized no limits on the exercise of sovereign power. The colonists phrased their protests in the republican language of British political opposition; lacking any other way to define constitutional limits to the exercise of metropolitan power, they virtually had to do so. There is nothing surprising in this. What *was* surprising—or at least what surprised British imperial authorities—was the intensity and indeed the violence of the colonists' responses. The emotional tenor of the Stamp Act riots and Townshend Acts protests can best be understood as reflecting feelings of betrayal rooted in the recent experience of war and victory. *What happened*, the colonists wondered, to the recent patriotic union that had won the war? *Why* is the ministry suddenly treating us as if we were Britain's conquered, instead of its fellow conquerors?

Over the twelve years between the end of the war and the outbreak of fighting at Lexington and Concord the colonists, through a series of crises, clarified their beliefs and articulated them in language sufficiently inclusive to build a broad base of support for opposition to the authority of the king-in-Parliament. These same political principles would eventually become the basis for a new political order, a republic, but they were not yet Revolutionary principles. Nor did anything that happened during those twelve years of controversy yet constitute a Revolution. Rather what took place between 1763 and 1775 was a prolonged, increasingly acrimonious debate over what the empire meant: a dispute over who belonged to it and on what terms of membership; a disagreement about the principles according to which it was supposed to function. The debates grew so bitter *not* because the colonists wanted independence and certainly not because they had acquired an American cultural identity, but because they thought of themselves as British.

They struggled with such conviction over the character of the empire not because they hated it, but because they loved it. It took more than a year of civil war to persuade the colonists that they were anything but Britons.

The irony here is intense, and worth pondering. A great victory—the most decisive outcome in a major European conflict between the end of the Hundred Years' War and the nineteenth century—turned out to have been a terrible thing for the victorious power, whereas defeat had much less severe consequences for the losers. It would seem clear that the experience of winning can carry with it great, if hard-to-recognize, dangers for the victor because the very fact of a decisive outcome in war can foster the illusion that military power is less limited and contingent than in fact it is. Britain emerged from the war as the closest thing the world had to a superpower in 1763, only to find that the other countries of Europe feared it enough to align themselves against it. Conscientious British administrators undertook imperial reforms that were obviously needed, only to mystify, then alienate the American colonists, uniting them against the authority of the metropolis. Then, when it finally applied its overwhelming military and naval power to cut the knot of colonial resistance by forcing the colonists to submit, it turned a resistance movement into a revolution. Force, and force alone, was the argument that finally convinced a majority of North America's Britons that shadowy metropolitan conspirators intended to enslave them and that the only way to preserve the British rights they cherished was by ceasing to be British.

Finally, the war's effect on the Indians who had played so great a role in determining its outcome was the most dramatic, and ultimately tragic, of all. By eliminating the French Empire from North America and dividing the continent down its center between Britain and Spain, the Peace of Paris made it impossible for the Iroquois and other major native groups to preserve their autonomy by playing empires off against each another. The former native allies of New France came to understand the tenuousness of their new position soon after the war when the British high command began to treat them as if they, not the French, had been conquered. They reacted with violence to Britain's abrupt changes in the terms of trade and suspension of diplomatic gift-giving, launching a pan-Indian insurrection to teach the British a lesson in the proper relationship of ally to ally. By driving British troops from their interior forts and launching raids that once again embroiled the frontier in a huge refugee crisis, the Indians compelled the British to rescind the offensive policies. Yet by 1764, when various groups began to make peace, native leaders understood that their ability to carry on a war was strictly limited. Without a competitor empire to arm and supply them, they simply could not sustain resistance once they ran out of gunpowder, lead, and spare parts to repair their muskets.

Meanwhile the bloodshed and captive-taking of the war and the postwar insurrection deranged relations between Indians and Anglo-American colonists. By 1764 most white Pennsylvanians, inhabitants of a colony that had never known an Indian war in seven decades before 1755, seethed with hatred for Indians. A decade later, when most native groups sided with the British in the Revolution, Indian-hating only became more prevalent. By 1783, Americans were willing to allow neither Indians nor the Loyalists with whom they had cooperated any place in the new Republic, except on terms dictated by the victor.

Indians in the eastern United States, of course, continued to resist the expansion of white settlement after the Revolution but could only do so if the British in Canada armed and supplied them. Unfortunately, the British proved inconstant allies. When they withdrew support for Indian resistance in the Ohio Country in 1794, the Miamis, Delawares, Shawnees, and others who had stood off the Americans with great success for the previous decade abruptly lost the ability to resist, and made peace. Within a year they were compelled to cede most of what became the state of Ohio to the U.S. government. Similarly, pan-Indian resistance animated by the religious visions of Tenskwatawa and the diplomacy of Tecumseh flourished before the War of 1812, when it suited the British in Canada to provide arms and supplies, but at the end of that war British support dried up forever. By 1820 Indian resistance east of the Mississippi was all but a memory, and Andrew Jackson, who made his military reputation fighting Indians at the Battle of Horseshoe Bend—a battle that ended in massacre—was well on his way to the White House.

In the classic narrative of the early national period, native peoples are acted upon far more than they are actors. To include the Seven Years' War in the story of the founding of the United States, however, makes it easier to understand Indians as neither a doomed remnant nor as noble savages but as human beings who behaved themselves with a canniness and a fallibility equal to those of Europeans; who acted with just as much courage, brutality, mercy, and calculated self-interest as the Euro-American colonists. In seeking security and hoping to profit from the competition between empires, native groups took actions that led to a world-altering war, which in turn produced the revolutionary changes that moved them from the center of the American story to its margins. No irony could be more complete, no outcome more tragic.

Repositioning the Seven Years' War as a turning point in American history thus allows us to understand the Revolution as emerging fortuitously, surprisingly, from an unintended set of *postwar* circumstances. But if the Revolution can be accurately seen as an unintended consequence of an imperial war, what does that mean for the rest of American history as we know it? Again, the answer depends on where the story begins and ends.

The story as outlined here begins in 1754 when a brash young Virginia colonel, further out of his depth than he knew, tried to exert military control over the geographical point, the Forks of the Ohio, that offered strategic command of the trans-Appalachian west. His failed attempt proved to be the catalyst for a world war and ultimately gave rise to circumstances that plunged the victorious empire into a civil war that in turn fostered a revolution. Oddly enough, that same brash young officer, grown older and (fortunately) wiser, proved to have the necessary qualities to lead an American Revolutionary army to victory, and then to lead the new American republic in the postwar era. Among the many challenges that the republic faced was armed Indian resistance to U.S. authority in the Ohio Valley and the even graver threat of armed resistance among white settlers on the upper Ohio and its southern tributaries—men who believed that they were being subjected to unjust taxation and who had taken up arms to defend their rights, as the Revolution had taught them to do. In 1794, as president of the United States and commander-in-chief of its armed forces, George Washington oversaw the military suppression of both the Ohio Indians' struggle for independence and the Whiskey Rebellion in the vicinity of Pittsburgh.[10]

In other words, George Washington finally succeeded, in 1794, in doing what he had first attempted in 1754—asserting imperial control over the Forks of the Ohio and the great river system that begins there. The movement of the story from 1754 to 1794, therefore, does not merely trace a trajectory from empire through revolution to republic, but a trajectory from empire through revolution to a new form of empire. This is an entirely different tale from the more familiar Revolution-centered narrative that begins in 1763 and ends in 1789.

What this story does that the familiar grand narrative cannot do is to explain the persistence of empire in American history. Our tendency to assume that the United States emerged from the Revolution as a fundamentally *anti-imperial* nation, wary of the exercise of state power of the sort commonly associated with empires, makes it difficult for us to integrate into the larger picture of national development those times—in 1812, 1846, and 1898, to name three—when the United States seems to have been bent on conquering and annexing territory that belonged to other polities; makes it difficult to see the dispossession of American Indians as more than the regrettable but inevitable by-product of an essentially peaceable expansion-by-settlement. What the story of American development recast in these unfamiliar terms encourages us to do is to imagine that empire has been as central to our national self-definition and behavior over time as liberty—that empire and liberty, in short, can be seen as complementary elements, related in as intimate and necessary a way as the two faces of a single coin.

None of this is to deny that political liberty *has* grown more widespread throughout American history, as the franchise has been extended from white adult property-holding males, to white adult males, to white and black adult males, to all adults without respect to sex. It is only to contextualize that story in a way that makes it possible to see those expansions of rights in relation to the parallel story of imperial expansion by means of war and conquest.

For in fact what we begin to see if we construe the Seven Years' War and the Revolution as equally central to the formation of American nationhood is a broader pattern that repeats itself in the century and a half between 1750 and 1900: the Age of Empires and Revolutions that begins with the colonies of the British Empire confined to the eastern seaboard of North America and ends with the United States in control not only of everything from the Atlantic to the Pacific between 49° North latitude and the Rio Grande, but of territories—colonies—in the Caribbean and the Pacific. The pattern of 1754 through 1794, as we have seen, is one in which an empire experiences a tremendous expansion in territory by virtue of military victory, then breaks down in about a dozen years' time because the rules and habits of mind that sustained the old empire as a consenting political community are no longer adequate to hold the new empire together. The upshot, civil war and revolution, enables the establishment of a successor empire capable of defining the terms of membership in such a way as to consolidate its control over the conquests that had so recently torn the old empire apart. By the 1820s, with Indian resistance all but a dead letter east of the Mississippi, seemingly nothing stood in the way of American expansion to the west, and the citizens of the Republic could begin to imagine that it was their destiny to spread liberty across the continent.

Then, in effect, it happened all over again with the Mexican-American War and its aftermath. Once again, a great conquest expanded the reach of a victorious empire beyond its grasp; once again postwar controversy exploded over the future of the conquests and the terms on which the newly enlarged empire would function. This time the dispute was over the expansion of slavery, and it was every bit as bitter, divisive, and irresolvable as the disputes of the 1760s and 1770s. Then it took twelve years for the victorious empire to collapse in civil war; this time it took thirteen years, from 1848 to 1861, to accomplish the same result. Once again, civil war produced revolutionary change; once again, the emergent empire consolidated its control over the lands gained by the previous imperial victory as between 1877 and 1890 the citizens of the re-United States overcame the last vestiges of Indian resistance in the trans-Mississippi west.

Twice, then, imperial victories created unanticipated, unsought revolutionary transformations in the victorious empire. When the next imperial victory occurred, in 1898, the result was not a third American Revolution, but rather a redefinition of the terms on which imperial power would be exerted—no longer as territorial control and incorporation, but as the exercise of hegemony, backed if need be by military power. This began the Age of Intervention, which is with us to this day; but to tell the story of that transformation in the relations between empire and liberty would take us even further from the era of the Seven Years' War than we have already come. Suffice it to say that empire is still very much with us, if only because wars fought to expand the reach of American power are still justified, as they have been since 1812, by the expansion of freedom's realm. For it is not, as many observers outside the United States believe, hypocrisy that leads the United States to employ coercive means in pursuit of liberating ends. Rather it is the deeply held, utterly sincere conviction, growing from roots struck deep in the soil of our historical experience, that other peoples will willingly embrace our political ideals if only they can be freed from the tyrannies of misrule and misperception that hold them fast.

In focusing as we typically do on the anti-imperial rhetoric of the Revolution and explaining our history to ourselves with so much emphasis on the War of Independence, the Civil War, and World War II, we have diminished our ability to see that wars for empire also made us the people and the nation we are. Those wars for the expansion of power fit less comfortably with the familiar justification of war by liberty than the three great wars for freedom commemorated on the centerline of the Mall.

Where are the monuments to these wars? Everywhere: you have only to look about you. You can see them on the hill above Winchester, where Fort Loudoun once stood, if you know where to look. With guidebook in hand you can find them up and down the Shenandoah Valley, where scores of tiny forts offered what security they could to the local inhabitants who confronted a terrifying enemy. You can see them at the Forks of the Ohio, in a handsome park where Fort Duquesne and Fort Pitt once stood. You can find them reconstructed at Fort Ligonier, preserved at Fort Ticonderoga, and in ruins at Crown Point. But most of all, you can *hear* them, everywhere across the United States, in the names of such notably unmilitary locales as Fort Lauderdale, Fort Wayne, Fort Worth, and Fort Collins—towns and cities whose names carry back, like the *ping* of sonar, echoes of a history formed no less in the pursuit of empire than in the defense of liberty. What these old forts can tell us about ourselves and how we came to be as we are is a kind of truth that we may find less comforting than those so prominently represented on the Mall. Yet it is in my view a truth that now, more than ever, we would do well to contemplate.

∼

The essays that follow originated as scholarly papers read at a conference on the Seven Years' War held at Shenandoah University in October 2004. The title of the conference, "Cultures in Conflict," was intended to encourage the participants to bring the perspectives of cultural history to bear on the motives and behavior of various groups that took part in this sprawling, complex, many-sided conflict. As these revised essays show, that invitation bore fruit that was both richer and more varied than perhaps the conference organizers anticipated. The culture concept, as it happens, proved most consistently useful in addressing the *consequences* of the war—a notoriously tricky issue to address in any historical case and a particularly difficult one when dealing with a war as large and complex as this one.

Paul Mapp's "British Culture and the Changing Character of the Mid-Eighteenth-Century British Empire" and Jonathan Dull's "Great Power Confrontation or Clash of Cultures? France's War against Britain and Its Antecedents" examine the war from European, metropolitan vantage points. Both scholars agree that while the culture concept can illuminate the character and consequences of the conflict, the calculations of power and advantage made by kings and their ministers played a decisive role in the causes, course, and effects of the war. In a European world rife with competition between empires and yet lacking in international institutions to contain violence, the men who directed affairs of state were apt to pay less heed to their own countrymen's views and convictions than to the suspected intentions and overt acts of their counterparts in other foreign ministries and courts. As a consequence, Mapp argues, we would be mistaken to conclude that the anti-French fervor of the British public influenced Britain's decision to retain Canada and Louisiana at the end of the war. Stripping France of its North American domain reflected less a desire to humiliate a hated enemy than a rational diplomatic calculation aimed at insuring that no future Anglo-French wars would erupt in North America. British chauvinism, in this case at least, was more a product of the war than a causal factor in shaping its outcome.

Jonathan Dull's close analysis of eighteenth-century European diplomacy and military policy similarly suggests that both the avoidance and the acceptance of war proceeded from fundamentally rational (or at least rationalized) causes: royal and ministerial calculations of advantage and anxieties concerning their own nations' vulnerabilities. Once undertaken, however, wars acquired a logic and a momentum of their own, creating consequences that echoed for decades in relations between states. Thus, Dull shows, French decisions to invade the Netherlands in 1744 may have been made "merely [as] military expedients" but influenced British kings' and foreign ministers' attitudes and policies toward France for the next seventy years. War, again, catalyzed cultural change; the eighteenth-century growth of national identities (and ultimately revolutionary ideologies as well) may be more accurately understood as the offspring than the progenitor of the competition for imperial advantage.

The cultural consequences of war and the exercise of state power in pursuit of imperial ends emerge strongly as themes in the remaining essays, all of which deal with North American groups. In "War, Diplomacy, and Culture: The Iroquois Experience in the Seven Years' War," Timothy Shannon assesses the cultural impact of the war on the peoples of the Six Nations, and finds that they were remarkably successful in avoiding the kind of devastation that the war visited on other Indian groups. The Iroquois managed this feat by adhering to a policy of neutrality for most of the war and then throwing in their lot with the British in 1759–1760, when an active alliance could bring them decisive material and diplomatic rewards at the lowest possible cost. In escaping the most direct adverse impacts of the war, however, the Iroquois could not avoid its larger consequences, for the destruction of New France deprived them of a competitor empire to play off against the British. As their options narrowed in postwar world, the Six Nations became steadily more dependent on the British, forgoing participation in pan-Indian resistance and increasingly adopting elements of Protestant Christianity in their spiritual lives. The Seven Years' War in this way diminished Iroquois independence and wrought significant changes in Iroquois culture: changes that were all the more insidious because they were *not* driven directly by violence and physical destruction, but rather by what seemed to be a sensible response to the opportunities for profit and power that the war seemingly afforded.

Eric Hinderaker's "Declaring Independence: The Ohio Indians and the Seven Years' War" describes the destructive consequences of the war for the native peoples of the upper Ohio Valley and explores the culturally creative way in which they responded. Hinderaker argues that by the late 1740s the disparate native groups of the region, distrustful of the Six Nations Iroquois who claimed suzerainty over them, were groping toward a kind of intercultural alliance in the hope of shaking off Onondaga's control. Their efforts only hastened the collision between French and British colonists in the region and hence the outbreak of war in 1754–1755. The stresses of war helped promote a nativist spiritual revival, which in turn became the basis of pan-Indian resistance to British authority in 1763–1764: a fulfillment, on a vastly wider scale, of the Ohio Indians' earlier efforts to overcome cultural divisions in a common endeavor. Ironically, however, that cooperation came too late to secure a lasting independence for them or the other native peoples of the interior. In the absence of a French ally to arm and resupply them, resistance to British power could last only as long as the Indians' limited stock of weapons and ammunition held out. The spiritual impulse toward pan-Indian cooperation, however, would endure, resurfacing in the early nineteenth century to organize resistance to the expansionist United States. For the Ohio Indians as much as for the Europeans, then, the violence of this war produced enduring cultural effects: it remade both the world they lived in and the terms in which they explained it to themselves.

Woody Holton's "How the Seven Years' War Turned Americans into (British) Patriots" interrogates the conflict's implications for the political culture of the Britons of North America, a group arguably made more conscious of their identity as subjects of the crown between 1755 and 1763 than they had ever been before. How could the colonists' participation in an imperial crusade of such magnitude and success create conditions that would break the empire apart in the Revolution? The connections that Holton sees are far less direct, and more contingent, than those posited by most previous commentators. The Seven Years' War changed the British imperial world in ways that no one fully grasped at the moment of victory, or for that matter in the years that followed. It altered the tenor of metropolitan-colonial relations and quality of allegiance, intensifying Anglo-American patriotism in ways that made resistance to imperial reforms more emotional, and more potentially explosive, than it could possibly have been without the shared experience of victory. In the end this great, transforming war did not make American colonists desire independence so much as make it possible for them to believe they had no choice but to accept it as the last desperate alternative to enslavement.

Finally, Catherine Desbarats and Allan Greer offer a wide-ranging assessment of the war's impact on *habitants* who saw their lives upended by war and invasion and on the binational Canadian political culture that emerged from a world transformed by *la guerre de la conquête*. "The Seven Years' War in Canadian History and Memory" frames the cultural effects of the conflict in two intriguing ways. On one hand, it describes a tradition of scholarly writing on the war deeply divided by language and religious affiliation, charged with emotion and inflected by nationalist mythologies; on the other, it introduces the findings of the late demographic historian Louise Dechêne concerning the war's effects on the people of the St. Lawrence Valley. Dechêne's clear-eyed, empirical, and resolutely anti-mythologizing approach to the war illuminates the social character of the Canadian militia, the experience of military service, and even the terms in which the militiamen understood the conflict. Here the cultural changes wrought by the war are made as unmistakably clear as the sufferings it inflicted on the militiamen and their families. The essay's final image, of "exhausted hungry refugee mothers, grandfathers, and children" struggling to survive in a homeland ripped apart by war and terror, reminds us with uncommon force of the toll that war exacts from those who do not choose it but merely find themselves unable to escape from its path: a cost as terrible for eighteenth-century Canadian peasants as for those of twenty-first-century Darfur.

What these excellent, provocative essays share, in my view, is a new and promising approach to understanding the Seven Years' War and its significance in North American and Atlantic history. Broadly speaking they participate in what has been called "the new imperial history," a reference to the approach to the colonial period practiced by Herbert Levi Osgood (1855–1918), Charles McLean Andrews (1863–1943), Lawrence Henry Gipson (1880–1971), and other scholars who for the most part published in the first half of the twentieth century. Their deep research in Colonial Office, War Office, and related archival groups in the Public Record Office imbued their work with a profoundly Anglocentric and Anglophilic quality; they saw Britain's empire essentially as British imperial administrators did. As a result they never managed to explain the American Revolution as anything but a terrible mistake on the part of the colonists—an approach to American history that accounts for their demise as a historiographical school.

Writers of the new imperial history take empire and warfare seriously, as these essays suggest, without being bound by the Eurocentrism that limited the perspective of the original imperial historians. The informing insight on which these scholars base their work is that empires should not be understood merely as hierarchical administrative institutions that project power from a metropolitan governing authority to an imperial periphery, but rather as "negotiated systems"—inherently unequal partnerships that create "sites for intercultural relations" and which express above all an attempt to impose and maintain order in a dangerous world.[11] Participants in imperial systems might enter into them by force or voluntarily, but no empire could long endure on the basis of coercion alone. The unequal political relationships characteristic of empires survive because they provide tangible benefits in the form of trade, defense, governance, and so on; they create consenting political communities.

Consent, of course, is always conditional, and rooted in cultural factors that are themselves shaped and reshaped by the experience of empire, especially as intensified by war. Because colonists and the colonized can withdraw their consent at any time, empires only superficially rest on the state power of the metropolis. Superior economic and military might can create a colonial relationship, but the continuing exercise of power by coercive means may well prove inimical to imperial control. In this sense, military force is only superficially the currency of empire, and even a highly successful war (one resulting in, say, the conquest of Canada) can produce unpredictable, destabilizing, even potentially revolutionary effects. The promise of the new imperial history, as these excellent essays suggest, is to illuminate those deeply ironic processes and to show in high relief the ways in which the history of North America has been shaped by the quest for power and the need for order, no less than by the more easily celebrated values of enterprise, egalitarianism, and republican political culture.

Notes

1. Luckily, such a guide exists, the result of many years of dedicated research by the local historian Norman Baker; see his French and Indian War in Frederick County, Virginia, with the Forts of the French and Indian War on the Northwestern Frontier (Winchester, VA: Winchester–Frederick County Historical Society, 2000). Most of the factual information in the paragraph above comes from this excellent source.

2. The first great scholarly work on the conflict, Francis Parkman's Montcalm and Wolfe, 2 vols. (Boston: Little, Brown & Company, 1884), was the best-selling history written by an American scholar in the nineteenth century. It has certainly had the most abiding influence; all subsequent histories of the war are in one way or another comments upon it. Of these, Lawrence Henry Gipson's magnum opus in fifteen volumes, The British Empire before the American Revolution (Caldwell, ID, and New York: Caxton Printers and Alfred A. Knopf, 1936–1970), remains the most significant and thorough in its treatment of the war and its contexts. It is also deeply Anglophilic and Anglocentric, radically underestimating the significance of native peoples to the war's outcome. Most of all, Gipson never managed to connect the war adequately to

its greatest legacy, the American Revolution, which appeared explicable to him only as a colossal mistake. (For particularly penetrating estimates of Gipson's monumental achievement, see John Shy, "The Empire Remembered: Lawrence Henry Gipson, Historian," in Shy, *A People Numerous and Armed: Reflections on the Military Struggle for American Independence* [New York: Oxford University Press, 1976], 109–32], and John M. Murrin, "The French and Indian War, the American Revolution, and the Counterfactual Hypothesis: Reflections on Lawrence Henry Gipson and John Shy," *Reviews in American History* 1 [Sept. 1973]: 307–18.)

Since Gipson some of the most illuminating and creative work on the war has taken precisely the opposite approach and examined the role of Native Americans in the war and in colonial North America generally. Among these, Francis Jennings deserves pride of place as the first to take on Parkman in a kind of career-long grudge match. His great work on the war was *Empire of Fortune: Crowns, Colonies, and Tribes in the Seven Years War in America* (New York: W.W. Norton, 1988). This was soon followed, and in many ways superseded, by a new generation of Indian scholarship. Among these important works see especially Richard White, *The Middle Ground: Indians, Republics, and Empires in the Great Lakes Region, 1650–1815* (New York: Cambridge University Press, 1991); Michael McConnell, *A Country Between: The Upper Ohio Valley and Its Peoples, 1724–1774* (Lincoln: University of Nebraska Press, 1992); James H. Merrell, *Into the American Woods: Negotiators on the Pennsylvania Frontier* (New York: W.W. Norton, 1999); Jane Merritt, *At the Crossroads: Indians and Empires on a Mid-Atlantic Frontier, 1700–1763* (Chapel Hill: University of North Carolina Press for the Omohundro Institute of Early American History and Culture, 2003); and a splendid synthesis by Daniel K. Richter, *Facing East from Indian Country: A Native History of Early America* (Cambridge, MA: Harvard University Press, 2001).

Significant modern works dealing with the war from the perspective of the empires that engaged in it include Eric Hinderaker, *Elusive Empires: Constructing Colonialism in the Ohio Valley, 1673–1800* (New York: Cambridge University Press, 1997); Timothy Shannon, *Indians and Colonists at the Crossroads of Empire* (Ithaca, NY: Cornell University Press, 2002); Richard Middleton, *The Bells of Victory: The Pitt-Newcastle Ministry and the Conduct of the Seven Years' War, 1757–1762* (Cambridge: Cambridge University Press, 1985); John Brewer, *The Sinews of Power: War, Money, and the English State, 1688–1783* (New York: Knopf, 1989); Eliga Gould, *The Persistence of Empire: British Political Culture in the Age of the American Revolution* (Chapel Hill: University of North Carolina Press for the Omohundro Institute of Early American History and Culture, 2000); and Jonathan R. Dull, *The French Navy and the Seven Years' War* (Lincoln: University of Nebraska Press, 2005). Scholarship that emphasizes warfare itself as a shaping influence includes a broad synthesis by Ian K. Steele, *Warpaths: Invasions of America* (New York: Oxford University Press, 1994), and Steele's complementary, tightly focused study, *Betrayals: Fort William Henry and the "Massacre"* (New York: Oxford University Press, 1990); also John Grenier, *The First Way of War: American War Making on the Frontier, 1607–1814* (New York: Cambridge University Press, 2005).

Several relatively new general works on the Seven Years' War in America have been published since 2000. These include William M. Fowler, Jr., *Empires at War: The French and Indian War and the Struggle for North America* (New York: Walker and Company, 2004); two volumes by William R. Nester, *The Great Frontier War: Britain, France, and the Imperial Struggle for North America, 1607–1755* (Westport, CT: Praeger, 2000) and *The First Global War: Britain, France, and the Fate of North America, 1756–1775* (Westport, CT: Praeger, 2001); and two works by Fred Anderson, *Crucible of War: The Seven Years' War and the Fate of Empire in British North America, 1754–1766* (New York: Alfred A. Knopf, 2000), and *The War That Made America: A Short History of the French and Indian War* (New York: Viking, 2000).

The writers of historical fiction have dealt with the war in many works of widely varying quality. Arguably the finest American novel published before the 1840s, James Fenimore Cooper's *Last of the Mohicans* (Philadelphia: Carey and Lea, 1826), centered on the war's pivotal moment, the "massacre" at Fort William Henry. The millions of copies it has sold over the intervening 180 years no less than its five film adaptations testify to this book's merits, as a story if not perhaps as a historical reconstruction. Twentieth-century novelists, notably Kenneth Roberts, also based best-selling works (in his case *Northwest Passage* [New York: Doubleday, 1936]) on the war, while those of the twenty-first century remain susceptible to the lure of the era. Among the latter, see especially Deborah Larsen's subtle and evocative fictional reimagining of Mary Jemison's experience of captivity and transculturation, *The White* (New York: Random House, 2002).

3. "Grand narrative" is a term derived from literary theory that historians have adopted to describe any overarching story that defines the shape and limits of the specific narratives of events that can be constructed to deal with specific events, periods, or persons. See Dorothy Ross, "Grand Narrative in American Historical Writing: From Romance to Uncertainty," *American Historical Review* 100 (June 1995): 651–77. The following attempt to characterize the American grand narrative by analogy to the placement of monuments on the Mall condenses a larger account in Fred Anderson and Andrew Cayton, *The Dominion of War: Empire and Liberty in North America, 1500–2000* (New York: Viking, 2005), ix–xxiv; a variant of it has also appeared as "The *Real* First World War and the Making of America," *American Heritage*, 56 (Dec. 2005), 6: 75–80.

4. Frederick Jackson Turner's 1893 address to the American Historical Association, "The Significance of the Frontier in American History," has been variously reprinted, ramified, glossed, disputed, dismissed, and celebrated. A version can be found in Frederick Jackson Turner, *The Frontier in American History* (New York: Henry Holt and Company, 1920). Important assessments can be found in John Mack Faragher, ed., *Rereading Frederick Jackson Turner: "The Significance of the Frontier in American History" and Other Essays* (New York: Henry Holt and Company, 1994); Wilbur R. Jacobs, *On Turner's Trail: 100 Years of Writing Western History* (Lawrence: University of Kansas Press, 1994); and Patricia Nelson Limerick, *The Legacy of Conquest: The Unbroken Past of the American West* (New York: W.W. Norton, 1987).

5. Richter, *Facing East*, 62–67; White, *Middle Ground*, 1–23; José António Brandão, *"Your Fyre Shall Burn No More": Iroquois Policy toward New France and Its Native Allies to 1701* (Lincoln: University of Nebraska Press, 1997); George T. Hunt, *The Wars of the Iroquois: A Study in Intertribal Trade Relations* (Madison: University of Wisconsin Press, 1967).

6. The best description of this "play-off" system in its mature eighteenth-century form is Daniel Richter's; see *Facing East*, 165–79.

7. James C. Riley, *The Seven Years War and the Old Regime in France: The Economic and Financial Toll* (Princeton, NJ: Princeton University Press, 1986), 3–37, 104–31, 224–26; Dull, *French Navy*, "Epilogue."

8. E. N. Williams, *The Ancien Régime in Europe* (New York: Harper and Row, 1970), 114–33; Mark Burkholder and Lyman L. Johnson, *Colonial Latin America*, 2d. ed. (New York: Oxford University Press, 1994), 194–97; Lester D. Langley, *The Americas in the Age of Revolution, 1750–1850* (New Haven, CT: Yale University Press, 1996), 147–65; Christon I. Archer, *The Army in Bourbon Mexico, 1760–1810* (Albuquerque: University of New Mexico Press, 1977); Lyle N. McAlister, *The "Fuero Militar" in New Spain, 1764–1800* (Gainesville: University of Florida Press, 1957).

9. The argument in the following paragraphs is principally derived from *Crucible of War*, 503–734; see also *Dominion of War*, 138–44, and *War That Made America*, 228–65.

10. *Dominion of War*, 160–201.

11. Hinderaker, *Elusive Empires*, xi.

CHAPTER TWO

~

British Culture and the Changing Character of the Mid-Eighteenth-Century British Empire

Paul Mapp

We naturally fixed our habitations along the coast, for the sake of traffick and correspondence, and all the conveniencies of navigable rivers. And when one port or river was occupied, the next colony, instead of fixing themselves in the inland parts behind the former, went on southward, till they pleased themselves with another maritime situation. For this reason our colonies have more length than depth; their extent from east to west, or from the sea to the interior country, bears no proportion to their reach along the coast from north to south.

—Samuel Johnson, 1756[1]

They ["the friends of the ministry"] expatiated on the great variety of climates which that country [North America] contained, and the vast resources which would thence arise to commerce. That the value of our conquests thereby ought not to be estimated by the present produce, but by their probable increase. Neither ought the value of any country to be solely tried on its commercial advantages; that extent of territory and a number of subjects are matters of as much consideration to a state attentive to the sources of real grandeur, as the mere advantages of traffic; that such ideas are rather suitable to a limited and petty commonwealth . . . than to a great, powerful, and warlike nation.

—Commons Debate, "Motion on the
Preliminaries of Peace," 9 December 1762[2]

One of the basic questions of mid-eighteenth-century British imperial history concerns the beginnings of a change in the empire's character between roughly 1748 and 1763. Britain was moving at this time from possession of an essentially "maritime," "commercial," or "mercantilist" empire to a more centralized and tightly controlled empire of territory and dominion. Historians often disagree about the labels to attach to this phenomenon, about its exact chronology, and about the extent to which it reflected the conscious intentions of British officials or simply the mute workings of larger historical trends, but they generally concur that a development of considerable significance occurred.[3]

Three aspects of this transition were especially important. The first was the effort by British officials to exercise greater control over existing British colonies, possessions which had enjoyed a high degree of autonomy under the long-standing policy of "salutary neglect."[4] This attempt to rationalize and tighten the administration of the British colonies merits attention, but, because of its relation to the chain of events that led to the outbreak of the American Revolution, it is better discussed in a volume focusing on the Revolution rather than on the Seven Years' War; so this essay will forgo discussion of this development in British imperial policy.

More important for an understanding of British actions during the Seven Years' War was a second expression of this change in British imperial policy: the extensive and unprecedented British governmental commitment to the defense of the backcountry of Britain's North American colonies in the years after the end of the War of the Austrian Succession. The dispatch of Major General Edward Braddock and his two regiments of Irish Infantry to Virginia in 1755 represented the most striking manifestation of this commitment. Braddock's arrival at Hampton Roads communicated the British government's refusal to cede the Ohio Valley region to French explorers, traders, and soldiers; and, more broadly, it bore witness to a British policy of countering perceived instances of French aggression and expansionism throughout continental North America and the Caribbean.

Still more significant as a sign of the changing character of the British Empire, and consequently most central as a subject of investigation in this essay, were the territorial decisions British ministers made at the end of the war that Braddock's expedition had helped to initiate. As the beneficiaries of a series of stunning British military victories on land and at sea, British diplomats in the early 1760s could reasonably expect major concessions from their French and Spanish counterparts at the negotiating table. With valuable portions of the French and Spanish empires seemingly within reach, the choices British statesmen made about which territories to grasp or relinquish provide important evidence of British imperial objectives. Surprisingly, in light of the British Empire's traditional focus on oceanic commerce and its corresponding preference for coastal and island colonies, British statesmen at the end of the Seven Years' War passed up the opportunity to acquire small, immediately profitable, maritime holdings such as the islands of Guadeloupe, Martinique, and Cuba, opting instead to obtain the vast, thinly populated, commercially underdeveloped, continental territories of Canada, Florida, and eastern Louisiana.[5] It was not simply that Britain had added new territories to its empire, but that it had taken on different kinds of territories, thereby creating a different kind of empire.

These British commitments to the defense and acquisition of North American territories before and during the Seven Years' War call for an explanation. In part, this is because such commitments seemed to many observers at the time, and have seemed to many historians since, to depart from traditional lines of British imperial conduct and, perhaps, to undermine British imperial interest.

The empire's assertive resistance to the French presence in the Ohio Valley in the early and mid-1750s, for instance, imperiled the shaky peace that prevailed between Britain and France after 1748. Decisions by British imperial officials in the early and mid-1750s to contest, contain, and counter the activities of French traders, explorers, and soldiers in the Ohio Valley; to dispatch diplomats to the French court to protest these French encroachments, and ships and soldiers to North America to repel them, rather obviously ran the risk of entangling Britain in another war with France. Nor was such a war an event that British officials could contemplate with equanimity. The struggle with France during the War of the Austrian Succession had cost Britain thousands of casualties, had left it with roughly £78,000,000 in national debt, and had offered Britain nothing in the way of territorial or commercial concessions as compensation.

Not only was Britain clearly risking a war, but it was unclear why. Part of what made British bellicosity so puzzling to many contemporaries was that the value of American territories such as the Ohio Valley seemed incommensurate with the risks Britain was running to defend them. The jingoistic aggression that had brought Britain into the War of Jenkins' Ear with Spain in 1739 could be explained by the allure of Spanish imperial markets and their silver-dispensing inhabitants. In the eyes of skeptics, the Ohio Valley of the early 1750s offered only furs, trees, and Indians. France's foreign minister was so puzzled by British belligerence regarding the region that he could only interpret it as a cover for the interest in Spanish territory that had been so evident sixteen years before.[6] If the Ohio Valley and the frontiers of the mainland Anglo-American colonies were the focus of attention, Britain seemed to many to be risking too much for too little.

Just as British decisions to defend marginal North American territories in the mid-1750s raise questions of historical explanation, so too do the choices at the end of the Seven Years' War that brought the British Empire to the heart of French Canada, the banks of the Mississippi River, and the tip of the Florida peninsula. While it is easy in retrospect to fall into the habit of thinking that all territorial acquisitions must have seemed desirable at the time, that larger tracts must have been still more appealing, and that areas such as eastern Canada, the eastern Mississippi Valley, and Florida—all of which have gone on to become rather significant pieces of real estate—must have been especially coveted, the value of these swathes of American land was less clear in the mid-eighteenth century. Many in Britain were neither well informed concerning nor especially enthusiastic about Britain's new western acquisitions. Samuel Johnson eloquently expressed this indifferent English sentiment when he averred, in speaking of the "large tracts of America" that "were added by the last war to the British dominions," that they were "at best . . . only the barren parts of the continent, the refuse of the earlier adventurers, which the French, who came last, had taken only as better than nothing."[7] The British government seemed to endorse the view with its October 1763 Royal Proclamation designating the lands west of the Appalachians and north of the Gulf Coast as an Indian reserve from which white settlers were to be excluded.[8] The general point to be drawn from comments such as Johnson's and from governmental acts such as the Royal Proclamation is that much of the New World territory gained by Britain in the Seven Years' War had been neither universally sought nor appreciated in old England, nor was there a consensus within the British government on the desirability of immediately expanding British settlement into it.

Moreover, even making allowances for Johnson's usual rhetorical vigor, Britons had good reasons to question the value of the territories acquired. Canada had generally lost money for France and had never been renowned for a pleasant climate. Nor did the territories between the Appalachians and the Mississippi comprising eastern Louisiana appear to be an unmixed blessing. Bringing the latter area into the British commercial system, for example, would depend on the ability to move commodities from it to England, but the region's crucial port, New Orleans, had not been included in the lands France ceded to Britain. Furthermore, in contrast with the islands of the West Indies, eastern Louisiana contained neither large and established markets for British goods, nor developed sources of lucrative commodities; nor was it, like the Newfoundland fisheries, a school for seamen. Some in

Britain worried that the need to move British settlers into new colonial possessions might harm the British economy by drawing valuable population
away from Britain itself.[9] Finally, the new acquisitions brought new lands
and non-British peoples to administer, and, as the subsequent history of
Pontiac's War, the Proclamation Line, and the Quebec Act would demonstrate, simultaneously governing French Catholics, unconquered American
Indian nations, and multiplying land-hungry Anglo-Americans would prove
neither simple nor cheap.

Beyond these practical questions, historians have noted recently that the
extension of imperial rule over non-British, non-Protestant, and often non-
Christian and non-European populations challenged pre-Seven Years' War
ideological justifications for the British Empire. In an attempt to contrast
this developing empire with the old and famously fallen empire of Rome,
and with the Spanish Empire of the "Black Legend," propagandists of British
maritime expansion spoke of a commercial empire, happily bringing together trade-craving and freedom-loving British Protestants for their mutual
benefit, rather than bloodily conquering hapless indigenes to enrich avari-
cious and cruel Latin overlords.[10] Wartime acquisition of direct rule over
French-Catholic Canadian *habitants* and American Indian nations, not to
mention Bengali peasants in the Indian subcontinent, challenged this older
imperial self-image.

British territorial acquisitions raised other problems as well. One was that
the scale of British successes might so alarm the other nations of Europe, and
so antagonize the defeated Bourbon powers of France and Spain, that the
British Empire would be confronted for years to come with the actively hostile policies of many European countries. Prominent figures in the British
government such as George III's closest advisor, the Earl of Bute, and British
diplomat, the Duke of Bedford, for example, feared the consequences that
might flow from the excessive abasement of France. Like Britain, France derived much of its maritime power from the revenues acquired and the ex-
pertise developed in colonial commerce. The loss of too many American
colonies might therefore undermine the foundation of France's naval power
and alarm other European nations with the prospect of an unrestrained and
unchallenged British naval hegemony.[11]

Finally, even before the Stamp Act and all that followed, and even before the end of the Seven Years' War, British officials and pamphleteers were
already contemplating the possibility that removal of the French threat to
the British colonies of the Atlantic seaboard through British acquisition of
Canada and eastern Louisiana would embolden the formerly security-
conscious colonists to challenge burdensome British imperial policies more

aggressively. That the colonists might eventually seek independence was not considered out of the question.[12]

In sum, Britain's moves to defend and acquire large tracts of American land in the years before and during the Seven Years' War and the resultant changes in the type of empire Britain possessed constitute puzzling events requiring explication rather than unexceptionable continuations of existing trends. British leaders seem to have had ample reason for doing something other than what they actually did, and this raises the historical question of why these officials pursued their particular and perhaps peculiar courses of action. This question in turn raises the historiographical issue of how recent scholars of the eighteenth-century British Empire have treated these curious events.

Since roughly the mid-1980s, some of the most intriguing works of British imperial history have considered what can loosely be called the relation between empire and culture. Scholars such as Gerald Newman, in *The Rise of English Nationalism: A Cultural History, 1740–1830* (1987); Nicholas Rogers, in *Whigs and Cities: Popular Politics in the Age of Walpole and Pitt* (1989); Linda Colley, in *Britons: Forging the Nation, 1707–1837* (1992); Kathleen Wilson, in *The Sense of the People: Politics, Culture, and Imperialism in England, 1715–1785* (1995); Eliga Gould, in *The Persistence of Empire: British Political Culture in the Age of the American Revolution* (2000); and Bob Harris, in *Politics and the Nation: Britain in the Mid-Eighteenth Century* (2002), have examined connections between popular beliefs and behaviors and the character and evolution of the British Empire. (In addition, though it is not strictly speaking a cultural history, Marie Peters's 1980 study of *Pitt and Popularity* is a fundamental examination of the dynamics of mid-eighteenth-century British public opinion). These scholars have explored brilliantly topics such as the cultural meaning of the British Empire, the role of popular opinion in shaping British politics, and the formation of national identities in the British Isles. Their books present a picture of a mid-eighteenth-century Britain in which imperial, cultural, and political matters were thoroughly intertwined. Such works merit examination to see if the cultural analyses they have undertaken can provide novel means of explaining the changing character of the mid-eighteenth-century British Empire.

To be fair to these works, it must be stated at the outset that the scholars just mentioned have generally tried to use the study of the British Empire and the Seven Years' War to understand mid-eighteenth-century British culture, politics, and nationalism, rather than to employ the study of British culture and politics to illuminate facets of the Seven Years' War. The question here is therefore not whether these scholars have met the burdens of proof appropriate for their individual works but rather whether scholars of the Seven Years' War can employ this recent scholarship to better understand their own topics of interest.

Combining the insights of the historians mentioned above, it is possible to assemble an explanation for Britain's mid-eighteenth-century imperial transition that enhances existing understandings of this historical development. Recent scholars have identified aspects of Seven Years' War-era British culture that could have contributed to the move to a more territorial empire: heightened distaste for French culture and growing fear of French imperial strength; a disdain for and disgust with Catholicism; a sense of shared identity with the colonists of British America and a desire to secure the safety of these overseas Britons; unease about creeping British effeminacy; and a corresponding desire for British victories and territorial conquests to allay this insecurity. These historians have, moreover, described means through which sentiments arising in popular culture could reach Britain's leaders: petitions, pamphlets, public celebrations, newspaper articles, instructions to members of Parliament, and even the odd riot. Finally, recent historians have provided at least some evidence that ministers and officials in a position to formulate imperial policy paid heed to these popular expressions.

Despite their considerable achievements in deepening understanding of the eighteenth-century British Empire these recent culturally oriented works provide a useful supplement to existing explanations of Britain's mid-eighteenth-century transformation rather than a logically necessary substitute for them. Earlier generations of scholars have argued that Britain moved to shield its North American colonies before the Seven Years' War and to expand its continental dominions at the end of that conflict because of a growing concern with colonial security. Such safety was deemed important because of concern for the welfare of Britain's colonists, because of weariness with having to defend these overseas possessions in every Anglo-French war, and because of a growing sense of the economic importance of these colonies as markets for British goods. These arguments retain their power.

What is interesting though, is that upon closer examination, old explanations for the mid-century British imperial transition emphasizing the importance of colonial markets and security and new approaches considering the cultural meanings of empire converge in important respects. Both treat manifestations of the same underlying phenomenon: British responses to the demands of the competitive European state system. The importance of colonial markets arose not merely because European merchants sought profits, but also because European governments needed the revenues and naval capacity generated in colonial trade to sustain state power; colonial commerce had accordingly to be nurtured and protected. At the same time, the public perils and sacrifices inherent in and the potential glory and lucre to be gained from the contest for overseas empire contributed to the ways in which European peoples such as the English imagined and conducted themselves.

In fact, both sets of explanations for Britain's mid-eighteenth-century move to territorial empire point to the significance of works on international relations by earlier scholars such as Walter Dorn and F. H. Hinsley.[13] Dorn and Hinsley tried to establish the fundamental importance of the rivalries among the states of early modern Europe, to show the manifold ramifications of what Dorn called the mid-eighteenth-century European "competition for empire." While recent scholarly works—with their nuanced, detailed, and comprehensive consideration of many dimensions of British culture among different parts of the British population in many parts of the British Isles—have gone beyond the achievements of earlier scholars, they have at the same time confirmed the importance of the workings of the European state system that scholars such as Dorn and Hinsley sought to understand.

Culture, Empire, and War

One reason for the possible pertinence of the recent works of British cultural history to the question of the Seven Years' War British transition from commercial to territorial empire is that these works explore the connections between the beliefs and behaviors of the populations of the British Isles and the possession and direction of the British overseas empire. Aspects of these beliefs and behaviors that are especially relevant for study of the Seven Years' War can be broken down into five categories: loathing for France; sympathy for Britain's American colonists; general insecurity about the mid-century state of Britain's military might and imperial vigor; a resultant support for aggressively anti-French British policies; and a delight in the fact and celebration of British imperial victories.

Because it was so evident before and during the Seven Years' War and because it underpinned other aspects of British attitudes and conduct, the deeply rooted and widely shared mid-eighteenth-century British loathing for France offers a good place to begin. Gerald Newman's elegant and subtle 1987 book on *The Rise of English Nationalism* provides the best starting point for discussion of this Gallophobia. Newman describes the character of anti-French sentiment among different parts of the English population. He begins with the views of those, such as English artists and writers, who aspired to prominence in the English cultural scene. Newman notes that these ambitious and talented figures frequently felt that the prestige of foreign artists

was overshadowing their own achievements and denying them the aristocratic and national preferment they craved. Faced with these unfavorable
features of the English cultural climate, English artists and authors, Hogarth
and Fielding, for example, responded by encouraging an English taste for the
homegrown products of English creators rather than for the elegant output of
foreign nations such as France and Italy. From at least the 1720s, English
artists such as Hogarth were trying to create a national space in which they
could achieve success and recognition; a necessary prerequisite for this development was the undermining of British prejudices against domestic art
and British preferences for the cultural achievements of nearby and culturally prestigious France.

In promoting this change of taste and in expressing their own sentiments,
English intellectuals launched vigorous critiques of French culture, critiques
that quickly evolved into acerbic attacks on the Frenchified English aristocrats who were most receptive to foreign fashions and who best exemplified
their pernicious consequences. With these aristocrats in mind, arguments
soon turned to the charge that French cultural imports were not simply excessive in quality and influence but also corrupting in effect; that they were
ruining native English virtue with the foppery and degeneracy of the continent. By the 1750s, this discourse had become something more than the un-
derstandable complaints of a small group of gifted and frustrated scribblers.
Newman speaks of "an emergent nationalist philosophy, anti-French and
anti-aristocratic, linked to sharpening moral, social and historical concerns
as well as aesthetic and commercial ones; the beginnings of a *Kulturkampf*."[14]

This evolving nationalist philosophy and cultural contest extended its influence to and drew its energy from circles wider than those of England's
community of arts and letters. Newman and the other cultural historians call
attention to a more general aversion for France among the common people
of Britain, an aversion which ran deep into the English past, which was sustained by folk tradition, and which provided an important point of reference
for English or British identity. The particular intensity of this anti-Gallic sentiment in the 1750s arose in part from the series of wars since 1689 that had
pitted British against French forces and had resulted in many British families
losing kith or kin. The stakes of these wars in the popular imagination, moreover, seem often to have included liberty as well as life; a French victory im-
plying the loss of the often-praised, less often-defined freedoms Britons cherished as their birthright. The feared and likely instrument of this loss was
thought to be a Jacobite prince supported and inspired by a despotic French
king and accompanied by a French army and fleet. Such a threat seemed especially plausible after the Jacobite uprising of 1745.[15]

Intensifying the magnitude of the threat that France and its armies seemed to pose to Britain were the religious differences between the two nations. The majority of Britons were, of course, protestant; the majority of French men and women Catholic. Linda Colley has emphasized with particular vigor the role this distinction played in arousing British feelings against France and in providing the English, Scots, and Welsh with some basis for a common identity. Protestantism gave ordinary Britons a sense of a special, providential destiny, of being modern Israelites under God's supervision. It also provided them with an enemy. Colley points out the wide popularity in eighteenth-century Britain of works such as Foxe's *Book of Martyrs*, with its vivid tales of Protestants suffering the most appalling persecutions by Catholics, and of Bunyan's *Pilgrim's Progress*, in which the Pope forms one obstacle between pious believers and the heavenly city. She notes further that the Jacobite restoration, which threatened Britain from across the channel in the first half of the eighteenth century, would have brought not merely a change of dynasty but also the introduction of a Catholic regime with a foreign Catholic army to help it enforce its will. France represented an ideological, cultural, and religious challenge to Britain, and British popular hostility toward France partook of these various elements.[16]

While such elements shaped popular attitudes in most decades of the eighteenth century, the authors of the recent cultural histories argue that the 1750s constituted a period of especially acute anti-French feelings. International tensions provide much of the explanation. The War of the Austrian Succession had ended in 1748 with little advantage for either Britain or France, the treaty terminating the war simply restoring prewar conditions. Anglo-French territorial and commercial disputes in India, Acadia, the Caribbean, and the Ohio Valley remained unresolved, and the underlying conditions pushing Britain and France against each other were growing more rather than less pressing. Both powers sought overseas sources of commodities for their own use and for resale to other nations; both hoped to sell goods produced by their own dominions to markets overseas, whether in their own colonies or in the colonies of their rivals. Both hoped that customs revenues from these activities would finance the fleets and armies needed to protect European territory, maritime trade, and overseas colonies. Both subscribed to a mercantilist philosophy holding that a gain on the part of one rival meant a corresponding loss on the part of the other. With so much at stake and so little resolved, it seemed clear to many that a new Anglo-French war could not be far off.

In light of these circumstances, observers in Britain in the late 1740s and early 1750s were especially concerned about what seemed to be the growth of French commercial and military might. Though French armies had not actually accompanied Charles Edward Stuart's 1745 march toward London, the French Navy had facilitated his arrival and he had expected French troops to be forthcoming. The whole episode had reminded Britons of the kind of threat a country of twenty million people with a peacetime standing army of more than a hundred thousand soldiers represented. And Britain's colonies in America, at no great distance from Canada and subject in each war to the murderous raids of French-Canadians and their Indian allies, seemed in British eyes to be in still greater peril. Press, pamphlets, and parliamentary speeches were filled with alarming reports of a growing French navy that could bring danger to British colonies or to Britain itself. Recent historical investigations suggest, in short, that what could have been an inchoate distaste for a cross-channel cultural other was instead a more immediate fear grounded in recent events. Within this volume, Jonathan Dull's treatment of the War of the Austrian Succession is especially important because it shows how events in the 1740s could reawaken certain kinds of British concerns about France that had been less prominent during the relatively pacific 1720s and 1730s.

Moreover, quite apart from the threat to the life and limb of British colonists, or perhaps to the much-vaunted liberties of Englishmen, in the public mind apparently increasing French maritime strength constituted a threat to British prosperity. The importance of colonial trades for the British economy of the mid-eighteenth century helps to explain this. Thousands of Britons profited directly from colonial commerce. They manufactured goods for the colonies, they loaded and unloaded ships to and from the colonies, they bought and sold products from the colonies, they invested in economic ventures in the colonies. Consequently, when they heard or read that French overseas trade was growing faster than that of Britain, that French sugar and coffee sold cheaper than that produced by Britain's own colonies, that French cloth was keeping English textiles out of Asian markets, Britons perceived a threat to their livelihood.

Commercial observations such as these become more worrisome still when filtered through the kind of pop-mercantilist ideology that historians such as Kathleen Wilson and Bob Harris have seen being spread by innumerable British pamphlets and newspapers. These written accounts of international commerce assumed that a finite amount of global wealth existed; they saw the necessity of aggressive, often exclusive and monopolistic policies to promote national wealth and to protect national trade; and they spoke of French commercial gains diminishing the revenues that sustained British naval power and enhancing the French threat to it.[17]

Overall, concern about French economic competition reinforced anti-French tendencies in English culture.

Further accentuating these Gallophobic inclinations and heightening the impact of anti-French writings was what seems by the 1750s to have been an increasingly prevalent sense among Britons of shared identity with the American colonists of the British Empire. Eliga Gould, in discussing British attitudes during the Seven Years' War, speaks of "the Anglicized character of Britain's colonies in North America" conjuring for many in Britain "the even grander prospect of a vast English-speaking empire founded on a shared religious, patriotic, and cultural heritage." Most of the white population of the mid-eighteenth-century British colonies could trace their ancestry back to the British Isles. Most were protestant. Most spoke English. They and the inhabitants of the British Isles lived at least nominally under a common king and Parliament; they observed and evaded the strictures of a common system of trade regulations; they exchanged the fruits of their labors with one another, increasingly aspiring to consume the same goods in the same way and depending on each other for their prosperity.[18] At the same time, the inhabitants of Britain's American colonies were, with the exception of small Huguenot communities in places like South Carolina, non-French; they were for the most part non-Catholic; and they were thus something distinct from Britain's main enemy. Britons in Britain could quite easily imagine that they were part of the same community as their colonial counterparts, taking offense and alarm as a result when French activities seemed to threaten them.

These different aspects of British aversion to France and its culture and of British concern about rising French power came together in a kind of generalized unease about the state of mid-eighteenth-century Britain. Newman, Harris, and, most creatively, Kathleen Wilson have called attention to one manifestation of this mid-eighteenth-century British insecurity about rising French power and corresponding British weakness; namely, worries about a kind of creeping British "effeminacy." This alleged effeminacy formed a widespread topic of conversation and lamentation in newspapers, plays, and pamphlets. Figures who felt they were observing the emasculation of British virtue traced this phenomenon to a decadent aristocracy; to the malevolent and insidious foreign—and especially French—influences to which the upper class was subject; and, in some cases, to the growing prosperity and luxury of commercial Britain and the urban corruption of London. This effeminacy, it was claimed, displayed itself in dandyism, foppery, impiety, dissipation, gambling, immorality, cowardice, and general spinelessness. To offer one example, the Reverend John Brown of Newcastle, frequent subject of the historians mentioned above and author of the 1757 *Estimate of the Manners and Principles of the Time*, spoke of "the ruling Character of the present times" being "that of 'a vain, luxurious, and selfish EFFEMINACY'"; opined that "this dastard Spirit of Effeminacy hath crept upon us, and destroyed the national Spirit of Defence"; and contended that France "hath allured her neighbour Nations, by her own Example, to drink largely of her circæan and poisoned Cup of Manners." He found the origin of this "Effeminacy of modern Manners" in "our present exorbitant Degree of Trade and Wealth." What made critiques such as this a matter of some urgency rather than a simple curmudgeonly screed was the perception that a creeping effeminacy was rendering Britain socially and militarily feeble at precisely the moment when strength was needed to overcome the challenge presented by French competition. Such worries became especially grave when defeats such as the loss of Minorca early in the Seven Years' War seemed to suggest a decline of Britain's martial prowess.[19]

Hostile to French culture, religion, and influence, fearful of growing French power, and worried about French threats to Britain's colonies and colonial commerce, significant parts of the British public in the mid-1750s favored endeavors to rescue the British colonies of North America from French encroachments. These efforts contributed to the chain of New World confrontations that transformed Anglo-French tensions into a global conflict. As the Seven Years' War unfolded, and events came to favor Britain, popular feelings increasingly pushed for the removal of France from the North American continent. Scholars have called attention to numerous indications of these sentiments, among which were the manifold expressions in newspapers, pamphlets, and private writings of concern about the security of the American colonies, of belief in the importance of these overseas possessions for British trade, and of support for the conquest of Canada as the best way to protect them. Kathleen Wilson, for example, has argued that newspapers generally served to publicize colonial issues in eighteenth-century Britain and that these newspapers "evinced a widespread interest in the processes of colonial acquisition and possession." During the latter years of the Seven Years' War, newspapers called often for the vigorous continuation of the conflict and trumpeted the importance of keeping the North American conquests because of that continent's value as a market for British goods.

Similar exhortations came from trade interests, cities, and regions. Nicholas Rogers has observed that in 1756, calls for an aggressive British maritime policy that would protect markets in America were heard in port cities, in textile-producing areas of Yorkshire and the West Country, and from the growing industries of the West Midlands. Later, the First Lord of the Treasury, the Duke of Newcastle, felt pressure from northern manufacturers to retain the French-American port of Louisbourg (captured in 1758), both to put an end to the raids of its French privateers and because manufacturers hoped that conquest of Canada in its entirety would create new markets for their products. Recent scholars have contended that opinion in London staunchly supported an assertive British policy in North America. One example was evident in October 1761, when the London Common Council instructed its members of Parliament "to insist on no peace without the retention of all or nearly all conquests, especially in North America and the fisheries."[20]

These aggressive British sentiments exhibited both positive and negative characteristics. On the one hand, sectors of British opinion imagined the advantages to be gained from acquiring American territories. On the other, many Britons emphasized the negative objective of crushing and humiliating the French enemy and of stripping the French empire of the colonies which augmented its prestige and enhanced its maritime strength. As the war went increasingly well for Britain, newspapers and pamphlets increasingly urged the importance of permanently reducing French power. As Gerald Newman has put it, "what was really new about the patriotic politics of the fifties was not its condemnations of 'corruption' and 'faction' nor even its vitriolic denunciation of ministerial dithering in foreign affairs. What was new was its strident insistence that the road to national greatness was the global expansion of British trade and the total destruction of . . . French economic and military power."[21]

Going beyond the practical dimensions of military victories and territorial dispossessions, both contemporary observers and recent historians have noted the sheer enjoyment the British public seems to have felt amidst the cascade of imperial triumphs in the latter years of the Seven Years' War. Recent historical studies paint a vivid picture of the British public's delight in military and imperial successes. The most visible manifestations of British enthusiasm for military victories were the popular celebrations succeeding them. Those following the capture of Louisbourg in 1758 provide a good example. These celebrations were especially spirited, perhaps because Louisbourg was the first major British success of the war and its seizure called to mind the earlier taking of the fort by New Englanders in 1745. (The British government had returned Louisbourg to France in 1748 in exchange for Madras in India, thereby alienating many New Englanders and their supporters in Britain.) Recovering Louisbourg washed away the sour aftertaste of its diplomatic sacrifice and inspired mafficks in towns throughout Britain. Bells rang, bonfires burned, cheers filled the air. Towns and various organizations sent at least fifty congratulatory addresses praising the victory and calling for retention of the prize. Newspapers, pamphlets, and poems lauded the triumph. A procession carried the captured French colors through the streets of London. More pageants, parades, bonfires, and drinking bouts greeted the stream of victories that followed, especially in the *annus mirabilis* of 1759 when the bells were "worn threadbare with ringing for victories" and when public celebrations and the acclamation of the press greeted the favorable news from the war.[22]

It seemed clear to observers at the time, and it has appeared evident to historians since, that the British public adored military triumphs and colonial acquisitions. Some scholars have gone further still in their assessments, indicating that British victories during the Seven Years' War responded to deeper emotional needs of the British public. A few observers at the time viewed this negatively and decried the public's tendency to allow the intoxications of victory to blind it to the sober realism of imperial interest. As Richard Rigby (a member of the political faction associated with the Duke of Bedford) put it: "Whilst we succeed and make conquests and bonfires, the value of the capture is no part of the consideration—fresh fuel is added to the delirium, and the fire is kept constantly fanned." A 1760 pamphlet discussing the advantages for Britain of keeping the French island of Guadeloupe rather than Canada averred that "The having all North-America to ourselves, by acquiring Canada, dazzles the eyes, and blinds the understandings of the giddy and unthinking people, as it is natural for the human mind to grasp at every appearance of wealth and grandeur."[23]

More recently, Kathleen Wilson has suggested that the military victories and colonial conquests of the latter stage of the Seven Years' War allayed earlier concerns about British effeminacy: "[e]mpire . . . was the means through which national potency could be nurtured and consolidated"; "colonial conquest was described and glorified as a *manly* [italics in original] occupation, the proving ground for national potency"; "Britain's spectacular successes clearly constituted a forceful repudiation of the anxieties of three years before, endorsing the masculinist version of the national character."[24] This seems a plausible account of at least part of the reason for the popular British enchantment with military and imperial triumphs at the end of the Seven Years' War. The earlier sense of national weakness could only make the later proof of national and imperial power more welcome.

Popular Sentiments and Imperial Policy

If the foregoing discussion of different aspects of popular British beliefs and attitudes is to elucidate British governmental decisions to defend and acquire hinterland territories of North America, however, it is necessary to establish the existence of some kind of mechanism through which these cultural sentiments could influence the actions of the British officials making key imperial decisions before and during the Seven Years' War. Scholars working in recent decades have succeeded in doing so.

Marie Peters has offered an especially strong account of the various means through which English public opinion could make itself felt. Employing, for example, the venerable petition, English subjects could use "addresses of congratulation on royal or national events . . . to make political points." Similarly, constituents could send instructions to their members of Parliament. Representatives had no obligation to follow such instructions, but they did at least provide a means for bodies such as borough corporations and county assemblies to communicate their views. Other expressions of opinion included newspapers and pamphlets. Pamphlets conveyed the opinions of their individual authors and when appearing and circulating in sufficient quantity, as was the case during the mid-eighteenth century, they disclosed to ministers the kinds of ideas constituting opinion more generally. Newspapers and magazines such as the *Monthly Review,* the *Critical Review,* and the *Gentleman's Magazine* were the pamphlets' close cousins, and they too were increasing in number, circulation, and geographical reach in the middle decades of the eighteenth century. It is estimated that by 1760 "London had four dailies, five or six tri-weeklies, and about four weeklies"; by 1760, provincial papers, usually weeklies, "numbered about thirty-five." Samuel Johnson thought that the *Gentleman's Magazine* sold about 10,000 copies per issue, and Peters suggests that the "total annual sales of all papers may have been ten million." Newspapers and magazines could of course influence the views of those who bought them, of those who read heavily used copies in coffeehouses, and of those who borrowed issues from friends. They could also reflect opinion inasmuch as, in the interest of selling copies, they often printed what they thought their audience wanted to read.[25]

Ample evidence indicates that British politicians attended to the sentiments of the nation expressed in these ways. The papers of leaders such as the Duke of Newcastle, the Duke of Bedford, and George Fox often say as much.[26] Specific examples make the nature of this ministerial attentiveness more clear. The loss of Minorca in June 1756 after Britain's Admiral Byng had chosen to abandon it shook the government, confronting it "with irreducible evidence of a harshly critical extra-parliamentary political opinion that was beyond its effective management or control."[27] Newspapers and magazines castigated Byng for cowardice and incompetence, and then, as the Ministry's initial efforts to lay all blame on Byng began to seem less than fair, publications pilloried British ministers, especially Newcastle, for the failure to hold the island. Pamphlets poured forth, beginning by attacking Byng, and then moving to an attack on the ministry as a whole for its scandalous mismanagement of Mediterranean naval affairs. For those already fretting about Britain's creeping effeminacy, the disgraceful loss of the island seemed a confirmation. Prints and ballads excoriated Britain's leaders. Crowds burned Byng in effigy, assaulted his country home, and mobbed Newcastle himself. Instructions flowed to members of Parliament and addresses made their way to the king; both called for investigations and punishments. In November 1756, in part because of the vehement public criticism of him, Newcastle resigned his position as First Lord of the Treasury and William Pitt, untouched by the fall of Minorca, came to power as Secretary of State.[28]

As popular outrage over the loss of Minorca helped to drive one minister from power, recent scholarship, especially that of Marie Peters, suggests that popular expectations may have shaped the way his successor used it. Pitt owed his reputation and position in large part to his ability to embody the anti-French sentiments of the British public and could therefore expect to pay a high political price should he antagonize his supporters by treating the Gallic enemy more gently than popular opinion demanded. It is possible to interpret Pitt's evolving positions regarding British territorial acquisitions in North America as a manifestation of his dependence on and concern with public sentiment. Initially, Pitt's goals were quite modest, and he aimed simply at obtaining on the ground in North America what he felt Britain had been given on paper by the Treaty of Utrecht in 1713. Until quite late in the war, he sought merely all of Nova Scotia and key points such as Fort Ticonderoga, Crown Point, Fort Frontenac, Fort Niagara, and Fort Duquesne. Pitt hoped for clear boundaries and a healthy distance between the colonies of Britain and any menacing foreign foe, but the annexations of Canada and eastern Louisiana do not seem to have formed part of his original design. Even as late as March 17, 1761, Hardwicke (a member of the cabinet without portfolio from 1757 to 1762 and a close confidant of Newcastle) was writing to Newcastle that Pitt had told him that "that *the Reduction of all Canada was of the utmost importance to the Security of our Colonies &c* [italics in original], and yet it might be wise & necessary. (tho' He hoped it would not become so) for the King, under certain circumstances, to give it up by a Treaty, either in whole or in part." By the spring of 1761, however, Pitt's position had become more rigid. Where before he had simply insisted on the establishment of a secure boundary following the lines drawn by the Treaty of Utrecht, and then on keeping parts of Canada; and more generally on the principle that no British conquest would be returned without compensation;

by the time Anglo-French peace negotiations began in the spring of 1761, he had instead come to see the retention of all of Canada as an essential British objective. Peters feels that Pitt's more draconian position was in part a response to the demands of the British public.[29]

In general, British ministers appear to have been cognizant of the opinions of the British public. They saw the celebratory bonfires and heard the jubilant bells and singing. They recognized that support for and opposition to government measures could be organized on a large scale in London and could extend to provincial cities as well. They knew that throughout Britain, subjects met in clubs, coffeehouses, and inns and discussed imperial issues there. Newspapers and pamphlets spoke of imperial concerns. Theaters presented plays treating imperial themes. Balladeers sang of imperial heroes. All of these mechanisms transmitted ideas and information to the general public and could easily arouse opposition to unpopular government policy and ministers.[30] And there was every indication that refusing to seize North American lands and failing to protect Britain's North American colonies would be widely unpopular.

In particular, British governments and British ministers who had to make their way through the London streets and the London crowds took public feeling, and the feeling of London especially, very seriously. While public opinion could express itself throughout Britain, London was the site of greatest concern for politicians. British leaders saw the city with its huge population, with its traditional independence of court and aristocracy, with its proximity to the seat of government, with its instructions, remonstrances, newspapers, pamphlets, petitions, and publishers, and with its influx of people from throughout the British Isles, as both index and influencer of imperial opinion. Governments had evinced throughout the century their fears that an unhappy London populace could become a riotous mob. Experience justified such fears. There had been pro-Tory riots in 1715 and a new anti-riot act in response. Nicholas Rogers recalls that in 1733, Robert Walpole's support of an Excise Bill resulted in him being roughly handled outside the House of Commons, his effigy being burned, and his associates being physically assailed. The crowd, some said, would have broken the windows of the Parliament House (while Parliament was in session) if it could have reached them. Upon taking up the reins of the British government in 1761, Lord Bute found immediately that the ire of the crowd could be aimed at him. Riotous demonstrations praised Pitt and vilified Bute. On the way to Parliament, Bute and his carriage endured not only the insults of the mob but also a pelting of dirt from it, and the "bruisers" Bute had hired for protection "were almost bruised to death themselves." The constables and peace officers at Guildhall brought Bute to safety, but one observer (Pitt's solicitor, Thomas

Nuthall), writing on November 12, 1761, of Bute's wild ride, opined that "had there been a furlong farther to go, the mob would certainly have cut the harnesses in pieces, and probably gone to greater extremity." Bute's worries continued in the year that followed. In contrast with Pitt, he was popularly thought to be too lenient toward France, and he felt increasing concern in the summer of 1762 about the storm of popular opinion and pamphlets criticizing him. As Bute and his representatives conducted negotiations with France, they had always to consider the consequences for their political lives, and, in Bute's case, perhaps for his personal safety, of failing to acquire concessions from France and Spain sufficient to sate the conquest-loving appetite of the British public.[31]

Stepping back for a moment, on the basis of this brief survey of recent cultural histories, it seems comfortably established that anti-French sentiments formed a prominent characteristic of mid-eighteenth-century British culture. It seems reasonable to assume that these sentiments contributed to popular desires for a vigorously anti-French policy, to the popular enthusiasm greeting British military victories, and to a popular wish to see French power crushed and French colonial territories taken and held. It appears also that ordinary Britons possessed a variety of means by which they could make their opinions known to their leaders, and that ministers often paid heed to them. Certainly this account of prominent features of British culture is compatible with the argument that popular beliefs and behaviors contributed to Britain's aggressive policy regarding the defense and acquisition of North American territories before and during the Seven Years' War. Kathleen Wilson provides a strong summary expression of this view: "Politically, ideologically and materially, the [Seven Years'] war thus enhanced the potency of that heady brew of empire, liberty and national aggrandizement that had been avidly consumed by large portions of the political public since the Vernon agitation. The ministry's orchestration of these well-entrenched sensibilities was evinced not least in the pursuit of an aggressive and expansionist policy in the New World and in the public, if not private, emphasis on the primacy of colonial over Continental campaigns."[32] (Jonathan Dull's essay offers a somewhat different assessment of these issues, agreeing on the unusual importance of public opinion in Britain in general but questioning the extent of its influence on British governmental conduct during the earliest phase of the Seven Years' War.)

Role of Strategic and Economic Considerations

Having laid out the pertinent points of the recent cultural histories, the question at issue becomes the extent to which they can contribute to an explanation of Britain's mid-eighteenth-century transition to a more territorially oriented empire.

One limitation of the recent cultural histories in this regard springs from the sources they have relied upon and the topics they have emphasized. For the most part, in the works discussed in this essay, scholars have examined British cultural issues quite broadly and have based their investigations on the kinds of public sources that shed light on popular beliefs: newspapers, pamphlets, works of literary and visual art, accounts of performances and demonstrations. It is entirely possible, even logically probable, that the sentiments of the British populace visible in these sources shaped the decisions of the British ministers, officials, and diplomats who articulated and implemented British imperial policy. To be certain, however, more close analyses of the ways in which the actions of key figures responded to their perceptions of public opinion are necessary. Marie Peters's work on William Pitt provides a good model for the kind of investigation that could be fruitfully pursued for other British officials. Such investigations could move the notion of popular beliefs' power to shape imperial events from likely hypothesis to well-grounded argument.

A more significant question concerns the degree to which the recent discussions of British culture are not simply logically compatible with Britain's mid-century imperial transition but logically necessary for an explanation of it. To put it differently, if we were to remove British cultural characteristics from consideration, could we nonetheless find logically sufficient and perhaps more fundamental reasons explaining the decisions that took Britain in the direction of a different kind of empire? The answer appears to be yes. Historical investigations antedating the recent wave of cultural histories make a strong case that the desires of British officials to protect Britain's North American colonies in the mid-1750s and to obtain a lasting and secure peace in North America in the early 1760s provide an adequate explanation for the mid-eighteenth-century changes in the character of the British Empire. These older works suggest that these adjustments of imperial policy were rooted in economic and strategic considerations that would have applied even if British culture had looked very different.

Many of these considerations were animating British policy in both the mid-1750s and early 1760s; some arose only in response to Britain's astonishing run of victories during the latter years of the Seven Years' War: a discussion beginning with and concentrating its efforts on British territorial decisions at the end of the "Great War for Empire" will encompass both sets of concerns.

A significant segment of the British public appears to have craved territorial conquests in the closing years of the Seven Years' War, in part because of a particularly mid-eighteenth-century British public desire to abase the French rival and exalt the British nation. The most prominent consideration in the minds of both British leaders and the British public, however, appears to have been the entirely reasonable and nonculturally specific wish to prevent future Anglo-French wars in North America and to ensure the safety of Britain's colonies on the Atlantic seaboard. Obtaining the vast French territories between the Appalachians and the Mississippi provided a logical way to accomplish this end because it removed potential French threats from the immediate vicinity of Britain's colonies and established clear boundaries between British territories and what British negotiators thought would be a continuing French presence on the other side of the Mississippi.[33]

Notwithstanding the favorable outcome of the war in which the British Empire was currently engaged, British officials in the latter part of the Seven Years' War possessed an abundance of reasons to seek to avoid a future Anglo-French conflict in North America. Though British officials were concerned at the end of the Seven Years' War that the scale of British successes would generate a hostile coalition of European powers, they could not, of course, predict with precision that the combination of French and Spanish forces and British diplomatic isolation would contribute decisively to Britain's defeat in the Revolutionary War. But British ministers and diplomats could see, even amid the torrent of Britain's triumphs late in the Seven Years' War, that any large-scale European and imperial war was a dangerous and uncertain proposition, and that a wise government would seek to avoid circumstances that might drag an unwilling empire into such a war in the future. Although Britain triumphed in the last years of the Seven Years' War, British statesmen were well aware that their empire nearly suffered defeat in the war's first phase: Braddock famously met disaster and death in 1755; Minorca, Oswego, and Calcutta fell in 1756; Fort William Henry followed in 1757; and Britain's Prussian ally Frederick the Great stood in constant danger of being overwhelmed by the French, Austrian, and Russian forces arrayed against him. As Lawrence Henry Gipson, one of the most distinguished historians of the Seven Years' War, put it, "as October 1757 drew to a close, there seemed to be little doubt that the two wars in which France was involved were being won by this nation and its numerous allies."[34] The situation was so grave that at the end of August 1757, William Pitt offered to return Gibraltar to Spain in a desperate attempt to induce that nation to enter the war on Britain's side.[35]

Moreover, even Britain's eventual successes came at an enormous cost. By early 1763, Britain's national debt had reached £146,000,000. During the war itself, when considering the expenses involved in supporting Frederick the

Great and funding British operations in North America, the Duke of New-castle had feared a national financial collapse.[36] Only in the future, when the American colonies resisted imperial attempts to tax them, would the full and disastrous import of the debts incurred during the Seven Years' War become entirely clear; but the danger of an unmanageably large public debt worried British officials well before the Stamp Act crisis. The point is simply that quite apart from an antipathy to French culture and religion, or a desire to affirm British national potency, British officials had good reasons to seek a territorial settlement in North America that would reduce the danger that Britain might be drawn into a future war in which fortune might favor Britain's opponents.

This hope to avoid future Anglo-French wars in North America by secur-ing a solid territorial settlement was evident in numerous public pronounce-ments and in more confidential discussions of peace terms. Colonial security figured prominently among the reasons that Britain allowed itself to become involved in fighting with France in North America in the opening years of the conflict, and it remained central throughout Anglo-French hostilities. British leaders repeatedly highlighted its importance. William Pitt, for ex-ample, having taken power as the nation's leading minister, declared in his inaugural speech of December 2, 1756, that "the succour and preservation of America cannot but constitute a main object of my attention and solicitude." When, after having been dismissed in April, he returned to power in June 1757, Pitt reiterated this statement before Parliament, and he repeated it on numerous occasions thereafter.[37]

Nor were such sentiments confined to Pitt and to Pitt's years in office. A debate that took place in Britain during the latter years of the Seven Years' War illustrates the centrality of this concern for colonial security and the way in which it was shaping British policy. The succession of British victories in 1759 and the years that followed put Britain in a position to de-mand significant concessions from France in peace negotiations. This raised the question of which French territories Britain should ask for; British pamphleteers sought to provide an answer. Between 1759 and 1763, no less than sixty-five British pamphlets discussed the specific question of whether Britain should demand that France yield Canada or the Caribbean island of Guadeloupe. The positions taken by various figures during the controversy are a valuable indication of some of the ideas roiling British opinion in the 1750s and early 1760s.[38]

A cluster of the factions and individuals powerful in British politics of the time preferred the continent to the island. Pitt came ultimately to favor the retention of conquered Canada to the acquisition of Guadeloupe. Early in the Canada-Guadeloupe debate, the court faction grouped around George III and led by the Earl of Bute pledged itself to support the acquisition of both the St. Lawrence and Mississippi valleys. George Grenville (he held a variety of posts, and was, for example, the secretary of state for the Northern Department from May 1762; he went on to become first lord of the Treasury) and his supporters also supported keeping Canada, as well as obtaining Louisiana. Other powerful figures such as James Morton, Earl of Douglas; the prominent London alderman Sir William Baker; and the seasoned diplomat the Earl of Chesterfield, wanted to acquire large tracts of French territory in North America to ensure the safety of the coastal colonies. In March 1762, Newcastle, Hardwicke, and the Duke of Devonshire supported the acceptance of France's August 1761 offer of Canada.[39]

In fact, as some of the references in the previous paragraph suggest, referring to the discussions of what territories Britain should demand from France as the Canada-Guadeloupe debate is somewhat misleading. The possibilities at stake were broader than reference to Canada and Guadeloupe alone indicates. France, for example, possessed other sugar islands, such as Martinique, and other North American territories, such as Louisiana, that Britain could ask for. For similar reasons, as Britain opted for Canada over Guadeloupe, it also preferred continental eastern Louisiana to Caribbean Martinique.[40]

What is significant here is that the objective of a secure peace settlement which would prevent future war appeared repeatedly in discussions of these possible territorial acquisitions. An October 14, 1760, Newcastle memorandum for the king, for example, indicated that William Baker felt "The Keeping Canada the most necessary for preserving The Peace; which cannot be done, whilst Canada, & Those Parts, are divided between Two Rival Powers, England and France, as the Indians will always be stir'd up one against the other." An unsigned April 13, 1761, "Memoir on Terms of Peace" advocated British acquisition of Louisiana and warned that without such an acquisition, "the possession of Louisiana will give the French the same means of encroaching upon our settlements of Georgia, Carolina & Virginia, as they had & exercised before the warr on the provinces of Pensilvania, Newyork, New England & Nova Scotia." Similarly, on June 15, 1761, the Earl of Morton wrote to Hardwicke that "I dont imagine we should people that immense Tract [eastern Louisiana] in Ten Centurys but unless we have the name of the whole we shall never be at rest in those parts that are peopled while the smallest Germ of French Government subsists from the Gulf of Mexico to Hudsons Bay. . . . we see what Disturbances a handful of Frenchmen have given us to the Southward by stirring up the Creeks and other Nations in those parts. . . . Upon the whole I think we should listen to no Terms of

Accommodation unless the French will agree to make an entire Cession of all their Claims and Possessions upon the Continent of North America from their Southermost to their Northermost limits." Security concerns pushed British officials to acquire both Canada and eastern Louisiana, the advantages of obtaining Canada being vitiated, for example, should a potentially hostile French presence remain between the Mississippi and the Appalachians. Hardwicke wrote to Newcastle on April 2, 1762, for example, that "The most material Argumt for retaining Canada has been the delivering your Northern Colonies from such bad Neighbours, & from the danger of French Encroachmts for the future; but some persons have thought That could never be securely attain'd witht conquering Louisiana also."[41]

Experiences during the Seven Years' War itself had given British officials ample reason for these kinds of concerns about the danger posed by a French presence in the vicinity of Britain's southern colonies. Lieutenant Governor Ellis of Georgia, Governor Lyttelton and Lieutenant Governor Bull of South Carolina, and Governor Dobbs of North Carolina had complained repeatedly to Pitt of French provocation of Indian attacks on their territories. Dobbs urged Pitt to drive the French off the North American continent, this being the only effectual means of ensuring that the southern colonies would be spared future Franco-Indian attacks; it would have the added benefit of giving Britain total commercial dominance in North America north of Mexico. Dobbs spoke on January 21, 1760, for example of his colony's "strong hopes that the Conquest of Mississippi and Mobile wou'd follow the Conquest of Canada which can only secure the future peace of these Southern Provinces, which will prevent any future American Wars with the French, and upon opening the Hudson Bay Trade will give us the whole Trade of the Northern Continent to Mexico."[42]

Others with a personal interest in Britain's North American colonies shared the views of governors such as Dobbs. Benjamin Franklin provided one of the clearest and best-known statements of concern about future French threats to the British colonies in the 1760 pamphlet "The Interest of Great Britain Considered, With Regard to Her Colonies and the Acquisitions of Canada and Guadeloupe." Franklin favored British annexation of both Canada and eastern Louisiana. Should France regain Canada and retain eastern Louisiana, he worried about future French encroachments on the territory of the British colonies and about continued French instigation of Indian raids. Franklin observed further that unless Anglo-French territorial limits were clearly delineated, a peace treaty with all its good intentions could not prevent a long and contested Anglo-French boundary in North America from providing future causes for a war that might once again spread from the

New World to the Old. (It should be remembered that British citizens and officials did not know that France was going to cede trans-Mississippi Louisiana to Spain in November 1762, and they therefore assumed that there would still be some kind of French presence in North America even if Britain acquired eastern Louisiana and Canada.) In such a war, British forces would have to repeat their bloody and expensive attempts to conquer Canada. If, in contrast, Britain held Canada and eastern Louisiana, Britain's colonies would be absolutely secure. The Indians would be dependent on the British for trade goods and would lack the European ally that had supported their attacks. France would no longer be able to reach Britain's American colonies and, consequently, Britain would not have to employ in colonial defense troops that could be more profitably used elsewhere.

Officials in Britain seem to have agreed with the ideas of Franklin and the British colonial governors. They saw that extending British territory to the Mississippi would not only move the French far from British possessions on the Atlantic, it would also provide a sharply defined boundary between the North American territories of the two nations. As mentioned earlier, Pitt had been especially concerned about establishing clear boundaries for the British colonies, though his initial ideas of what these would be were fairly modest. Numerous documentary references attest to the continued importance of such boundaries for his successors. Bute wrote to Bedford on May 1, 1762, for example, that "to prevent all future disputes, the Mississippi should be the boundary between the two nations."[43] Commenting on the proposal that the Mississippi River constitute the line of demarcation between British and French possessions in North America, the Earl of Egremont (secretary of state for the Southern Department and thus one of the key British officials conducting relations with France) wrote on July 10, 1762, that the British object "was not to draw any advantage from the extension of our territory into a country a great part of which is waste, and which we shall probably never clear nor people. It was to reëstablish peace on solid and lasting foundations and to forestall all disputes respecting the boundaries of the two nations on the American Continent."[44] In short, British statesmen hoped that the westward expansion of British territorial dominion would free Britain from future North American entanglements.

There is nothing surprising about an empire's desire to protect its overseas possessions and subjects from attack, particularly in the latter years of a war whose immediate causes lay on the poorly protected frontiers of those colonies, a war that Britain had begun so disastrously and conducted so expensively. It may be worthwhile, nonetheless, to consider some of the reasons why British ministers in the 1750s and early 1760s had become especially concerned about the security of these particular colonies. One of these reasons was the growing importance of Britain's North American colonies as markets for British goods. The historian George Louis Beer wrote in 1907 that the 1763 Treaty of Paris marked a "turning-point" in the colonial policy of the British Empire inasmuch as the colonies were important thereafter primarily as markets for British manufactures rather than as suppliers of raw materials and agricultural products.[45] One finds numerous documentary references to these American markets. Pitt believed in the "importance of America" as a market for British goods, speaking of it as "a double market, the market of consumption and the market of supply." Pulteney, the aged Earl of Bath who had become famous as leader of the opposition to Walpole, argued strongly for the British retention of conquered Canada. He contended that it was essential to keep Canada so as to avoid leaving the foundation for another Anglo-French war that would jeopardize again Britain's valuable North American possessions, and he stressed the economic value of the populous British continental colonies as markets for the manufactures of Great Britain. Other authors, such as John Douglas (a follower of the Earl of Bath and later the Bishop of Salisbury), echoed these arguments about the importance of the continental colonies as future markets for British goods, and therefore the importance of ensuring their security.[46]

Economic developments promoted such sentiments. Up until about the middle of the eighteenth century, prevailing mercantilist sentiments held that the ideal British colony produced staple commodities and raw materials that were not found in England and that were not competitive with the products of the mother country. The sugar islands of the West Indies, and, to a lesser extent, the southern colonies of North America, furnished models of such colonies. Jamaica, for example, produced a commodity, sugar, that England could not produce for itself. Without its own colonial supply of sugar, Britain could obtain the commodity only by enriching an imperial rival such as France. Moreover, because no producers of sugar existed in the British Isles, no domestic interest groups existed to complain about competition from Britain's colonists. Furthermore, if British colonies concentrated on the production of export crops such as sugar, rather than on the production of a variety of goods for local use, they would also serve as markets for British manufactures and agricultural produce. To this way of thinking, the northern and middle colonies seemed far less desirable possessions. Instead of tropical commodities not found in the British Isles, they generated products such as wheat, fish, and even ships that England produced itself, and constituted, therefore, potential rivals for England's farmers and manufacturers.

Beginning in the middle decades of the eighteenth century, however, a change in ideas about colonial value become evident in Britain. Over the course of this century, England was becoming increasingly a manufacturing rather than an agricultural nation. By 1763, England was, for example, no longer a regular exporter of wheat, and England became a net importer of foodstuffs sometime after the Seven Years' War. In contrast, British exports of manufactures were growing substantially, with the bulk of the increase going to consumers in America, Africa, and Asia, rather than to traditional markets in Europe, which were difficult to penetrate because of tariffs and other barriers. Woolen cloth was by far England's most significant industrial activity and export, but exports of other textiles, hardware, leather goods, and a variety of other products were also growing. As English manufacturing production grew, its manufacturers and the middlemen who made fortunes selling their products abroad grew increasingly interested in finding new markets for British goods. Limited space and plantation agriculture limited the populations and thus the market potential of the islands of the West Indies, but the continental North American colonies were large and their populations were already growing at a phenomenal rate. The population of the British West Indies went from roughly 147,000 in 1700 to about 330,000 in 1750; that of the British mainland colonies from 265,000 to 1.2 million. Relative rates of export growth to these areas reflected their different rates of population increase. Annual exports of English home produce and manufactures to the West Indies went from £205,000 in 1700 to £449,000 in 1750; to the thirteen colonies from £256,000 to £971,000. As a result, thousands of Britons in ports like Manchester, Bristol, and Liverpool drew income from trade with the colonies and invested in ships bound for them, and market-oriented thinkers found their attention drawn away from the Caribbean and toward the expanding colonies of North America's Atlantic seaboard.[47]

Economic developments of this nature were mentioned earlier in this essay to show the way in which matters of pounds and pence could reinforce popular dislike for the cultural and commercial rival France. What is important to note here, however, is that considerations of the economic importance of the British North American colonies and therefore of the importance of protecting them would in all likelihood have exercised a considerable influence upon British officials even had Britons been less averse to French culture and less uneasy about the state of British masculine vigor. Mercantilist imperatives played upon official minds in all the great European imperial powers, regardless of whether the predominant imperial culture was British, French, Spanish, Portuguese, or Dutch.

In fact, one way to elucidate the importance of these distinctively British cultural issues is to look briefly at the policies of some of Britain's rivals. Such a comparison is immediately suggestive. It is certainly true that Britain aggressively defended its claims in contested regions of North America, such as the Ohio Valley and Acadia, and that prominent features of British culture contributed to a popular climate that supported such pugnacity. But on the other side of those disputes stood a French Empire with a significantly different national culture and with different, and perhaps less satisfactory ways for popular opinion to influence governmental decisions, and this French Empire pursued a course of action as belligerent as Britain's. Similarly, at the end of the Seven Years' War, the fortunes of war and the vagaries of French diplomacy put Spain in a position to receive from France those portions of Louisiana lying west of the Mississippi, as Britain was receiving the lands to the east of the river. Spain, like France, a nation and empire with a culture and political system quite different from Britain's, also chose to acquire large tracts of the North American hinterland, and also hoped to secure a peace settlement that would protect its vulnerable American colonies from future hostilities. Such observations are in no way meant to deny the potential importance of cultural issues in shaping imperial policy.[48] But they do suggest that we should perhaps be directing investigation of the territorial transfers at the end of the Seven Years' War and the bellicose maneuvers that began the conflict to include consideration of the conditions that brought Britain, France, and Spain together, rather than focusing uniquely on the factors that distinguished them.

National Cultures and State System

In fact, if one considers the interrelated acts of the British, French, and Spanish governments, and if one examines the full range of popular and official concerns within these empires as discussed by both recent and past historians, it appears that the most basic phenomenon, the underlying issue that most usefully enriches understanding of Britain's imperial transformation, was Britain's inclusion within the competitive European state system of the mid-eighteenth century.[49] A number of the features of this period of international relations merit particular mention here. First of these was international anarchy, in the sense that no power or effective system of law stood above the nations of Europe and could dictate or mediate resolutions of their conflicts; only their own force, guile, and diplomacy could do so. Related to this anarchic context was the essentially individualistic orientation of state policy. Though the many western European nations seem to have felt a general sense of belonging to a common European culture, they swore allegiance to no overarching body or binding league. The "egotisms of the individual states" drove events, not the collective actions of a cohesive community. One consequence of this anarchy and this state selfishness was that "a general feeling of insecurity of territorial possession" shaped the conduct of foreign relations: The Habsburgs might hold Silesia one year, for example, only to find that Frederick the Great had conquered it in the next. States could only count on keeping what they could protect from their potentially aggressive rivals. Where insecurity and state egotism prevailed, wars were naturally frequent; peace might be desirable, it might even be long-lasting, but its continuance could not be assumed by the wise, only maintained by the wary. Where peace was uncertain and war probable; where states fought as much as they cooperated; where alliances shifted and enmities lingered long or arose unexpectedly; and where territorial acquisitions could bring power, territorial possessions invite aggression, and territorial losses underscore weakness, each state had to be attentive to the distribution of power. Any decline in a state's power relative to that of its potential adversaries was genuinely threatening; any enhancement potentially useful. Finally, and perhaps most crucially for understanding the nature of the imperial rivalry of France and Britain, within this world of jostling and competing states and empires economic vitality was seen as the foundation of state power. Consequently the sources of national and imperial wealth needed to be developed and protected; the springs that fed the wealth of rivals diverted, seized, or sullied.

These general features of European international relations illuminate phenomena discussed above. It was not just that Britons dependent on colonial trades found their preexisting hostility to French culture accentuated by the economic threat of French competition; it was that these feelings were an entirely logical response to the character of the particular international system in which both empires operated. Economic interest groups within innumerable historical contexts have feared the loss of business to their rivals. What made this context special was the tight connection thought to exist between economic well-being and state power. It is one thing when a rival steals the key customer, supplies the lucrative market, or buys up the best raw materials, and then uses the profits to build a nicer house and wear fancier clothes: irritating, but not existentially threatening. It is quite another matter when an imperial rival uses economic gains to acquire the tools of state power for the purpose of seizing the sources of national wealth and thereby fundamentally altering economic circumstances in its favor. This was the course of action that mid-eighteenth-century Britain and France feared where they had to and followed where they could. The British Empire opened, expanded, and protected imperial markets and sources of supply for its subjects; it tried to exclude the subjects of other empires from these markets. To the extent that Britain was successful, its imperial power grew, thereby providing the means to acquire further economic advantages, and its subjects prospered. On the other hand, France was naturally fearful of the gains of its rival and tried to take economic assets from it and to exclude British subjects from enjoying their profits. So long as both empires perceived the absolute economic gains of the other as dangerous, they had reason to try to undercut their rival's economic welfare. Under these conditions, Britons had every reason to oppose French imperial aims, to detest the French subjects who sustained French power, and to band together as Britons to support British imperial expansion. The competitive nature of the state system in which both France and Britain existed thus helps to explain both the cultural animosities highlighted by recent historians and the official economic concerns emphasized by an earlier generation of scholars.

Similarly, both the British public and British officials in the early and mid-1750s fretted about an apparent increase in French power and apparently aggressive French conduct in North America because rising state power often facilitated and encouraged expansionism, and because territorial encroachments constituted a usual feature of the international relations of the period. Toward the end of the war, the British public sought to despoil the French Empire and British officials to fashion a secure peace settlement for their colonies precisely because the anarchic character of the competitive state system meant that future wars could be expected unless vigorous measures were taken to forestall them either by rendering the colonies too well-protected to invite attack or the French Empire too weak to contemplate aggression. Both ministers in power and people on the British street were responding to the nature of European state and imperial competition, to conditions within what Jonathan Dull refers to as the "jungle of eighteenth-century diplomacy."

Such an assertion in no way diminishes the achievements of the recent generation of cultural historians, but it does point to the importance of earlier works by historians such as Walter Dorn, F. H. Hinsley, and Patrice Higonnet which described and analyzed Europe's state system.

It points, moreover, to another type of question. Ernest Gellner once hypothesized that the dictates of national economic units force modern educational systems toward a national orientation, and that this in turn forms a basis in common experiences and common attitudes for nationalism itself. Linda Colley and Gerald Newman note in their discussions of British and English national identities that some form of nationalism appeared to be developing in other parts of Europe, such as France, at roughly the same time.[50] This essay has suggested that because the subjects of states often gained or lost as a national body, they had reason to think in terms of national unity. With such notions in mind, we might ask if the demands of state competition among the different political entities of mid-eighteenth-century Europe were not in fact contributing to the formation of national sentiments among the peoples living within these units; if that is, national culture was not arising in part in response to international structures.

Notes

1. "An Introduction to the Political State of Great Britain," in *Political Writings*, Donald J. Greene, ed. (New Haven, CT: Yale University Press, 1977), 147–48.

2. *Proceedings and Debates of the British Parliaments Respecting North America, 1754–1783*, R. C. Simmons and P. D. G. Thomas, eds. (Millwood, NY: Kraus International Publications, 1982), 422–23.

3. For classic descriptions of this transition, see Charles M. Andrews, *The Colonial Background of the American Revolution*, rev. ed. (New Haven, CT: Yale University Press, 1924), 123–26; George Louis Beer, *British Colonial Policy, 1754–1765* (New York: Macmillan, 1907), 139–40, 155; Lawrence Henry Gipson, *The Triumphant Empire: The Empire Beyond the Storm, 1770–1776* (New York: Alfred A. Knopf, 1967), 181–82. For recent discussions, see Daniel Baugh, "Maritime Strength and Atlantic Commerce: The Uses of 'a Grand Marine Empire,'" in *An Imperial State at War: Britain from 1689 to 1815*, Lawrence Stone, ed. (London: Routledge, 1994), 185–86, 201–3; Jeremy Black, *America or Europe? British Foreign Policy, 1739–1763* (London: UCL Press, 1998), 149; Eliga H. Gould, *The Persistence of Empire: British Political Culture in the Age of the American Revolution* (Chapel Hill: University of North Carolina Press, 2000), 58; Steven G. Greiert, "The Board of Trade and Defense of the Ohio Valley, 1748–1753," *Western Pennsylvania Historical Magazine* 64 (1981): 1–2, 6; Bob Harris, *Politics and the Nation: Britain in the Mid-Eighteenth Century* (Oxford: Oxford University Press, 2002), 4; P. J. Marshall, "Britain and the World in the Eighteenth Century: I, Reshaping the Empire," in *"A Free though Conquering People": Eighteenth-Century Britain and its Empire* (Aldershot, Hampshire, Great Britain: Ashgate Publishing Limited, 2003), 4–5, 9; Timothy J. Shannon, *Indians and Colonists at the Crossroads of Empire: The Albany Congress of 1754* (Ithaca, NY: Cornell University Press, 2000), 57–61, 65–72, 79–82; Kathleen Wilson, "Empire of Virtue: The Imperial Project and Hanoverian Culture, c. 1720–1785," in *An Imperial State at War*, 144. Note that Wilson begins her period of imperial transformation in 1739, earlier than the other authors.

4. For the fundamental discussion of this imperial initiative, see Jack Greene, "An Uneasy Connection: An Analysis of the Preconditions of the American Revolution," in *Essays on the American Revolution*, Stephen G. Kurtz and James H. Hutson,

eds. (Chapel Hill: University of North Carolina Press, 1973). For an astute recent analysis of one event pertaining to it, see Shannon, *Indians and Colonists*, 52–82.

5. By eastern Louisiana, I mean those portions of the French colony lying between the Mississippi and the Appalachians. At the same time that the British government was acquiring territories in North America, the British East India Company assumed a set of territorial and revenue rights in India; by 1765, it exercised direct rule over the province of Bengal. While these Indian acquisitions are related to British territorial expansion in America, the reasons for and consequences of them are sufficiently distinct to justify separate treatment. This chapter will focus, therefore, on North America alone. On British activities in India, see P. J. Marshall, "The British in Asia: Trade to Dominion, 1700–1765," in *The Eighteenth Century*, ed. P. J. Marshall (Oxford: Oxford University Press, 1998), 498–503; Marshall, "Britain and the World in the Eighteenth Century: I," 12–13.

6. Rouillé to Duras, Feb. 25, 1755, in French Archives des Affaires Étrangères, Correspondance Politique, Espagne, 517, 154–55: "One need only cast ones eyes on a map to be left with no doubt about the designs of England. The territory of the Ohio which forms the subject of the current discussions does not approach in value the amount that the court of London is expending on armaments, and the nation would not pardon the ministry for engaging in a war of which all the advantage was limited to a portion of a barren and wild country where it is not possible to establish a lucrative commerce. The supposed rights to the Ohio are nothing but a mask artificially contrived to cover the true objective intended. It is at the possessions of Spain that the English wish to arrive. [Nos possessions en Amerique sont elles l'unique objet de la jalousie, de l'ambition et de la cupidité des Anglois?. . . Il n'y a quà jetter les yeux sur une carte géographique pour ne laisser aucun doute sur les vues de l'Angleterre. Le territoire de la belle riviere qui fait le sujet des discussions actuelles, ne vaut pas à beaucoup près la dépense que la Cour de Londres fait pour ses Armemens, et la Nation ne pardonneroit pas au Ministère de l'engager dans une guerre dont tout l'avantage se borneroit à une portion du pays stérile et désert, où il n'est pas possible d'établir un commerce intéressant. Les prétendus droits sur l'Ohio ne sont qu'un masque artificialement imaginé pour couvrir le véritable but qu'on se propose.]"

7. Samuel Johnson, "Thoughts on the Late Transactions Respecting Falkland's Islands," in *Political Writings*, 373.

8. See Fred Anderson, *Crucible of War: The Seven Years' War and the Fate of Empire in British North America, 1754–1756* (New York: Knopf, 2000), 565–71.

9. Black, *America or Europe?*, 162–63; Samuel Johnson, "Review of Lewis Evans," in *Political Writings*, 210–11; Anthony Pagden, *Lords of All the World: Ideologies of Empire in Spain, Britain, and France, c. 1500–1800* (New Haven, CT: Yale University Press, 1995), 108–9.

10. See especially Linda Colley, *Britons: Forging the Nation, 1707–1837* (New Haven, CT: Yale University Press, 1992), 109.

11. Bedford was British secretary of state for the Southern Department from 1748 to 1751 and British plenipotentiary to France during the final phase of the negotia-

tions of the Peace of Paris. Anderson, *Crucible of War*, 479–84; Zenab Esmat Rashed, *The Peace of Paris, 1763* (Liverpool: University Press of Liverpool, 1951), 118, 161, 167, 174; Max Savelle, *The Origins of American Diplomacy: The International History of Anglo-America, 1492–1763* (New York: Macmillan, 1967), 490, 500, 502, 505.

12. Clarence Walworth Alvord, *The Mississippi Valley in British Politics: A Study of the Trade, Land Speculation, and Experiments in Imperialism Culminating in the American Revolution* (Cleveland, OH: The Arthur H. Clark Company, 1917), vol. 1, 59–60; Beer, *British Colonial Policy,*171–73; Harris, *Politics and the Nation*, 145.

13. Walter Dorn, *Competition for Empire* (New York: Harper Torchbooks, 1963); F. H. Hinsley, *Power and the Pursuit of Peace: Theory and Practice in the History of Relations between States* (London: Cambridge University Press, 1963).

14. Gerald Newman, *The Rise of English Nationalism: A Cultural History, 1740–1830* (New York: St. Martin's Press, 1987), 63–73. See also Jeremy Black, "Ideology, History, Xenophobia and the World of Print in Eighteenth-Century England," in *Culture, Politics and Society in Britain, 1660–1800*, Jeremy Black and Jeremy Gregory, eds. (Manchester: Manchester University Press, 1991), 199–200.

15. Newman, *Rise of English Nationalism*, 74–6.

16. Black, "Ideology, History, Xenophobia," 191–94; Colley, *Britons*, 19–29, 57; Harris, *Politics and the Nation*, 124.

17. Colley, *Britons*, 26, 76, 83–84, 92–94; Harris, *Politics and the Nation*, 122, 237, 246–47; Bob Harris, "War, Empire, and the 'National Interest' in Mid-Eighteenth-Century Britain," in *Britain and America Go to War: The Impact of War and Warfare in Anglo-America, 1754–1815*, Julie Flavell and Stephen Conway, eds. (Gainesville: University Press of Florida, 2004), 14, 16, 18, 30; Kathleen Wilson, "Empire of Virtue: The Imperial Project and Hanoverian Culture, c. 1720–1785," in *An Imperial State at War*, 129, 132, 144, 154; Wilson, *Sense of the People*, 178. Jeremy Black notes that some of the vigor and alarm of these press accounts derived from an attempt by opponents of the ruling ministry to discredit it for failing to protect Britain's national interest. See Black's *Natural and Necessary Enemies: Anglo-French Relations in the Eighteenth Century* (London: Duckworth, 1986), 57.

18. Colley, *Britons*, 74–76; Gould, *Persistence of Empire*, 66; Shannon, *Indians and Colonists*, 57–60. See also Stephen Conway, "War and National Identity in the Mid-Eighteenth-Century British Isles," *English Historical Review* 116 (Sept. 2001): 893.

19. John Brown, *An Estimate of the Manners and Principles of the Times* (London, 1757), 30, 67, 91, 140, 209; Harris, *Politics and the Nation*, 123–24; Newman, *Rise of English Nationalism*, 80–83; Wilson, "Empire of Virtue," 137, 141, 145–46; Wilson, *Sense of the People*, 185–88.

20. Quotation is from Marie Peters, *Pitt and Popularity: The Patriot Minister and London Opinion during the Seven Years' War* (Oxford: Oxford University Press, 1980), 209, (see also 164 and 245 in the same volume); Alvord, *Mississippi Valley in British Politics*, 48–49; Julian S. Corbett, *England in the Seven Years' War: A Study in Combined Strategy* (London: Longmans, Green, and Co., 1907), vol. 1, 373–74; Nicholas Rogers, *Whigs and Cities: Popular Politics in the Age of Walpole and Pitt* (Oxford:

Clarendon Press, 1989), 94–95, 104, 110, 115–16, 120–21; Wilson, "Empire of Virtue," 133, 144–45, 150; Wilson, *Sense of the People*, 178–79. It should be noted that Bob Harris has questioned the existence of this British interest in acquiring large tracts of overseas territory, taking particular aim at "Wilson's claims about imperial expansion as a cry of popular opinion" (Harris, *Politics and the Nation*, 117, 126); Harris, "'American Idols'": Empire, War, and the Middling Ranks in Mid-Eighteenth Century Britain," *Past and Present* 150 (Feb. 1996): 138–39; Harris, "War, Empire, and the 'National Interest'"). At present, I find Wilson's claims more persuasive, primarily because Harris, although he repeatedly displays a truly impressive knowledge of the sources for mid-eighteenth-century British imperial history, asserts the contrary without, in my view, adequately addressing the specific evidence on which Wilson bases her conclusion. I would like to see Harris explain in greater detail, for example, why we should not consider the numerous addresses, newspapers, pamphlets, and demonstrations calling for the retention of conquered overseas territories as an indication of popular British interest in imperial expansion.

21. Newman goes on to mention that the new popular politics also suggested that "England's vital affairs were in the hands of hardened Francophiles, addicted by both taste and fashion to the superiority of the national enemy." Newman, *Rise of English Nationalism*, 169. See also Alvord, *Mississippi Valley in British Politics*, vol. 1, 48–49; Harris, *Politics and the Nation*, 145; Peters, *Pitt and Popularity*, 165–67.

22. The famous Horace Walpole quotation appears in Rogers, *Whigs and Cities*, 110. See also Harris, "'American Idols,'" 115–18; Harris, *Politics and the Nation*, 113–14; Peters, *Pitt and Popularity*, 125–27; N. V. Russell, "Reaction in England and America to the Capture of Havana, 1762." *Hispanic American Historical Review* 9 (Aug. 1929): 303–15; Wilson, *Sense of the People*, 196–98.

23. Mr. Rigby to the Duke of Bedford, Aug. 27, 1761, in *Correspondence of John, Fourth Duke of Bedford* (London: Longman, Brown, Green, and Longmans, 1846), vol. 3, 43; Pamphlet quoted in Alvord, *Mississippi Valley in British Politics*, vol. 1, 61.

24. Wilson, *Sense of the People*, 195, 197, 201–3. See also Harris, "'American Idols,'" 119–20; Wilson, "Empire of Virtue," 137, 141, 145–46, 155–56.

25. Peters, *Pitt and Popularity*, 3–4, 16–21.

26. Peters, *Pitt and Popularity*, 3; Rogers, *Whigs and Cities*, 127–28.

27. Wilson, *Sense of the People*, 185.

28. Peters, *Pitt and Popularity*, 46–62; Rogers, *Whigs and Cities*, 95–104; Wilson, *Sense of the People*, 180–85.

29. Hardwicke quoted in Theodore Calvin Pease, ed., *Anglo-French Boundary Disputes in the West, 1749–1763* (Springfield: Illinois State Historical Library), 289. For additional primary material, see Pease, *Anglo-French Boundary Disputes*, 286–87; Philip C. Yorke, *The Life and Correspondence of Philip Yorke, Earl of Hardwicke*, vol. 3 (Cambridge: Cambridge University Press, 1913), 245, 313–15. For secondary discussions of Pitt, see Jeremy Black, *Pitt the Elder* (Cambridge: Cambridge University Press, 1992), 192–93; Corbett, *England in the Seven Years' War*, vol. 1, 374–75, vol. 2, 141–43; Richard Middleton, *The Bells of Victory: The Pitt-Newcastle Ministry and*

the Conduct of the Seven Years' War, 1757–1762 (Cambridge: Cambridge University Press, 1985), 22, 135, 183–84, 211–12; Richard Pares, *War and Trade in the West Indies, 1739–1763* (Oxford: Clarendon Press, 1936), 186, 224; Peters, *Pitt and Popularity*, 167–69, 196; Marie Peters, "The Myth of William Pitt, Earl of Chatham, Great Imperialist: Part I: Pitt and Imperial Expansion, 1738–1763," *Journal of Imperial and Commonwealth History* 21 (Jan. 1993): 31–74; Marie Peters, *The Elder Pitt* (Harlow, Essex: Addison Wesley Longman Limited, 1998), 115–16, 118–19; Rogers, *Whigs and Cities*, 126–28; Jack M. Sosin, *Whitehall and the Wilderness: The Middle West in British Colonial Policy, 1760–1775* (Lincoln: University of Nebraska Press, 1961), 6–9; Basil Williams, *The Life of William Pitt, Earl of Chatham* (London: Longmans, Green, and Co., 1914), vol. 2, 77–78, 83–84. Opinion about the timing and nature of Pitt's intentions is divided. Corbett argued that the "conquest of Canada and the expulsion of France from North America" was a "dominant note" of Pitt's plans in autumn 1758. Corbett contended further that by the end of 1760, Pitt wanted to crush France so completely that it would not be able to restore its naval power. Black sees Pitt as willing to return Louisbourg in negotiations in late 1759 but as seeking "to retain the whole of Canada" in February 1760. Peters avers that by April 1760, Pitt "was probably beginning to contemplate more far-reaching demands in America" and that his terms for peace had "hardened" by May 1761; Williams sees Pitt making up his mind to retain much of Canada by December 1760; Sosin places Pitt's decision some months later; Middleton in April 1761. I should point out, following a discussion with one of the other contributors to this book, Jonathan Dull, that Pitt's changing territorial demands can also be seen as a pragmatic response to the changing circumstances of the war. Independent of popular opinion, Pitt may simply have asked for more from France as British military victories made it possible for him to do so.

30. Wilson, *Sense of the People*, 11–12, 29–31, 34–40, 65–67, 71.

31. Nuthall to Lady Chatham, Nov. 12, 1761, in William Stanhope Taylor and John Henry Pringle, eds., *Correspondence of William Pitt, Earl of Chatham* (London: John Murray, 1838), vol. 2, 166–68; Corbett, *England in the Seven Years' War*, vol. 2, 213, 353–54; Pares, *War and Trade in the West Indies*, 609; Peters, *Pitt and Popularity*, 5; Rogers, *Whigs and Cities*, 14, 25–31, 53–54, 127–28.

32. Wilson, *Sense of the People*, 193.

33. British diplomats, such as the Duke of Bedford, began by December 1762 to suspect that France had ceded trans-Mississippi Louisiana to Spain, but these suspicions arose after Britain's November 3 acceptance of preliminary peace proposals. See Bedford to Egremont, Dec. 24, 1762, *Correspondence of John, Fourth Duke of Bedford*, vol. 3, 180.

34. Lawrence Henry Gipson, *The Great War for the Empire: The Victorious Years, 1758–1760* (New York: Alfred A. Knopf, 1949), 125.

35. Pares, *War and Trade in the West Indies*, 561; Williams, *Life of William Pitt*, vol. 1, 339–40.

36. Anderson, *Crucible of War*, 481, 493, 562.

37. Quotation from Williams, *Life of William Pitt*, vol. 1, 288. See also 312 and 353 in the same volume; Middleton, *Bells of Victory*, 97, 148; Rogers, *Whigs and Cities*, 109–10.

38. Alvord, *Mississippi Valley in British Politics*, vol. 1, 49–78; William L. Grant, "Canada versus Guadeloupe, An Episode of the Seven Years' War," *American Historical Review* 17 (July 1912): 735–43; Philip Lawson, "'The Irishman's Prize': Views of Canada from the British Press, 1760–1774." *Historical Journal* 28 (Sept. 1985): 575–96; L. B. Namier, *England in the Age of the American Revolution* (London: Macmillan, 1930), 317–27; Pares, *War and Trade in the West Indies*, 216–19, 223–26; Sosin, *Whitehall and the Wilderness*, 9–10. It must be admitted that the extent to which these pamphlets influenced government officials is unclear. There are some indications that British statesmen, already committed to the safety of the British colonies, naturally fell into the choice of Canada, which could do more than Guadeloupe to protect British possessions on the continent. For purposes of this essay, the Canada-Guadeloupe controversy is valuable primarily as an indication of the views of a variety of figures interested and involved in British imperial policy.

39. Alvord, *Mississippi Valley in British Politics*, vol. 1, 33, 35–37, 45, 55–58, 70; Sosin, *Whitehall and the Wilderness*, 6–7, 11, 17.

40. Rashed, *Peace of Paris*, 141; Savelle, *Origins of American Diplomacy*, 491–94.

41. Quotations from Pease, *Anglo-French Boundary Disputes*, 286, 291, 302–4, 412.

42. See letters from Pitt, Ellis, Lyttelton, Bull, Dobbs, Atkin, and Amherst, Dec. 10, 1757 to April 28, 1761, in Gertrude Selwyn Kimball, ed., *Correspondence of William Pitt, when Secretary of State, with Colonial Governors and Military and Naval Commissioners in America* (New York: Macmillan, 1906), vol. 1, 129–32, 198–200, 376–77, vol. 2, 37–38, 67, 183–86, 205–6, 245–46, 254–56, 259–60, 268–72, 277–79, 286–87, 300–1, 316–17, 344–47, 420–25.

43. *Correspondence of John, Fourth Duke of Bedford*, vol. 3, 76. The official September 4, 1762, instructions to Bedford for his mission as minister plenipotentiary to France, after telling him to take great pains to establish the center of the Mississippi River as the boundary between the dominions of France and Britain, and to ensure British rights to navigate the Mississippi, stated that ". . . the great object We propose by the limits above described, besides the acquisition of an extended territory, is the establishing a certain, fixed boundary between Our dominions in North America and those of the Most Christian King [Louis XV], which may ascertain beyond all possibility of doubt the respective property of the two Crowns in that part of the world, and which may by that means remove forever the source of those unhappy disputes which always arise from an equivocal and unsettled frontier, and from which the miseries and calamities of the present war have sprung." "Instructions for . . . John, Duke of Bedford . . . Appointed Minister Plenipotentiary to . . . the Most Christian King," Sept. 4, 1762, in Wickham Legg, *British Diplomatic Instructions*, 57. See also "Charles, Earl of Egremont, Secretary of State, to Bedford," Sept. 7, 1762, in same volume, 65.

44. Quoted in Pease, *Anglo-French Boundary Disputes*, 452–53. See also "Egremont's Memoir of June 26, 1762," quoted in Pease, *Anglo-French Boundary Disputes*, 436–37.

45. Alvord, *Mississippi Valley in British Politics*, vol. 1, 56–57; Beer, *British Colonial Policy*, 139, 155. Scholars such as Jack Sosin and Ronald Hyam criticize those emphasizing the importance of economic considerations in Britain's decision to retain Canada and eastern Louisiana at the end of the war. In my view, these critics do not adequately address the evidence on which historians such as Alvord and Beer rest their arguments. See Sosin, *Whitehall and the Wilderness*, 23–24; Ronald Hyam, "Imperial Interests and the Peace of Paris, 1763," in *Reappraisals in British Imperial History*, Ronald Hyam and Ged Martin, eds. (London: Macmillan, 1975).

46. Alvord, *Mississippi Valley in British Politics*, vol. 1, 56–57; Beer, *British Colonial Policy*, 142–43; Pitt quotation in Williams, *Life of William Pitt*, vol. 2, 83.

47. Alvord, *Mississippi Valley in British Politics*, vol. 1, 52; Baugh, "Maritime Strength and Atlantic Commerce," 196, 211; Beer, *British Colonial Policy*, 134–39; Patrick K. O'Brien, "Inseparable Connections: Trade, Economy, Fiscal State, and the Expansion of Empire, 1688–1815," in *The Eighteenth Century*, P. J. Marshall, ed. (Oxford: Oxford University Press, 1998), 53–54, 56, 58, 70–72; Pares, *War and Trade in the West Indies*, 217–18; Jacob M. Price, "The Imperial Economy," in *The Eighteenth Century*, P. J. Marshall, ed. (Oxford: Oxford University Press, 1998), 80, 82, 87, 98, 100–1, 103; Shannon, *Indians and Colonists*, 56, 64–65; Wilson, *Sense of the People*, 56, 158–60.

48. In a different essay I have argued that a set of French and European intellectual developments concerning techniques for evaluating uncharted territories influenced the French decision to cede Western Louisiana to Spain. See "French Geographic Conceptions of the Unexplored American West and the Louisiana Cession of 1762," in *French Colonial Louisiana and the Atlantic World*, Bradley G. Bond, ed. (Baton Rouge: Louisiana State University Press, 2005).

49. For seminal discussions of this state system, see Dorn, *Competition for Empire*, 1–12; Hinsley, *Power and the Pursuit of Peace*, 153–85. Among recent historians of the mid-eighteenth-century British Empire, two who call attention to the importance of the state system are Marie Peters in "The Myth of William Pitt," 56; and Bob Harris in "War, Empire, and the 'National Interest,'" 16, 30. Harris, in particular, in a critique of Kathleen Wilson's work, notes the manner in which rivalry with France shaped British perceptions of empire.

50. Colley, *Britons*, 91–92; Ernest Gellner, *Nations and Nationalism* (Ithaca, NY: Cornell University Press, 1983); Newman, *Rise of English Nationalism*, 162.

~

CHAPTER THREE

Great Power Confrontation or Clash of Cultures? France's War against Britain and Its Antecedents

Jonathan R. Dull

All wars are a clash of cultures. They almost always involve group hatred, and usually they also involve the fear or greed of the general public. Sometimes these emotions can force a government to fight a war it does not want. In 1739, for example, the English public's hatred of Spain chiefly was responsible for a war the ministry of Sir Robert Walpole did not wish, the so-called War of Jenkins' Ear. The English people were outraged by Spanish mistreatment of the crews of British ships in the Caribbean seized on the suspicion of smuggling, Captain Jenkins being the master of one of the ships. To placate the public, the British government forced King Philip V of Spain into a corner, thereby dooming Walpole's hopes for a peaceful resolution of the dispute.[1] The subsequent war lasted for nine years and became so entangled with parallel conflicts in Italy, Germany, and the Low Countries that its causes gradually became forgotten. The issues that had led to war in 1739 were not even mentioned in the peace treaties of 1748. Soon thereafter Britain conceded its right to bring slaves and trade goods to the Spanish Empire. By then the British public's ingrained anti-Catholicism had found a new outlet in its suspicion of another Catholic power, France.

Franco-British relations thus also were affected by public opinion, although its impact was far greater on British foreign policy than it was on French. As Paul Mapp demonstrates so brilliantly, British diplomacy throughout the eighteenth century was influenced not only by the aims of the king, the cabinet, and Parliament, but also by various interest groups and even the prejudices of the public at large. This was unusual. Elsewhere in Europe, except perhaps for the Netherlands, the opinion of the general public was far less influential. Unlike Britain, protected by its navy, the states of the European continent were vulnerable to invasion. Thus in early modern Europe, questions of security were paramount even over the economic interests and religious beliefs of the public. This became evident as early as the Thirty Years' War of 1618 to 1648.[2] That war began chiefly as a religious conflict but ended with Cardinals Richelieu and Mazarin, the successive chief ministers of France, helping the Protestant princes of Germany against their Catholic overlord, the Holy Roman Emperor. Thereafter it was clear that *raison d'état* or reason of state dictated the actions of the rulers of Europe. Alliances were made regardless of religion or the wishes of the general public. By the end of the seventeenth century, even the rulers of the Islamic Ottoman Empire had been befriended by France, even if the two states were not quite allies. Reason of state was a euphemism for whatever actions European rulers took out of greed, fear, or suspicion of their neighbors. In this nearly lawless world, many rulers were, of necessity, as ruthless as today's drug lords.[3] It is from this perspective that we need to discuss the so-called French and Indian War of 1754 to 1760 and the interrelated struggle in Europe, the Seven Years' War of 1756 to 1763.

It is customary to regard these wars as part of a century-long conflict between Britain and France, sometimes called by historians the Second Hundred Years' War.[4] This characterization of British-French relations is a misnomer. Relations between the two states were not necessarily hostile in spite of the cultural, social, and religious differences between the average Briton and the average Frenchman. What made the establishment of cordial relations between their countries difficult were the differences between English political culture and the culture of the court of France.

Here, too, the Thirty Years' War was a crucial turning point. France played a major role in preventing Emperors Ferdinand II and Ferdinand III from making a unified, centralized state out of the Holy Roman Empire (which included what today is Germany, Austria, the Czech Republic, Belgium, Luxembourg, Slovenia, and parts of France, Italy, and Croatia). Ferdinand II was successful in imposing substantial political and religious unity on the eastern third of the empire, the hereditary lands of the House of Habsburg, which he ruled as Archduke of Austria. (The Habsburgs also ruled the Kingdom of Hungary which adjoined the Holy Roman Empire.) The potential unification of the entire Holy Roman Empire posed a great risk to French security because Ferdinand II and Ferdinand III were allies of their cousin King Philip

IV of Spain, the head of a collateral branch of the House of Habsburg. Philip ruled not only Spain and its huge overseas empire but also a substantial part of Italy and also Franche Comté (now part of France) and the Spanish Netherlands (today's Belgium, which at that time was nominally a part of the Holy Roman Empire). The Habsburgs had been rivals and often enemies of France for a century and a half. In 1635 France declared war on Spain, which implicitly meant war against the Austrian Habsburgs as well. The following year a Spanish army advanced from the Spanish Netherlands to Corbie, only seventy miles from Paris.[5] Eventually, however, the French prevailed. A peace was concluded in 1648 with the Austrian Habsburgs, leaving the Holy Roman Empire disunited and giving France and its Protestant ally Sweden the right to intervene to prevent its unification. The war with Spain continued, however, and in 1648–1652 a civil war called the Fronde convulsed parts of France. Opponents of the monarchy among the aristocracy and law courts (Parlements) even forced Cardinal Mazarin, the young King Louis XIV, and the Queen Mother to flee Paris. Mazarin eventually restored order and in 1659 made a favorable peace with Spain. As part of the treaty Mazarin arranged the marriage of the twenty-one-year-old Louis XIV to his second cousin, Princess Maria Teresa of Spain. Two years later Mazarin died, and Louis began personally ruling France.[6]

For the next 130 years French court culture would follow the pattern Louis established. His successors, his great-grandson Louis XV and his great-great-great-grandson Louis XVI tried in vain to live up to the standard he set. Ironically in a cultural sense, it was Spain that defeated France. In a number of ways, Louis's style of ruling resembled that of his mother's grandfather, King Philip II of Spain, who had ruled from 1556 to 1598.[7] Not only did Louis learn from his beloved mother rules of kingship established by Philip II, but he had some personal similarities to his great-grandfather. Each was obsessed with ceremony and built a gigantic palace as a symbol of his power (the Escorial and Versailles respectively). Each was renowned for courtesy and industriousness. Each showed great courage in the face of adversity. Each created simultaneously the most powerful army and the most powerful navy in Europe. Each was defeated at sea by the English.

There were important differences between them, however. Philip II was as concerned with the well-being of the Catholic Church as he was with the well-being of Spain. Louis XIV was willing to ally with the Protestant princes of the Holy Roman Empire and the Protestant states of Sweden and the Netherlands in order to defeat his fellow Catholics, the Habsburgs. Louis, in spite of a rather scandalous personal life, was a traditional Catholic who eventually suppressed Protestantism in France, but his chief concerns were the security of France and the strength of the monarchy. Remembering the Fronde, he was obsessed with the threat of anarchy posed by potential rivals among the aristocracy and in the courts. It was partly to overcome this danger that he created a huge army both to overawe potential rivals and to provide patronage. The higher nobility was not so much intimidated as co-opted. Louis provided it wealth and power by allowing it to staff the upper ranks of his army, navy, and bureaucracy. Although Louis was an authoritarian, he was not a tyrant but a traditionalist who preferred ruling by consent.

The creation of an extremely large army also protected France from invasion. Remembering the war against the Habsburgs, Louis sought to expand France's borders to the north and east, particularly against the Spanish Netherlands, which was dangerously close to Paris. In so doing he undertook a series of increasingly large wars which provided employment for his armies, and at least initially increased his prestige and reputation. Ultimately his wars led to financial disaster and public misery and undermined his popularity; it is not coincidental that many of the greatest writers of his reign, such as Molière, Racine, La Bruyère, La Rochefoucauld, La Fontaine, and Fénelon, did not celebrate martial glory but wrote directly or indirectly of man's weaknesses and failings.

Louis's culture of war, Catholic orthodoxy, and state power eventually brought him into conflict with England, whose political culture, although also aggressive and warlike, emphasized trade, wealth, and suspicion of monarchs, even English ones. This hostility toward the French model of government had an even greater impact on English domestic history than it did on the history of English foreign policy. Fear that the Stuart monarchs of England would impose such a French model helped lead both to the execution of King Charles I in 1649 and to the overthrow of his son, King James II, in 1688. This suspicion was all the greater because Charles I was Louis XIV's uncle (he was married to the sister of Louis's father) and James II was his first cousin.

When James was forced into exile in 1688, he was welcomed by Louis and the French court. Louis was all the more anxious to restore his cousin to the English throne because James had been replaced by his daughter Mary and her husband William, Prince of Orange, ruler of the Netherlands and Louis's most bitter enemy. For most of the next twenty-five years England and France were at war, first in the Nine Years' War of 1688–1697 and then in the even more bloody War of the Spanish Succession of 1701–1714. (During the latter England and Scotland were unified, becoming Great Britain.) During his earlier wars, Louis had used brutal methods to achieve extremely limited objectives. In his final war he fought successfully to save the Spanish throne for his grandson Philip, who had inherited it from the previous king (who had died without children of his own). At war's end, however, Spain did have to surrender the Spanish Netherlands and part of Italy to the Austrian Habsburgs, who also were able to defeat the Turks and greatly expand their territory in Hungary, thereby reestablishing themselves as a rival to France.

With the end of the great wars and the death of King Louis XIV in 1715, there arose the possibility of not only better relations between Britain and France, but also of a more secure and peaceful Europe at large. After the death of Louis XIV, power passed to his nephew Philippe, duc d'Orléans, the regent of France, who acted on behalf of his young cousin, the child king Louis XV.[8] Meanwhile with the death of Queen Mary's sister (and William and Mary's successor) Queen Anne, there was a transfer of power in Great Britain, too. Anne's closest Protestant relative was a distant cousin, Elector George of Hanover, a principality in northwest Germany. He became King George I of England. Although he and the duc d'Orléans never met face to face and seem to have been rather suspicious of each other, they had much in common. Both were accomplished former generals. Each had dangerous dynastic rivals, respectively James Edward Stuart, the son of the former king, James II of England, and King Philip V of Spain, the victor in the recent war, who had designs on ruling France too. (He was Louis's uncle.) Finally George I and Philippe of Orléans had a family connection. George's beloved late mother had been the great-aunt of Philippe. When she visited the French court in 1679, she had been amused by her young nephew.[9]

The personal bonds and shared needs of George and Philippe were strong enough to overcome the cultural differences between their countries. Britain and France became allies and soon thereafter something amazing occurred.[10] For the dozen years between 1721 and 1733 Europe was free of war. This was the longest period of peace it had ever known. There even was a primitive forerunner of the United Nations, a system of diplomatic congresses to resolve disputes. A major reason for this prolonged peace was the unwillingness of Britain and France, the two richest states in Europe, to bankroll other states to make war on their behalf. Sadly the alliance and the peace eventually came to an end, partly because of the deaths of George and Philippe. George's son, King George II, lacked his father's wisdom and vision, while Cardinal André-Hercule de Fleury, Louis XV's tutor and chief minister, lost interest in the British alliance once George II began providing diplomatic support to France's old rival Austria.[11] Nevertheless relations between Britain and France remained proper, and Britain remained neutral during the Franco-Austrian war of 1733 to 1735.

The Franco-British alliance ended as it began, with little input from the public of either country. Both Fleury and George's prime minister, Sir Robert Walpole, would have been happy to keep public opinion quiet and see their countries remain at peace. What turned their countries into open enemies? To answer that question we must return to the war of 1739 with which we began this discussion.

The War of Jenkins' Ear was caused not only by the English public's anger at Spain, but also by the hope of Englishmen, particularly merchants, that war would permit Britain to seize Spanish treasure ships or even part of the Spanish Empire. This was a threat to the balance of power in the Caribbean, where Spain, Britain, and France all had colonies. Philip V of Spain had become a French ally a few years earlier; moreover, France did not wish to see Britain, an economic competitor and potential military enemy, become wealthier and hence more powerful. In 1740 Fleury sent most of the French Navy to the Caribbean to help Spain. This help was not needed and the fleet returned to Europe early the following year.[12] War between Britain and France was narrowly averted, but the French government had come to regard the British as aggressive and greedy.

In 1741 the situation was reversed. King Frederick II of Prussia had just invaded Silesia, one of the provinces ruled by Maria Theresa, the new Archduchess of Austria. France was obligated to recognize Maria Theresa's right to inherit the possessions of Austria, but, disregarding the advice of Fleury, King Louis XV decided to attack Austria, too. This attempt to plunder and permanently weaken a rival was popular with the French public, but it was the most serious mistake of Louis's reign.[13]

By joining the war, France helped spread it, as well as reviving British fears of French aggression. Soon Britain was indirectly involved in the war as an auxiliary of Austria. Spain joined the war in hopes of taking Austrian territory in Italy to confer on Philip V's youngest son. By 1743 the French Navy was helping Spain convoy troops to Italy while the French Army was fighting British troops in Germany. Britain and France did not declare war on each other, however, until the following year. During 1744 the French government took a number of actions that poisoned relations with Britain for many decades: it supported the efforts of the Stuarts to regain the English throne,[14] it joined with the Spaniards in attacking the British Mediterranean fleet,[15] it attempted to invade England,[16] and it began the conquest of the Austrian Netherlands, now Belgium, a potential staging point for future invasion attempts. All of these operations failed, except for the last one. Fortunately for France its great general, the comte de Saxe, was able to conquer all of the Austrian Netherlands, to invade its northern neighbor, the United

Provinces of the Netherlands, and to force the Dutch and British to the peace table. In 1748 they signed with France the Treaty of Aix-la-Chapelle; the signatories then forced the other participants in the war to accept its terms. The French returned the Austrian Netherlands to Maria Theresa, while the British government, to the dismay of the public, returned the captured fortress of Louisbourg on Cape Breton Island to the French.[17] France did achieve one major war objective. By keeping Silesia, Prussia so increased its strength that a balance of power was established in Germany between it and Austria, thereby greatly reducing the Austrian threat to France.

To France the decisions taken in 1744 were merely military expedients. To British politicians and the English public, however, they seemed designed to eliminate Britain as a French rival and to destroy British independence. For them, as Mapp notes, France had shown it was still the expansionist, menacing power it had been under Louis XIV. The decisions of 1744 would not soon be forgotten; even when British politicians, such as the Earl of Shelburne in 1782, were amenable to better relations, the hostility of the public made it almost impossible.[18] It was not until after the Battle of Waterloo, when French seizure of the Low Countries ceased to be a menace, that cordial relations with France became possible.

In America the war of 1744–1748 (here called King George's War rather than the War of the Austrian Succession) also was poisonous to relations. During the thirty years prior to the war the British colonies and New France had coexisted as rivals in the fur trade but not as military enemies. British-Americans objected to the French building of Fort St. Frédéric on Lake Champlain just as the French objected to New York's building a post at Oswego on Lake Ontario. The French-British border, however, was less tense than was the border between Georgia and Spanish East Florida. Relations deteriorated quickly, though, once the war of 1744 spread to North America. British-Americans were outraged by Canadian participation in Indian raids on frontier settlements. Meanwhile Frenchmen and Canadians were terrified by the capture of Louisbourg by Massachusetts troops and a British Navy squadron in 1745. The following year a British force even prepared to attack Quebec, but it had to be diverted to the French coast when a large French squadron put to sea with its own army, hoping in vain to recapture Louisbourg.[19] Also of concern to the French was the penetration of Canada's Upper Country (*pays d'en haut*) by British traders. This happened because the war disrupted the supply of trade goods to Canada's Indian allies.[20]

When the traders did not leave after the war ended, the French governors general at Quebec panicked. For sound economic reasons the French hitherto largely had neglected the part of the Upper Country that today forms western Pennsylvania and Ohio. Now it was flooded with British-American traders.[21] Acting Governor General the Marquis de La Galissonnière in particular was obsessed with the supposed threat this penetration posed to the lake and river link between Canada and Louisiana that passed through the western part of this region (along the Maumee and Wabash Rivers to the Ohio), particularly should the British establish a post like Oswego along the Ohio River.[22] This dispute with the traders was a trade rivalry that the French attempted to resolve by bluster combined with parsimoniousness, eventually culminating in an attempted military solution—a combination familiar to students of Britain's American policy after 1763, if not to students of more recent disputes. It did have a cultural component, however, that of how the French government regarded Canada and its peoples.

From the viewpoint of France, the Canadian heartland was less important than Louisbourg and the Newfoundland fishery. The fishery was extremely valuable economically, as there was an enormous reexport market for cod. Canada's main export was furs, particularly beaver, which had a very limited market. Well before the middle of the eighteenth century Canada had become an economic liability.[23] Its main purpose, as even La Galissonnière admitted, was military, that of forcing the British to divert resources from Europe or the Caribbean to protect their valuable North American colonies. Not only Canada but all of New France (including Cape Breton Island and Louisiana) was organized along military, or more properly naval lines, with its governor general being a senior naval officer. This was because the colonies were part of the responsibility of the French naval minister. It was chiefly defended not by soldiers, but by some 1,500 marines, who were French troops with Canadian officers and reported to the navy department.[24] Hence it is not surprising that the governors general saw British trade rivalry not as a commercial problem but as a military one. Rather than attempting to regain the allegiance of the Indian nations of the Upper County by treating them with respect and generosity they attempted to drive out the British by force, while intimidating native peoples. This culminated in the building of a string of forts from Lake Erie to the junction of the Monongahela and Allegheny Rivers, which in the long run angered powerful native nations like the Shawnee and Delaware; they came to see the French as no different than the English, that is as enemies to be driven out.

It should be noted that average Canadians participated reluctantly in the fort building south of Lake Erie and that the French policy was essentially defensive; it was aimed at potential British-American expansion rather than at existing British-American settlements. This expansion was even more of a threat than the French realized, but this threat was driven less by demographic or cultural pressures than by the greed of Virginia Lieutenant Governor Robert Dinwiddie and his cronies in the Ohio Company of Virginia, who sought to sell land near the forks of the Ohio for settlement.[25] At least in the short run, the attempt of British-Americans to settle in the area could have been countered by the Indian nations of the region had France treated them properly, just as in 1752 Chippewas, Ottawas, and Potowatomis destroyed Pickawillany, the chief British trading post in the Ohio Country.[26] Instead the folly of the governors general brought about the danger it was meant to avert, the British sending regular troops from home that posed a far greater threat than the schemes of the Ohio Company.

Why did the French government condone, even encourage, a military solution to its problems in the Upper Country? Although the nobility with its emphasis on military virtue still had enormous influence in France, French policy after 1748 was driven less by aggression than by fear. Its military, colonial, and diplomatic policies were basically defensive. True, the French Navy did build a fairly large number of ships during the six years after the war, but they were designed for convoy protection.[27] Moreover, when a new war broke out in 1755, the French Navy was unprepared, having cut back for reasons of economy the purchase of supplies such as timber.[28] French colonial policy did not directly threaten existing British settlements. The British were correct that in search of furs, Canadian traders had pushed to the edge of the mountains, but the British had the mountains wrong—it was the Rockies not the Appalachians that attracted French interest.[29] The British also were right that French postwar diplomacy was active and focused, but it was aimed not at Britain but at Russia, which had replaced Austria as France's chief rival in eastern Europe. Indeed, the French were interested in better relations with Britain, although their actions in the recent war made this difficult.[30]

One serious problem affecting the making of French policy was turnover among the governors general, foreign ministers, and naval ministers, the naval ministers also being in charge of colonies. None of the four governors general or acting governors general of the period had time to gain the experience necessary for acquiring a measured and broad-minded approach to the problems of the Upper Country.[31] There also were three naval ministers during the period. The comte de Maurepas, who had directed the navy and colonies since 1723, was relieved of office shortly after the end of the war as a result of court politics. His successor, Antoine-Louis Rouillé, a timid bureaucrat, was good at building ships but knew nothing of North America and was easily won over by the alarmist La Galissonnière. In mid-1754 he was shifted to the foreign ministry. His successor was the former finance minister Jean-Baptiste Machault d'Arnouville. Machault eventually proved one of the greatest, if not the greatest naval minister of the century, but he was too new in office to have much impact on the effort to avert war.[32] There also were three foreign ministers between 1748 and 1755. The first, the wise and prudent marquis de Puyzieulx, failed to achieve the reconciliation with Britain he sought, but he did win the respect of the Earl of Albemarle, the British ambassador. Unfortunately Puyzieulx resigned for health reasons in 1751, and his lackluster successor died in office three years later. Rouillé, who then took over, was sincere, well meaning, and anxious to avoid war with Britain, as even the Duke of Newcastle, the British prime minister, admitted.[33] Rouillé, however, was hampered by his own legalism, pedantry, and lack of imagination. The only continuity in the French government was provided by King Louis XV, who had acted as his own first minister since the death of Fleury in 1743. As yet, however, Louis lacked the self-confidence and forcefulness necessary to impose consistency on his fractious royal council of state.

The British had their own problems with divided counsels, turnover of key personnel, and excessive delegation of power to local hotheads. In spite of his suspicion of French intentions, Newcastle too worked to avert war. He was undercut not by the public as Walpole had been fifteen years earlier, but by the machinations of warmongers like the Duke of Cumberland (King George II's brutal son) and the Earl of Halifax, head of the Board of Trade.[34] The British public seems to have had little impact on the negotiations. Not until France went to war with Prussia, a fellow Protestant state, did the war become a full-blown religious crusade. The French public too had little initial enthusiasm for war. Parisians were mesmerized by an ongoing religious dispute between the archbishop of Paris and the Jansenists, a group of Catholics with Calvinist leanings. The Jansenists were particularly influential because some of them were serving in the Parlement of Paris, a judicial body that also served as a center of resistance to royal taxation. Most Frenchmen seem to have been more violently opposed to tax increases than to the English, although the government used the death of Ensign Junonville, a Canadian officer killed by Washington's patrol, to propagandize them.[35] It was not until the crippling defeat of the French Navy in the 1759 Battle of Quiberon Bay that a wave of patriotism swept the French people.[36] As other chapters in this book discuss Canadian and British-American feelings about the war, I will only note that the British and French governments were not very concerned about the feelings of their respective colonists. Prewar Canadians and British-Americans had more in common than they realized; two of the things they shared was being patronized by the governments of their mother countries and being treated brutally by their enemies. British-Americans along the frontier were driven from their homes by Indians raids, while the French-speaking population of Acadia was brutally expelled by the British.[37] Since the governments of France and Great Britain were not pressured by the public into war as the British government had been in 1739, how did two skirmishes in the backwoods of Pennsylvania lead to a war that spread to Europe, Asia, Africa, and South America? The answer is that the war was caused by a mixture of international politics and governmental culture. In the jungle of eighteenth-century diplomacy, to show weakness was to invite attack. France was particularly vulnerable because of its dependence on its allies, who in many cases looked to it for protection. This made it difficult for Foreign Minister Rouillé to offer major concessions during the abortive negotiations of 1755. Conversely, Newcastle, whose political position was threatened by more bellicose rivals, did not have enough influence with King George II to make significant concessions himself. As a result Rouillé and Newcastle were forced into a war neither wished.

British and French treatment of their colonists improved after the outbreak of war, even though generals like Braddock and Montcalm looked down on Americans and Canadians. Better strategists such as British Secretary of State William Pitt felt differently; Pitt even was willing to pay for large numbers of American provincial troops. For its part the French government made massive efforts to feed and protect an endangered Canada. It realized from the beginning, however, that the best for which it could hope was buying time in order to win the war elsewhere. War is a matter of culture, but it also is a matter of geography. Canada simply could not grow enough food to feed a large army and the French Navy, outnumbered two, three, and eventually four to one, could not assure the arrival of food from France. Hence the British were assured of eventual victory; when a two to one superiority in soldiers proved insufficient, they sent enough soldiers from home and raised enough soldiers in America to increase that superiority to three to one.[38]

It often is assumed that France neglected Canada to pursue gains in Europe. The exact opposite is true—France went to war in Europe in the hope of saving Canada. Once again the culture of eighteenth-century diplomacy was involved—defeat was an even more dangerous sign of weakness than was eagerness to avoid war. When the royal council of state learned that on June 10, 1755, a British squadron had seized French warships en route to Canada, it debated French options. France had to respond to the attack in order to preserve its credibility, without which its own security and the security of its allies would be at risk. It could not remain on the defensive, given the superiority of the British Navy and the population disparity in North America. It

had two major offensive options. France could invade the Austrian Netherlands as it had done in 1744 in the hope that gains there could be exchanged
for losses in North America (the way Louisbourg had been recovered). Although some in the council proposed doing so, Louis, doubtless remembering
the difficulties of the last war, rejected that option. Instead he leaned toward
the other option, that of attacking King George II's beloved Electorate of
Hanover in northwestern Germany. Because the invasion route would skirt
the Austrian Netherlands, however, Louis had to obtain Maria Theresa's
consent to the attack.[39] He waited, however, in the hope that capturing the
British-held island of Minorca in the Mediterranean would induce the
British to make peace. The French were successful in driving off a British
fleet and capturing the island; the French admiral in charge was La Galissonnière, a better fleet commander than colonial governor. The loss of Minorca did not make the British public defeatist. It made it so angry that
George used the British admiral, George Byng, as a scapegoat. The defeat
cost Byng his life.[40] Another defeat, the French capture of Oswego, cost
Newcastle his job.

France now decided to attack Hanover. Maria Theresa demanded an alliance against Prussia as her price for consenting to the attack. The first step
was a defensive alliance, signed on May 1, 1756. The abbé de Bernis, who
had negotiated it, later attributed it to the king's religious views, as Austria,
like France, was Catholic.[41] Historians generally have seen it as an attempt
to avert the war's spreading to Europe. Neither explanation is tenable. The
defensive treaty was merely a way station on the road to war. Negotiations
for an offensive treaty began immediately and were greatly assisted by King
Frederick II of Prussia who decided to attack Austria before it could attack
him. Once again a preventive military action backfired. In 1757 Louis and
Maria Theresa signed an offensive alliance. Soon a French Army captured
Hanover, while an Austrian army captured Breslau, the capital of Silesia. All
was undone by Frederick's miraculous victory over the Austrian Army at
Leuthen.[42] Thus the fate of Canada was decided by a battle in what today is
Poland, a battle in which no British or French troops participated.

The tide of war turned, as 1758 and 1759 were years of French defeats.
The French persisted in their strategy of using the German war to exhaust
the British and in 1760, too late to save Canada, the strategy began to work.
The French began winning some of the battles. Particularly important was
the Battle of Clostercamp near the Rhine, that saved France's chief bridge-
head into Germany.[43] The object of the war had now changed. The French
government now had a real if unofficial chief minister, the courageous and
ruthless duc de Choiseul. Reluctantly Choiseul abandoned hope of saving

Canada or obtaining its restoration at the peace, the initial goal of France's war in Europe. What now was at stake was French access to the Newfoundland and St. Lawrence fisheries, without which, as both Pitt and Choiseul realized, the French Navy could not be rebuilt after the war. Neither the French nor the British Navy could afford to train its own sailors. Both depended on merchant sailors who were taken into service when wars broke out. Many of the best sailors in the French Navy were trained in the harsh conditions of the North American fisheries. The future of the French Navy depended on France's retaining a share in the fisheries.

Ultimately the French prevailed. The British taxpayer tired of the interminable war in Germany. Spain entered the war in 1762. Its new king, Charles III, feared for the Spanish Empire if Britain crushed France; he told the French ambassador that the news of the capture of Quebec made his blood run cold.[44] This too played a part in Britain's consenting to French access to the fisheries, as the interruption of trade with Spain led to unemployment and discontent in England.[45] Unlike France, the wealthy of Britain shared in directly running the government. This was a mixed blessing. When things went well, the British government was able to raise loans at a low interest rate, but the patience of the British taxpayer was limited. In 1748, 1762, 1782, and 1802 public pressure forced concessions on British negotiators. Representative governments are unbeatable in unlimited wars like the one Britain fought against Napoleon, but they do less well in limited wars of attrition. At the end of 1762, the French and British agreed to a peace that transferred Canada and all of Louisiana east of the Mississippi to Britain. (The French were able to exclude New Orleans from the transfer by pretending it was an island between two channels of the river; at the same time as they made peace with Britain, they secretly gave New Orleans and the portion of Louisiana west of the Mississippi to Spain.) On the other hand, Britain agreed to permit France access to the Newfoundland and St. Lawrence fisheries. This made possible the eventual rebuilding of the French Navy and hence French participation in the American War of Independence. At the time of the Battle of Yorktown the head of the French Navy was the marquis de Castries, the head of the French Army was the marquis de Ségur, and the commander of the French expeditionary force was the comte de Rochambeau. Ironically, all three had been present at Clostercamp, Castries as commander of the army and Rochambeau as a regimental commander and the hero of the battle. If Canada was lost at Leuthen, the possibility of foreign assistance to the United States was saved at Clostercamp.

Did the Seven Years' War make the French participation in the American Revolution inevitable? The answer is complicated. For the French public, particularly officers like Lafayette, the war was in good part one of revenge, although the Enlightenment too played a part by making the cause of America the cause of mankind—an opinion that has lost some of its popularity in France recently. Louis XVI, the new French king, was not forced into the war by public pressure, but by the advice of his own royal council of state, particularly his foreign minister, Charles Gravier, comte de Vergennes. For Vergennes the war was one of revenge, but not for Britain's taking Canada. Vergennes and his chief assistants at the foreign ministry were experts on central Europe and, like Puyzieulx a generation earlier, strongly anti-Russian. Vergennes seems to have made war on Britain because of Britain's support of Russia during the interwar years. He hoped Britain, once weakened, would be amenable to French direction and even before the war was over began looking for British help against Russia.[46] He was a prisoner of his culture which saw enemies become allies (and vice versa) as soon as self-interest encouraged it. He misjudged Britain where politicians feared the prejudices of the public and could not reconcile with France.

The Franco-British wars of 1744, 1755, and 1778 illustrate a point that is valid even today. Cultural differences are important in understanding wars but not always because of their impact on the public. Instead they often do damage by influencing the fears, prejudices, and calculations of the leaders, statesmen, and politicians who send young men (and now women) into battle. Sometimes the results are worth the sufferings of these young people. This was not the case, however, with the Seven Years' War, whose results were as universally tragic as were its human costs. Like World War I, defeat was a catastrophe for the losers, but even for the winners, victory was hollow. The Americans soon saw their path to expansion blocked by the British crown and their long-standing quasi-independence within the British Empire challenged. Britain gained new colonies only to see their old ones grow disaffected and eventually rebel. Canadians saw themselves subjected to an alien culture, while to dozens of Indian nations their entire world became imperiled. The culture of war thus led to the wounding or even destruction of cultures.

Notes

1. The best account is Philip Woodfine, *Britannia's Glories: The Walpole Ministry and the 1739 War with Spain* (Woodbridge, UK and Rochester, NY: Boydell Press for the Royal Historical Society, 1998).

2. C. V. Wedgwood, *The Thirty Years' War* (Garden City, NY: Doubleday and Co., Anchor Books, 1961), provides a good introduction.

3. For a brilliant critique of eighteenth-century international relations by one of the greatest of all diplomatic historians see Albert Sorel, *Europe and the French Revolution: The Political Traditions of the Old Régime*, trans. Alfred Cobban and J. W. Hunt (Garden City, NY: Doubleday and Co., Anchor Books, 1971).

4. One example is Jean Meyer and John Bromley, "The Second Hundred Years' War (1688–1815)" in Douglas Johnson, François Crouzet, and François Bédarida, eds., *Britain and France: Ten Centuries* (Folkestone, UK: Dawson, 1980), 139–72.

5. For the Spanish side of the war see J. H. Elliott, *The Count-Duke of Olivares: The Statesman in an Age of Decline* (New Haven and London: Yale University Press, 1986), 457–673.

6. For the reign of Louis XIV see John B. Wolf, *Louis XIV* (New York: W. W. Norton & Co., 1968) and Andrew Lossky, *Louis XIV and the French Monarchy* (New Brunswick, NJ: Rutgers University Press, 1994).

7. Henry Kamen, *Philip of Spain* (New Haven, CT: Yale University Press, 1997) is a sympathetic biography.

8. The best study of George I is Ragnhild Hatton, *George I, Elector and King* (Cambridge, MA: Harvard University Press, 1978; reissued under the title *George I* by Yale University Press, 2001). There are numerous biographies of Philippe; a readable recent one is Christine Previtt, *Philippe, Duc d'Orleans, Regent of France* (New York: Atlantic Monthly Press, 1997).

9. Hatton, *George I, Elector and King*, 36–37.

10. For the working of the alliance, see Arthur McCandless Wilson, *French Foreign Policy during the Administration of Cardinal Fleury, 1726–1743: A Study in Diplomacy and Commercial Development* (Cambridge, MA: Harvard University Press; London: Humphrey Milford, Oxford University Press, 1936); Jeremy Black, *British Foreign Policy in the Age of Walpole* (Edinburgh: John Donald, 1985) and "Interventionism, Structuralism, and Contingency in British Foreign Policy in the 1720s," *International History Review* 26 (Dec. 2004), 734–64.

11. See Jeremy Black, *The Collapse of the Anglo-French Alliance, 1727–1731* (Gloucester, UK: Alan Sutton; New York: St. Martin's Press, 1987).

12. See Richard Harding, *Amphibious Warfare in the Eighteenth Century: The British Expedition to the West Indies, 1740–1742* (Woodbridge, UK and Rochester, NY: Boydell Press for the Royal Historical Society, 1991).

13. Two recent surveys of the ensuing war are Reed Browning, *The War of the Austrian Succession* (New York: St. Martin's Press, 1993) and M. S. Anderson, *The War of the Austrian Succession, 1740–1748* (New York and London: Longman, 1995).

14. F. J. McLynn, *France and the Jacobite Rising of 1745* (Edinburgh: University of Edinburgh Press, 1981); Christopher Duffy, *The '45* (London: Cassell, 2003); Sir Herbert W. Richmond, *The Navy in the War of 1739–48* (3 vols., Cambridge: Cambridge University Press, 1920), 2: 58–119, 146–67.

15. Richmond, *Navy*, 1: 197–240; 2: 1–57.

16. Jean Colin, *Louis XV et les Jacobites: Le Projet de débarquement en Angleterre de 1743–1744* (Paris: R. Chapelot et Cie., 1901).

17. Jack M. Sosin, "Louisbourg and the Peace of Aix-la-Chapelle, 1748," *William & Mary Quarterly*, 3rd ser., 14 (Oct. 1957), 516–35.

18. Jonathan R. Dull, *The French Navy and American Independence: A Study of Arms and Diplomacy, 1774–1787* (Princeton, NJ: Princeton University Press, 1975), 296–97, 338.

19. For a good brief summary of the siege of Louisbourg, see Julian Gwyn, *An Admiral for America: Sir Peter Warren, Vice Admiral of the Red, 1703–1752* (Gainesville and elsewhere: University Press of Florida, 2004), 75–99. For the abortive attempt to recapture Louisbourg, see the superb book by James Pritchard, *Anatomy of a Naval Disaster: The 1746 French Naval Expedition to North America* (Montreal, Kingston, London, and Buffalo: McGill-Queen's University Press, 1995).

20. A brilliant history of cultural conflict and culture accommodation between the governors general of Canada and the nations of the *pays d'en haut* is Richard White, *The Middle Ground: Indians, Empires and Republics in the Great Lakes Region, 1650–1815* (New York: Cambridge University Press, 1991).

21. An excellent study of this region is Michael N. McConnell, *A Country Between: The Upper Ohio Valley and Its Peoples, 1724–1774* (Lincoln: University of Nebraska Press, 1992).

22. The key document is a December 1750 memoir by La Galissonnière, which is translated in E. B. O'Callaghan et al., eds., *Documents Relative to the Colonial History of the State of New York* (15 vols., Albany, NY: Weed, Parsons & Co., 1853–87), 10: 220–34.

23. For Canada in the early eighteenth century, see James S. Pritchard, *In Search of Empire: The French in the Americas, 1670–1730* (New York: Cambridge University Press, 2004).

24. There were thirty companies of approximately fifty men each: W. J. Eccles, "The French Forces in America during the Seven Years' War," in Francess G. Halpenny, ed., *Dictionary of Canadian Biography*, vol. 3, *1741 To 1770* (Toronto: University of Toronto Press, 1974), xvii.

25. For Dinwiddie, see John Richard Alden, *Robert Dinwiddie, Servant of the Crown* (Charlottesville: University Press of Virginia, 1973).

26. Francis Jennings, *Empire of Fortune: Crown, Colonies, and Tribes in the Seven Years' War in America* (New York: W. W. Norton, 1988), 49; Fred Anderson, *Crucible of War: The Seven Years' War and the Fate of Empire in British North America, 1754–1766* (New York: Alfred A. Knopf, 2000), 28–29.

27. Jonathan R. Dull, *The French Navy and the Seven Years' War* (Lincoln: University of Nebraska Press, 2005), 11–12, 258–60.

28. James Pritchard, *Louis XV's Navy, 1748–1762: A Study of Organization and Administration* (Kingston and Montreal: McGill-Queen's University Press, 1987), 137–53, 216, 218, and "Fir Trees, Finances, and the French Navy during the 1750's," *Canadian Journal of History*, 23 (1988), 337–54.

29. W. J. Eccles, *The Canadian Frontier, 1534–1769* (rev. ed., Albuquerque: University of New Mexico Press, 1969), 145–47.

30. Dull, *French Navy and the Seven Years' War*, 6–9.

31. White, *Middle Ground*, 186–242.

32. Dull, *French Navy and the Seven Years' War*, 20–26.

33. Dull, *French Navy and the Seven Years' War*, 23. Newcastle also praised the duc de Mirepoix, Rouillé's minister to the British court: Dull, *French Navy and the Seven Years' War*, 25.

34. T. R. Clayton, "The Duke of Newcastle, the Earl of Halifax, and the American Origins of the Seven Years' War," *Historical Journal* 24 (Sept. 1981), 571–603.

35. David Bell, "Junonville's Death: War Propaganda and the National Identity in Eighteenth Century France," in Colin Jones and Dror Wahrman, eds., *The Age of Cultural Revolution: Britain and France, 1750–1820* (Berkeley, Los Angeles, and London: University of California Press, 2002), 33–61.

36. See Edmond Dziermbowski, *Un nouveau Patriotisme français, 1750–1770: La France face à la puissance anglaise à l'époque de la guerre de Sept Ans* (Oxford: Voltaire Foundation, 1998).

37. Matthew C. Ward, *Breaking the Backcountry: The Seven Years' War in Virginia and Pennsylvania, 1754–1765* (Pittsburgh: University of Pittsburgh Press, 2003); John Mack Farragher, *"A Great and Noble Scheme": The Tragic Story of the Expulsion of the French Acadians From their American Homeland* (New York and London: W. W. Norton, 2005).

38. Dull, *French Navy and the Seven Years' War*, 54–56, 107–9, 144–45, 174–75, 261–84. For the propagation of the myth that France abandoned the Canadians, see the essay by Catherine Desbarats and Allan Greer in this book.

39. Dull, *French Navy and the Seven Years' War*, 36–37, 41–42.

40. Dudley Pope, *At Twelve Mr. Byng was Shot* (Philadelphia: J. B. Lippincott, 1962).

41. Philippe Bonnet, ed., *Mémoires du Cardinal de Bernis* (Paris: Mercure de France, 1980), 145. For a critique of Bernis's veracity, see Léon Cahen, "Les Mémoires de Bernis et les débuts de la guerre de sept ans," *Revue de histoire moderne et contemporaine* 12 (Jan.–Mar. 1909), 73–99.

42. See Christopher Duffy, *Prussia's Glory: Rossbach and Leuthen, 1757* (Chicago: The Emperor's Press, 2003).

43. Sir Reginald Savory, *His Britannic Majesty's Army in Germany during the Seven Years' War* (Oxford: Clarendon Press, 1966), 259–79; Dull, *French Navy and the Seven Years' War*, 180–81.

44. Dull, *French Navy and the Seven Years' War*, 155.

45. T. S. Ashton, *Economic Fluctuations in England, 1700–1900* (Oxford: Clarendon Press, 1959), 124–25, 187.

46. Dull, *French Navy and the Seven Years' War*, 252–54. For an extended study of Vergennes's part in the War of American Independence see Dull, *French Navy and American Independence*.

$\sim$

War, Diplomacy, and Culture: The Iroquois Experience in the Seven Years' War

Timothy J. Shannon

The story of Iroquois participation in the Seven Years' War is at once familiar and irretrievable. The familiar part comes to us from the military narrative of the war; it is a story of campaigns and diplomatic councils, of efforts by colonial officials to recruit Iroquois as allies or at the very least to ensure that they remained neutral while European armies fought it out. In this story, the Iroquois appear mostly as shrewd negotiators or fickle allies, depending on the observer's assessment of Indian character: calculating or cowardly, independent or mercenary. The irretrievable part of the story concerns the perspective of the Iroquois themselves. European soldiers, missionaries, and agents did their best to ascribe motives to Iroquois actions (and inaction) during the war, and they did occasionally record the explanations offered by the Iroquois themselves at treaty councils. But these materials can be maddeningly opaque for the historian. Filtered as they were through interpreters and secretaries with their own agendas and circumscribed by the Indians' reticence to speak disruptively when conducting diplomacy, the words Indians spoke to their colonial contemporaries rarely described in explicit terms the Iroquois's understanding of how the war started, what it meant to them, or what they hoped to come from it. Furthermore, the war disrupted the customary flow of people, goods, and information between the Iroquois and their colonial neighbors, making it hard for historians to get a clear picture of life within Iroquois communities during this conflict.

Adding further complication is the question of what exactly constituted "Iroquois" in the mid-eighteenth century. For scholars and laypeople alike, the term "Iroquois" usually conjures a map of modern upstate New York and the five nations originally joined in the Iroquois League: from east to west, the Mohawks, Oneidas, Onondagas, Cayugas, and Senecas (the Tuscaroras migrated from North Carolina into the upper Susquehanna Valley in the 1710s and were adopted by the others as the "sixth" Iroquois nation). But this definition is too narrow for the purposes of describing the eighteenth-century Iroquois. Contemporaries spoke of a bewildering array of native peoples stretching from the St. Lawrence River to the Ohio Valley who were attached in some manner to the New York Iroquois. Some were descendants of Iroquois converts to Catholicism who had resettled in mission villages near Montreal; others were displaced peoples such as the Tuscaroras, Mahicans, and Delawares who established new homelands in territory nominally under Iroquois control; still others were Iroquois who had left traditional homelands for the Ohio Country or Susquehanna Valley, where they intermixed with other Indian peoples (see map). This combination of amalgamation and diaspora gave the name "Iroquois" a fluid cultural meaning in the eighteenth century that makes it difficult for modern scholars to speak of a single Iroquois experience during the era of the Seven Years' War.[1]

If words and their definitions make it difficult to retrieve the Iroquois perspective on the Seven Years' War, then perhaps it is better to look at actions. Two scenes of dramatic encounter from the war offer an opportunity to reconstruct some of the cultural patterns and values that shaped Iroquois participation in this conflict. The first one comes to us from the Battle of Lake George in September 1755. William Johnson, a New York militia officer and Indian agent from the Mohawk Valley, commanded an army composed mostly of New England provincials and charged with laying siege to the French Fort St. Frédéric on Lake Champlain. Johnson's considerable effort in recruiting Iroquois warriors for this expedition had yielded only about two hundred Mohawks, the easternmost Iroquois people and the ones with the closest ties to the British. On the morning of September 8, the Mohawks and provincials marched into an ambush planned by the French and Indian forces that had come south from Canada to intercept Johnson's army. In that engagement, Johnson's Mohawk allies suffered considerable casualties, the most famous of whom was Theyanoguin, also known as Hendrick, purported to be the most steadfast friend of the British among the Iroquois. Eyewitness accounts of the battle placed the aged Hendrick on horseback, dressed in the laced hat and coat that Johnson typically gave as diplomatic presents to Indian leaders. Despite his rather ignominious death, Hendrick's stock rose posthumously in Britain, where news reports, prints, and maps describing the Battle of Lake George used his sartorial finery as visual shorthand to convey his loyalty to the British.[2]

Let us fast forward to a council at Johnson's home in July 1757 and another episode involving an Iroquois ally of the British. Nickus, an Oneida leader of a war party outfitted by Johnson a few days earlier, returned to inform Johnson of the murder of two Indians by colonial fur traders. As he related the details of this crime, Nickus "stripped off a Scarlet Laced Coat, Gorget, Laced Hat, and everything Sir William had given him . . . and threw them all down at his Feet and said he would not keep or wear them any longer as his regard for the English was now at an end." The following day, Johnson told Nickus, "It surprized me to see you (whom I looked upon as one of my sincerest Friends) cast away all the marks of Distinction and regard w[hi]ch I had given you heretofore." Johnson then expressed sympathy for the murdered Indians and their families, granted "10 black Strouds, 10 Shirts, and 7 Silk handkerchiefs" as condolence presents to cover their graves, and returned to Nickus all of "his Cloaths, Jewells, &c." so that he would "rest easy in his Mind."[3]

What can the actions of these two Indians, one of whom died a well-dressed death in the British cause and the other of whom got naked in abandoning it, tell us about the Iroquois perspective on the Seven Years' War? Both of these episodes offer revealing glimpses into the means by which colonial agents, such as Johnson, tried to recruit Iroquois support for the war and the limited success they had in doing so. In the first instance, Hendrick's death at Lake George symbolized the ill-fated alliance between his people and the British. Johnson's personal bond with many of his Native American neighbors helps explain why the Mohawks were among his forces at Lake George, even while other Iroquois stayed home. This was a relationship cemented by the material generosity Johnson showed the Mohawks; Hendrick literally wore the evidence of Johnson's esteem on his back. But even that personal bond had its limits when it came up against the cultural values and practices that shaped Iroquois warfare.

Shortly after the engagement at Lake George, the surviving Mohawks in Johnson's forces informed him that they were going home. They did so not because they were fickle or scared but because they were acting on certain cultural practices that informed how they made war. Iroquois warriors went to war to assert their manhood, to gain trophies and plunder that would serve as physical evidence of their courage, and most importantly, to gain captives who could replace recently deceased members of their families and communities. Large-scale engagements in which they sustained heavy casualties

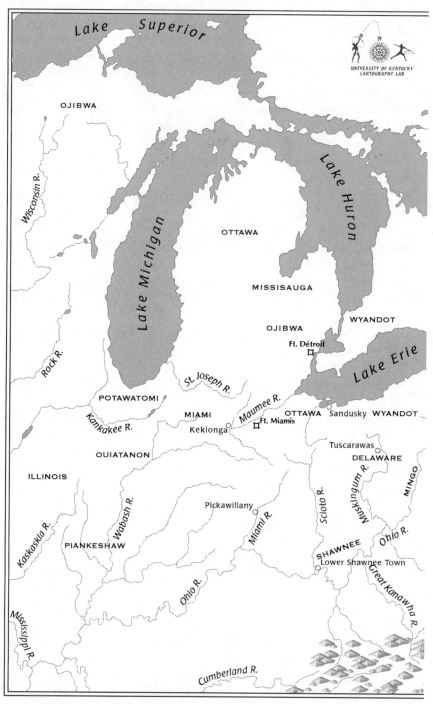

Native North America at the Time of the Seven Years' War. (Maps by Dick Gilbreath at the University of Kentucky Cartography Lab)

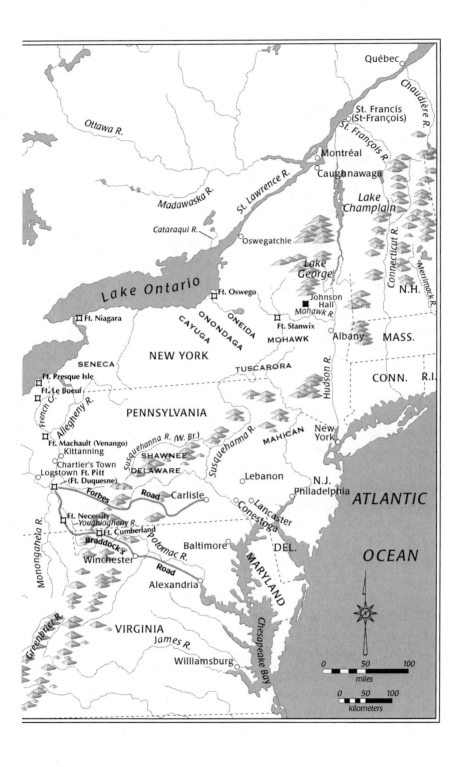

defeated the purpose of such warfare.[4] Johnson tried to convince the surviving Mohawks to stay, but the resignation with which he greeted their departure is indicative of his recognition that the Mohawks fought on their own terms and for their own reasons. In a report to his London superiors, Johnson explained his inability to control the Mohawks by observing that it was their "constant Custom" to act in such a manner "after an Engagement wherein they had met with any considerable Loss."[5] Johnson later learned that the Mohawks would not be rejoining him anytime soon. Their clan matrons—the elder women of their villages whose support was necessary to organize and provision war parties—thought the losses at Lake George too steep, and they told the men to stay home "to take Care of their Wives and children." Four years passed before Johnson was able to recruit another sizable contingent of Iroquois for a British campaign.[6]

The symbolic striptease by which Nickus divested himself of his allegiance to the British likewise illustrated the limits of Johnson's influence over his supposed Indian allies. While Johnson may have provided the material wherewithal by which Nickus could make war, the Oneida warrior was still enough of a free agent to decide where, when, and with whom he would fight. When it came time for Johnson to appease Nickus, he did so by following the Iroquoian custom of making a condolence present to mourn the murdered Indians and honor their families. As in the case of the Mohawks after Hendrick's death, Johnson's ability to manipulate Nickus and his fellow Oneida warriors was checked by their insistence on conducting war and diplomacy by their own rules. Johnson may have had the goods with which to lure Iroquois warriors to the British cause, but the ways in which he did so followed a decidedly native, not European, blueprint. Hendrick's Mohawks and Nickus's Oneidas still had the cultural autonomy to resist playing the role of pawns to British interests.

As these two episodes indicate, one dimension of the "cultures in conflict" in the Seven Years' War involved the dissonance between Iroquoian and European notions of warfare and diplomacy. Differing values create differing expectations and behaviors in warfare and diplomacy, as much for allies as enemies. All actors in the Seven Years' War moved within parameters set by their cultural backgrounds; the rules of war, the meaning of victory or defeat, and the definition of atrocity all differed across cultural lines. Despite attempts by Europeans to impose their own standards on their Native American allies, the Iroquois held fast to their rules for making war and peace, allowing them to weather this conflict with less sustained damage than either the Ohio Indians of the Pennsylvania frontier or the Iroquois of the Revolutionary Era. They did so by sticking to familiar patterns of diplomacy and warfare that had helped expand Iroquois power during the first half of the eighteenth century: keeping open channels or "paths" of communication with colonial governments, even as war raged around them; playing off British and French imperial powers against each other, so as to avoid being attached too firmly to either; and judiciously observing the shifting tides of war to prevent ending up on the losing side.

The war did have its share of negative ramifications for Iroquois society. It diverted precious manpower away from subsistence activities to diplomacy and warfare; it deepened Iroquois dependence on material goods acquired as diplomatic presents; and it increased the flow of alcohol and firearms into their communities. Nevertheless, by the war's end, the Iroquois Confederacy, if not intact, at least remained politically viable, a force to be reckoned with by Indian and colonial neighbors alike. Much of this resilience can be attributed to accommodations the Iroquois had been making to the rising power of their European neighbors well before 1754, but it is also important to recognize the creeping challenge that William Johnson's largesse presented to their cultural integrity during and after the war. In the final analysis, the Seven Years' War did not turn the Iroquois world upside down, but it did plant seeds of disruption that would bear fruit a generation later during the American Revolution.

Warfare and Military Culture

British agents and military officers who regarded the Iroquois as colonial subjects to be recruited, organized, and deployed in the service of the empire were invariably disappointed in their schemes. Especially after the losses sustained by the Mohawks at the Battle of Lake George, Iroquois warriors were reluctant to join Anglo-American forces, preferring instead to rely on their own well-established methods of raising and conducting war parties. Likewise, Iroquois from French mission communities in Canada participated in the war but only as allies who needed to be persuaded to fight on behalf of the French, never as conscripts forced to serve. This response to Anglo-French warfare continued a pattern that had been established in 1701 when the Iroquois negotiated dual treaties in Montreal and Albany, asserting their neutrality between the French and the English.[7] What changed for the Iroquois practice of warfare over the long course of the Seven Years' War was not method or motivation but a deepening reliance on the political benefits they realized from flirting with alliance with either European power.

As one historian has described it, European powers expended much energy and treasure during the colonial era trying to recruit a "usable Indian" who could serve as a reliable ally in times of war.[8] Colonial governments and agents offered a variety of incentives—scalp and prisoner bounties, diplomatic presents, even regular wages—to woo Indian warriors to their cause as scouts or auxiliaries to regular troops or militia forces. The very limited success colonial governments had had with this practice before 1754 did not prevent British officers from pursuing it during the Seven Years' War, especially after Braddock's defeat illustrated the risks of fighting a frontier war without Indian support. In two subsequent major campaigns, British commanders took pains to solicit Indian assistance, but in both instances, the experience left them grousing that it was not worth the time or expense. During the 1758 campaign against Fort Duquesne, Cherokee warriors abandoned Brigadier General John Forbes when they grew impatient with the slow pace of his advance through the Pennsylvania wilderness. During General Jeffrey Amherst's campaign against Montreal in 1760, seven hundred Iroquois warriors recruited by Johnson gradually deserted the expedition in such numbers that Johnson felt it necessary to chastise them for their conduct during treaty conferences the following year.[9]

Perhaps the best example of the British inability to comprehend Iroquois motives and methods of warfare was that provided by William Shirley, the royal governor of Massachusetts charged with raising an expedition against Fort Niagara in 1755. For several months, Shirley and Johnson competed intensely in the upper Hudson and Mohawk valleys for Iroquois auxiliaries. Shirley, using the Albany fur trader John Henry Lydius as his agent, found it difficult to wean Indian warriors away from Johnson, who had a long-standing reputation for showing a cultural affinity toward his Iroquois neighbors. Shirley, on the other hand, had organized a successful intercolonial expedition against the French fortress of Louisbourg in 1745, but he was a novice at Indian relations. He regarded Indians as if they were provincial recruits, expecting them to be lured into the king's service by offers of regular pay and then to endure the same sort of laborious duty and harsh discipline that were the lot of British and Anglo-American soldiers. Despite the many blandishments offered by Lydius, the Iroquois refused to serve as cannon fodder for Shirley, and the Niagara campaign stalled at Fort Oswego on the eastern shore of Lake Ontario.[10]

The dream of turning the Iroquois into "usable Indians" died hard for the British. In 1756, colonial official Thomas Pownall published a pamphlet titled *Proposals for Securing the Friendship of the Five Nations*. Pownall had occupied a series of positions in colonial administration since arriving in North

America in late 1753, and he fancied himself an expert on the Iroquois because he had attended a treaty conference with them in Albany in 1754.[11] In
his pamphlet, Pownall suggested creating a system of storehouses, settlements, and garrisons among the Iroquois for the mutual defense of the king's
colonial and Indian subjects. The officers charged with supervising this system would also "keep an exact Account of all the fighting Men in each [Iro-
quois] Nation, and . . . form them into Companies, under proper Officers,
each Nation to have its proper Uniform, to distinguish them from one another, and from all other Indians."[12] Pownall's scheme for turning Iroquois
warriors into uniformed soldiers in Britain's imperial service betrayed his lack
of familiarity with their military culture, but it was also typical of colonial administrators' hopes to subject independent Indian allies to British-style discipline, leadership, and objectives in military matters.

Pownall's plan sank without a trace, and a sizable number of Iroquois did
not take part in another British campaign until the expedition launched
against Niagara in 1759. Once again, William Johnson played a central role
in recruiting warriors, but this time it was the Senecas, the westernmost Iroquois nation, who led the way. Niagara was in Seneca country, and its importance as a trading post as well as military garrison accounts for the
Senecas' pro-French sympathies up to that point in the war. However, during the previous year's campaigns, the French posts of Louisbourg on Cape
Breton Island, Fort Duquesne on the Forks of the Ohio, and Fort Frontenac
on the northeastern shore of Lake Ontario had fallen to the British, leaving
Niagara dangerously isolated and even more significantly to the Senecas,
bereft of trade goods. The tide of the war had turned decisively against the
French in the Great Lakes region, and the western Iroquois were ready to see
the fur trade restored by way of the British.[13]

About one thousand Iroquois warriors accompanied Johnson and the
British commanding officer of the expedition, Brigadier General John
Prideaux, to Niagara. Once the siege of the fort got underway, a wrinkle developed in the British plans. Seneca warriors among the French forces inside
the fort insisted on holding a diplomatic council with their kin among the
British. The commanding officers on both sides consented, anxious not to
alienate their Indian allies and hoping to neutralize the other side's Indian
support. After several councils conducted under a flag of truce, the French-
allied Senecas withdrew from the fort and encamped some distance away at
La Belle Famille on the Niagara River. A portion of Johnson's warriors also
joined the encampment at La Belle Famille (Johnson used the promise of pil-
lage to keep others from going). A little more than a week later, a French and
Indian force from the Ohio Country arrived to lift the siege. The Iroquois

warriors who had apparently declared their neutrality by moving to La Belle Famille then joined the British in delivering a devastating blow against these reinforcements, but not before engaging in some more diplomacy across enemy lines to avoid fighting their kin.[14] Shortly after, the fort surrendered.

The turn of events at Niagara was a testimony to Iroquois autonomy in conducting their military affairs. Neither the French nor British officers were able to exert any kind of coercive power over their Indian allies, and the Iroquois exhibited an unchallenged ability to turn their neutrality between the French and English on or off as they saw fit. It is also worth noting that at both the siege and engagement at La Belle Famille, the Iroquois took pains to avoid shedding the blood of their cultural cousins, conducting their own inter-Indian diplomacy independently of whatever negotiations were going on between the Europeans. Such conduct had also occurred at the Battle at Lake George, where French-allied Caughnawagas, Catholic Mohawks who lived in mission villages near Montreal, forced the French commander Baron Dieskau to alter his battle plan because they did not want to engage their kin among Johnson's forces.[15]

This refusal to engage in intra-Iroquois violence had precedents as old as the Iroquois League itself, which according to oral tradition, had been founded as a type of mutual nonaggression pact between its original five nations. Iroquois communities and even individual warriors acted independently in matters of war or peace, but all also followed the principle of keeping the peace among each other. Furthermore, this *pax Iroquoia* extended to other Indians beyond the original Iroquois League.[16] As witnessed at the battles at Lake George and Fort Niagara, the Iroquois definition of who was Iroquois rarely matched British or French notions of friends and enemies. The Enlightenment idea of the nation-state, which fundamentally altered British and French notions of national identity in the eighteenth century, held little meaning to Native Americans.[17] Iroquois political identity was rooted first and foremost in kinship ties that easily transcended geographic borders drawn in North America by European imperial powers. More than a century's worth of migrations and religious conversions had been occurring among the Iroquois since their first contact with Europeans; these changes made the cultural meaning of "Iroquois" adaptable, and as new Iroquoian populations and identities emerged in distant places, kinship bonds developed between them that were resilient in the face of European imperial rivalries and wars. The durability of these bonds constantly confounded the British and French when they tried to mobilize their supposed Iroquois allies in the field of battle.

Iroquois reluctance to commit fully to either side in the Seven Years' War had a practical political dimension as well. In treaty conferences with colonial powers, the Iroquois claimed sovereignty over the Ohio Country by right of wars they had fought against native enemies during the seventeenth century. By 1748, however, it was clear to everyone involved in that region that the balance of power had tipped to the Indians who actually lived there, mostly Delawares, Shawnees, and Senecas who had migrated there during the previous thirty years. The Iroquois Grand Council in Onondaga designated "half-kings" Tanaghrisson and Scarouady to represent its interests in the Ohio Country, but these men acted more as observers for the New York Iroquois than as enforcers of any policy dictated by them.[18] When the French withdrew from Fort Duquesne in late 1758, they left behind a power vacuum in the Ohio Country the New York Iroquois were anxious to fill, even if they lacked the means to do so. They had good reason to seek British help in shoring up their presumed authority over the Ohio Indians. British officer Hugh Mercer recognized as much in early 1759, when he wrote of the Iroquois, "they are by no means that powerfull and Warlike People they were on our first Settling America; and should the Shawnese and Delawares join in [a] Confederacy against them, their ruin would soon be completed."[19] But custom and good sense dictated against shedding Iroquois blood in the British cause if it could be avoided. Thus, from the Iroquois perspective, the Niagara campaign was an elaborate exercise in shadow boxing, making a show of support for the British while positioning themselves to play a prominent role in the postwar settlement of the Ohio-Niagara region.

The ability of the Iroquois to respond to the Seven Years' War according to their own cultural imperatives affected significantly the conflict's outcome for others. When Iroquois warriors failed to materialize for expeditions or abandoned them before their completion, they acquired a reputation as unreliable partners in empire. In response, British officers developed a nearly universal contempt for native allies, which contributed to the air of distrust between redcoats and Indians that fueled Pontiac's War in 1763. Had the Iroquois proven to be the loyal soldiers of empire that William Shirley and Thomas Pownall envisioned at the war's outset, then perhaps the British war effort would not have involved committing thousands of regular troops to North America, and those troops would not have been such a point of friction in Anglo-American relations after 1763. The French, like the British, found their efforts to utilize Iroquois allies limited by the refusal of such warriors to make war on their cultural kin, as illustrated by the episodes at Lake George and Niagara noted above. Of all the war's participants, the Ohio Indians were the ones most affected by Iroquois neutrality. As Eric Hinderaker relates in his essay in this book, the Ohio Indians assumed a militant posture in the Seven Years' War that was boldly defiant of the French, the British, and the Iroquois who claimed sovereignty over them. Had the New York Iroquois taken a similar stance against the extension of British power after the fall of Canada, the Ohio Indians would have stood a much better chance of maintaining their territorial and political integrity.[20]

The fighting of the Seven Years' War left the Iroquois relatively unscathed. Some Iroquois may have been among those Indians killed by colonial scorched-earth raids on Kittanning, St. Francois, and Conestoga—all of which were polyglot native communities on the outer reaches of Iroquois territory—but no marching army or marauding militia unleashed similar violence in the heart of Iroquoia in modern upstate New York.[21] As they had managed to do since 1701, the Iroquois weathered an Anglo-French war by refusing to commit wholeheartedly to either side. What European commanders saw as inconstancy and fecklessness, the Iroquois (had it been possible for them to be readers of Tocqueville) would have described as self-interest rightly understood: by refusing to be recruited into the ranks of regular troops or militias, by refusing to wait endlessly for marches to start or sieges to end, and by refusing to fire upon each other or destroy each other's homes, they kept themselves out of harm's way. In retrospect, this strategy worked well. The Iroquois population appears to have been on the rise during the tumultuous war years of 1755 to 1763.[22] Some Iroquois may have chosen to go to war, but for the most part, the war did not come to them.

Diplomacy and Material Culture

In reviewing the relevant sources, it is fair to conclude that Iroquois men spent far more time in diplomatic councils than on the warpath during the Seven Years' War. Following precedents established in previous Anglo-French wars in North America, the Iroquois maintained open diplomatic channels with each side, even as individual warriors cast their lot with one or the other. Furthermore, the means of conducting this diplomacy remained Iroquoian in practice: whether in Montreal, New York, or Pennsylvania, colonial agents observed the condolence ritual that provided a framework for Iroquoian diplomatic encounters, used wampum beads and belts to convey their points in speech-making, and gave trade goods as presents to convince the Iroquois of their friendship and faithfulness. As was the case in warfare, the cultural motives and methods for Iroquois diplomacy seemed to weather the war undamaged, suggesting that the Iroquois remained in control of their political destinies, regardless of the shifting fortunes of war among their native and colonial neighbors.

This conclusion appears sound, save for one factor: William Johnson's appointment as the British crown's Superintendent of Indian Affairs in 1755.

To assess Johnson's impact on Iroquois diplomacy, it is best to return briefly to the stories of Hendrick and Nickus. Hendrick and Nickus were eastern Iroquois who lived close enough to Johnson's home in the Mohawk Valley to visit him frequently for private and public councils. These encounters, as recorded in Johnson's accounts and official papers, invariably followed Iroquoian precedents, in which Johnson provided hospitality for his guests and made them presents of trade goods. Johnson recognized the cultural significance of gift-giving among the Iroquois, and he used it to practice an intensely personal form of diplomacy, welcoming Indians into his home, entertaining and outfitting them from his stores, and provisioning their families when they went off on war parties he sponsored. While contemporaries often described Johnson as the single most influential colonial agent among the Iroquois, the roots of his power at the outset of the Seven Years' War were actually much more local, extending hardly beyond his Mohawk and Oneida neighbors. During his tenure as New York's Indian agent from 1746 to 1751, Johnson rarely visited Iroquois villages west of the Mohawk Valley, and he exerted very little influence among them.[23]

After Johnson received his appointment from the crown in 1755, he extended his personal style of diplomacy to the rest of Iroquoia and beyond. During the Seven Years' War and its aftermath, he or his agents convened treaty conferences in Pittsburgh, Detroit, Montreal, and the Pennsylvania towns of Easton and Lancaster. Johnson also turned his home in the Mohawk Valley into a site of treaty conferences on a grand scale, drawing Indian audiences there from throughout the Great Lakes and trans-Appalachian frontier. Intercolonial treaty conferences were not uncommon before the Seven Years' War, but those convened by Johnson during the war years readily eclipsed any precedents in terms of their frequency, the number of Indians who participated, and the amount of material wealth they distributed as diplomatic presents.[24] Johnson's personal largesse, made possible by his ability to charge expenses directly to the crown, opened a Pandora's box for those Indians who encountered it. The clothing Hendrick and Nickus wore on their backs did more than symbolize their alliance with Johnson; it represented the deepening dependency of the Iroquois on Johnson for the material necessities of life. Diplomacy, the means by which the Iroquois negotiated and preserved their political and territorial autonomy, became during the Seven Years' War the primary avenue by which their economic independence eroded, leaving them dangerously exposed to the vagaries of British imperial policy by the war's end.

On the eve of the Seven Years' War, there was plenty of evidence that the eastern Iroquois were already economically dependent on their colonial neighbors for the stuff of life. Since the establishment of Oswego on the southeastern shore of Lake Ontario in the 1720s, the fur trade had bypassed the Mohawks and Oneidas. Many of these Indians earned a seasonal living by assisting in the portage of furs and trade goods between the Mohawk River and Oswego, although this employment generated complaints on both sides of fraud, abuse, and ill will. The easternmost Mohawks at Fort Hunter on the Schoharie River had acculturated to European forms of production in their housing, dress, and farming, but the Mohawks of Canajo-harie, Hendrick's village, were generally described by Johnson and his con-temporaries as impoverished and desperate, relying on land sales and diplomacy with colonial governments to supply their material necessities.[25] Johnson employed many of them personally during the ginseng boom of the early 1750s, paying them to harvest the valuable root in the wild.[26] Far-ther west, the Onondagas, Cayugas, and Senecas were still active partici-pants in the fur trade, but they too depended on diplomacy with the French and British to supplement their subsistence.

For the Iroquois, especially those living east of Onondaga, Johnson's ele-vation as the crown's Indian Superintendent could not have come at a bet-ter time. He provided a lifeline to the material goods necessary to sustain lo-cal economies made even more precarious by the outbreak of war. Johnson's accounts from the Seven Years' War reveal the myriad ways he supplemented Mohawk and Oneida subsistence patterns: scalp and prisoner bounties paid to their warriors; entertainments hosted at their treaty councils and confer-ences; fortifications for their towns; clothing, provisions, and medicine for their families given out in presents made at treaty conferences and in count-less piecemeal disbursements to Indians who showed up at his home.[27] For Iroquois chiefs and warriors, Johnson became a valuable ally and benefactor; his Indian name of Warraghiyagey, which contemporaries translated as "doer of great things," might in fact have been more accurately rendered as "keeper of deep pockets."[28]

The generosity Johnson showed the Iroquois had significant repercussions for their material culture. Johnson may have provided much needed clothing and food to Indian families during wartime, but he also increased the flow of firearms and liquor into Iroquois homelands. In a 1771 letter to a London cor-respondent, Johnson recognized the way in which European firearms had transformed Indian warfare and political leadership, making "every man . . . his own general" and lessening the power of traditional chiefs in matters of peace and war.[29] The adoption and spread of European firearms in Indian war-fare and hunting also increased the Indians' dependency on colonial traders and agents to keep them supplied with ammunition and gunpowder. By the 1740s in Iroquoia, access to blacksmiths capable of maintaining and repairing

firearms became indispensable to Indians, and it was frequently a point of negotiation with missionaries and colonial agents at treaty conferences.[30] Johnson's distribution of firearms during the Seven Years' War deepened this dependency and helped create the circumstances that led to Pontiac's War
when British commander-in-chief Jeffrey Amherst tried to limit the amount
of powder and shot disbursed to the Indians after the fall of Canada.[31]

Liquor was another good freely distributed by Johnson that had a destructive impact on the cultural integrity of the Iroquois. As with firearms, rum
already played a significant role in Iroquois trade and diplomacy in the mid-
eighteenth century, but the Seven Years' War intensified its negative consequences for Iroquois communities. Johnson and his agents treated Iroquois
chiefs, warriors, and their families liberally at diplomatic councils and conferences, quickly filling the lapse in supply caused by the wartime disruption
of the fur trade. The provisioning of thousands of British and provincial
troops stationed in the upper Hudson Valley also stimulated alcohol production in New York. Albany merchants opened their first distillery in 1758–
1759, responding to the demand created by the influx of regular and provincial troops into that region.[32] During the war, Johnson complained of the
negative impact alcohol had on his Indian diplomacy, even as he continued
to dole it out at innumerable councils and treaty conferences. He reported
that Indians sold "the necessaries they receive from the Crown thro me for
Rum, to the infinite detriment of His Majestys service & the increase of Indian Expences." The Mohawk towns, home to those Indians with the most
regular contact with Johnson, had become "scenes of perpetual riot."[33] After
the war, Johnson's laments about Indian abuse of alcohol continued unabated, but he refused to curb the supply because of the importance he as-
signed to liquor in expanding the fur trade and pacifying western Indians.[34]

Even more subtle were the changes that Johnson's distribution of material
goods wrought in traditional patterns of Iroquois politics and leadership. By
the mid-eighteenth century, a shift in power was already well underway in
Iroquois politics away from the traditional hereditary chiefs, selected by clan
matrons to represent their lineages at the Iroquois Grand Council in
Onondaga, to "pine tree chiefs," men acknowledged as leaders because of
their personal powers of influence and persuasion. Iroquois headmen such as
Hendrick and Nickus became influential within Iroquois communities in
part because colonial agents perceived them to be influential and loaded
them with diplomatic presents that reinforced their power when redistrib-
uted among their kinsfolk and neighbors at home.[35]

By the eve of the Seven Years' War, Johnson had already knit himself into
Iroquois politics by distributing presents to those chiefs and warriors with

whom he cultivated close alliances. Those "marks of Distinction" worn by Hendrick and Nickus—laced coats and hats, ruffled shirts, silver gorgets and medals—were tangible evidence of Johnson's insertion of himself into the internal dynamics of Iroquois leadership. Johnson referred to his distribution of medals he commissioned from Albany and New York City silversmiths as "making Sachems," and he made great ceremony out of such occasions.[36] By the end of the Seven Years' War, recognition from Johnson by the bestowal of a medal and certificate had become *de rigueur* for Iroquois chiefs conducting diplomacy with the British.

Evidence of Johnson's manipulation of the objects and rituals that signified Iroquois leadership can be found in any number of contexts from this era. In Onondaga in 1766, an Iroquois chief offered his credentials to visiting Moravian missionaries by allowing them to "look through his documents, among which was his Warrant from Sir William Johnson, appointing him the Chief and Speaker of the Onondago [sic] Nation, together with the great Seal."[37] On some occasions, friends and relatives of deceased sachems returned silver medals or gorgets to Johnson so that he might award them to an appropriate successor. At a conference at Johnson's home in 1758, a half dozen or so Oneida sachems met privately with Johnson and returned to him a medal he had granted to a recently deceased Oneida, asking him to give it "to such of the Oneidas as he thought deserving or qualified for a Sachem."[38] On a similar occasion in 1767, the brother of a recently deceased Iroquois sachem presented to Johnson the dead man's son along with a silver gorget Johnson had previously given to the deceased. The uncle asked Johnson to raise up his nephew in the dead man's place by giving him the gorget. Johnson had no objection to doing so but promised to wait until a general treaty council, "so that all Nations might be privy and see that it was done by him."[39] The ceremony hinted at here, a sort of public investiture at which Johnson presided, became commonplace during the 1760s. It was visually depicted on a certificate Johnson distributed to his Indian allies, allowing them safe passage between British posts. In the scene, Johnson and a group of Indians are gathered under the Tree of Peace, a symbolic chain hanging from its limbs. Johnson stands at the center, presenting a medal over the council fire to an Indian (see figure 4.1).

The more systematically Johnson knit himself into the fabric of Iroquois leadership, the greater the material dependency those Iroquois leaders had on him. That dependency in turn eroded Iroquois political autonomy during the 1760s. After the fall of Montreal, the Iroquois lost their ability to maintain a parallel diplomatic relationship with the French, and with the centralization of colonial Indian affairs under the crown's Indian superintendencies during

Figure 4.1. *Indian Certificate*, by Sir William Johnson, engraved by Henry Dawkins, April 1770, original impression made from copper plate, negative number 2611. (Collection of The New-York Historical Society). The scene depicted on this certificate shows Johnson presenting a peace medal to an Indian ally.

the war, Johnson became the only game in town. As Johnson's diplomacy with Indians from the Great Lakes and Ohio regions took him farther and farther afield from the Mohawk Valley, the eastern Iroquois who had served as his original powerbase in Indian affairs were reduced to serving as members of his entourage, symbolizing his wealth and power but possessing little influence on his decision-making.

The marks of the transformation wrought within Iroquois society by Johnson's rise to power were everywhere in the 1760s. Onondaga, the traditional seat of Iroquois power, was eclipsed by Johnson's home as the center of Iroquois diplomacy. In exchange for his protection and material assistance, Johnson sought and received from his Iroquois neighbors land grants of increasing size and value, on which he settled German and Scots-Irish tenants. Rum trafficking continued unabated in Iroquois villages, as did outmigration for other Iroquois communities in the St. Lawrence and Ohio river valleys more distant from Johnson's interference. Gradually, the tone of the intercultural diplomacy conducted between Johnson and the Iroquois changed from exchange to extraction. Before the Seven Years' War, colonial and Iroquoian parties came to treaty conferences seeking a variety of services or concessions from each other: better prices or regulation in the fur trade, military alliance or at least neutrality, adjudication of disputes and reparations for grievances. The Fort Stanwix Treaty of 1768, the most important intercolonial treaty conference Johnson presided over in his postwar tenure as Indian Superintendent, offered a much starker display of diplomatic tit for tat. More than three thousand Indians attended, drawn by the promise of cash and presents valued in the thousands of pounds, to witness the Iroquois cede to the British crown their land claims in western Pennsylvania, Virginia, and modern Kentucky.[40] This simple equation of land for loot provided the template by which the United States conducted its diplomacy with the Iroquois during the following generation, demanding land cessions in exchange for annuities of cash or material goods that the Indians would need to sustain themselves as they were confined to small, unproductive reservations.[41]

Conclusion

The cultural impact of the Seven Years' War on the Iroquois cannot be measured strictly in terms of the usual casualties of war: blood and treasure expended, lives lost, homes destroyed. Indeed, by relying on a system of warfare that had protected them against British or French domination since 1701, the Iroquois emerged from the military conflict relatively unscathed. Far more subtle but also pernicious were the changes wrought in their lives by their increasing material dependence on the British crown via William Johnson. In brief, Iroquois military culture proved to be remarkably resilient during the war, but Iroquois material culture underwent profound stress, in a way that abetted their eventual dispossession during the Revolutionary Era.

The Iroquois experience in the Seven Years' War comes into sharper relief when compared to that of other Indian groups. In the Ohio Country, the brutal frontier warfare of the Seven Years' War put in motion a culture of violence that gave rise to racist "Indian hating" on the part of the whites and nativist movements that preached rejection of white ways among the Indians.[42] The war failed to produce these same circumstances in the homelands of the Iroquois nations, where no armed colonial mobs akin to Pennsylvania's Paxton Boys conducted murderous raids against Indian towns, and no Indian prophets emerged to fire Indian resistance. Among the Ohio Indians, prophets such as Neolin appeared in the mid-eighteenth century, preaching a message of collective Indian revival by rejecting Christianity, liquor, and dependence on European trade goods. While this message first gained currency among the mixed Indian populations of the upper Susquehanna Valley in the 1730s and 1740s, it appears to have moved west into the Ohio Country during the era of the Seven Years' War, rather than north into the Iroquois homelands. By the time of Pontiac's War in 1763, the nativist message of separate paths for Indians and whites had taken firm root among the Indian communities of the Allegheny and Ohio rivers, uniting and militarizing their resistance to Anglo-American western expansion, but the Iroquois of New York would not witness a similar movement until the Handsome Lake revivals among the Senecas in the early years of the nineteenth century.[43]

There is no doubt that social conditions were ripe for such a nativist movement to emerge in Iroquoia on the eve of the Seven Years' War. The Mohawks were alienated by land frauds perpetrated by colonial New Yorkers; the Oneidas and Onondagas complained of abuses at Oswego and threatened violence against the traders there; and everywhere the liquor trade was fracturing Iroquois communities. Moravian missionaries living in Onondaga in 1754 attended a council meeting at which Nanticokes from the northern Susquehanna Valley preached an antiliquor message to the local men and women, urging them to stop drinking rum so that famine might end and their population be replenished. The Nanticokes conveyed their argument "by a letter, written on wood with black paint," depicting the all-seeing eye of God and the punishments inflicted by the Devil on drunkards in the afterlife.[44] This message had much in common with that preached by Neolin and other Indian prophets in the Ohio Country: a rejection of rum as an agent of the devil, a call for spiritual renewal, a promise of restored strength and prosperity. Yet, with the exception of the western Senecas, the Iroquois remained aloof from the anti-British militancy of Pontiac's War.

One reason for this may have been that the Iroquois were already so acculturated to the Anglo-American presence in their lives that it was impossible to contemplate the nativist alternative of a world in which Indians and Europeans came from separate creations and walked separate paths. Among the Mohawks, a syncretic religious faith that combined native and Anglican forms of worship was already well established by 1750. The Oneidas, although less exposed to missionary work in the early eighteenth century than the Mohawks, developed a strong partnership with Congregationalist missionary Samuel Kirkland in the 1760s. Moravians from Pennsylvania lived and traveled among the Onondagas and Cayugas periodically during the 1740s, 1750s, and 1760s. It is also worth noting that in the years preceding the Seven Years' War, many inhabitants of Onondaga chose to resettle at the French missionary community of Oswegatchie (modern Ogdensburg) on the St. Lawrence River.[45] As all of these examples attest, a pattern of religious and cultural adaptation to colonial peoples had a firm foundation in eighteenth-century Iroquoia, making it less fertile ground for the kind of nativist movements that militarized the Ohio Indians and preached a rejection of European goods and Christianity.

In the years between the Seven Years' War and the American Revolution, this acculturation continued apace. In some respects, the Iroquois experience in this era paralleled that of the colonial Americans described by Woody Holton elsewhere in this book. They participated in an eighteenth-century "consumer revolution" that reshaped their material lives and drew them into a tighter economic orbit around Great Britain.[46] Some of them (although admittedly a small minority) were swept up in the tide of evangelical Christianity known as the Great Awakening and formed new alliances with colonial preachers or fellow converts in mission communities.[47] Commerce and religion, two of the revolutionary forces that transformed eighteenth-century Anglo-America, also had their impact on the Iroquois. Unlike colonial Americans, however, the Iroquois did not find in these forces new bonds of political and cultural unity that enabled them to break free from their material and political dependence on Great Britain. Rather, the range of choices they could exercise in their economic and political lives grew narrower in the years after the Seven Years' War. The British conquest of New France and the rise of Johnson as Indian Superintendent closed off the diplomatic paths they had maintained with other colonial governments before 1760. Their material dependency on diplomatic presents acquired from Johnson continued to grow, at precisely the time when Johnson's attentions shifted to Indians farther west in the Great Lakes and Ohio regions.

Ever the astute observers of geopolitics, the Iroquois quickly realized what was at stake here. When Johnson visited Onondaga while en route to Detroit to meet with the Ottawas, Chippewas, Shawnees, and other western nations in 1761, the Onondaga chiefs expressed surprise that he was traveling so far to convene a treaty conference with Indians recently allied with the French. "You know that the chief and only council fire burns at your house and

Onondaga," they told him, "besides, these Indians you are going to, ought rather, as being aggressors, to come to you." Johnson responded to this thinly veiled assertion of Iroquois primacy in British Indian affairs by reminding them that the fall of Canada had changed everything: "As our conquests in this country are now great . . . it will be necessary to have other meetings and places of trade, than Oswego and Onondaga." In his capacity as the crown's Indian Superintendent, he had to "keep up a good understanding" with those western Indians now joined to the British interest, and, he warned the as-sembled Onondaga chiefs, "it will be for your good to keep up a good under-standing with them also."[48]

Just a few years earlier, Johnson had depended on Iroquois such as Hen-drick and Nickus to preserve and extend his influence among the Indians; now he could confidently chide chiefs and warriors in Onondaga, the tradi-tional seat of Iroquois power, for assuming a preeminence in Indian affairs that they no longer commanded. In the end, it was not warfare that undid the Iroquois, but their own diplomacy that reduced them from partners to clients in Britain's expanding empire.

Notes

I would like to thank Eric Hinderaker, Warren Hofstra, Greg Nobles, and the other participants in the "Cultures in Conflict: The Seven Years' War in North America" conference for their comments on earlier drafts of this essay.

1. Two works that elaborate on this expansive definition of "Iroquois" in the eigh-teenth century are Daniel K. Richter and James H. Merrell, eds., *Beyond the Covenant Chain: The Iroquois and Their Neighbors in Indian North America, 1600–1800* (Syra-cuse, NY: Syracuse University Press, 1987), and Jon William Parmenter, "At the Wood's Edge: Iroquois Foreign Relations, 1727–1768" (PhD dissertation: University of Michigan, 1999).

2. *Documents Relative to the Colonial History of the State of New York*, eds. E. B. O'Callaghan and Berthold Fernow, 15 volumes (Albany, NY: Weed, Parsons, and Company, 1853–1887), 6:1003–4, 1006–9 (hereinafter *NYCD*). For the Battle of Lake George, see also Ian K. Steele, *Betrayals: Fort William Henry and the "Massacre"* (New York: Oxford University Press, 1990), 28–56; Fred Anderson, *Crucible of War: The Seven Years' War and the Fate of Empire in British North America, 1754–1766* (New York: Alfred A. Knopf, 2000), 115–23; and William M. Fowler, *Empires at War: The French and Indian War and the Struggle for North America, 1754–1763* (New York: Walker and Company, 2005), 77–85. For a description of Hendrick's death, see Soci-ety of Colonial Wars in the State of New York, *Daniel Claus' Narrative of His Relations*

with Sir William Johnson and Experiences in the Lake George Fight (New York: Society of Colonial Wars, 1904), 13–14.

3. James Sullivan, et al., *Papers of Sir William Johnson*, 14 volumes (Albany: University of the State of New York, 1921–62), 9:796–97. Hereinafter *WJ Papers*.

4. See José António Brandão, *Your Fyre Shall Burn No More: Iroquois Policy Toward New France and Its Native Allies to 1701* (Lincoln: University of Nebraska Press, 1997), 31–61 and Daniel K. Richter, "War and Culture: The Iroquois Experience," *William and Mary Quarterly*, 3rd ser., 40 (October 1983): 528–59.

5. NYCD, 6:1010.

6. *WJ Papers* 2:80, and Steele, *Betrayals*, 54.

7. On the 1701 Grand Settlement, see Daniel K. Richter, *Ordeal of the Longhouse: The Peoples of the Iroquois League in the Era of European Colonization* (Chapel Hill: University of North Carolina Press, 1992), 190–215, and José A. Brandão and William A. Starna, "The Treaties of 1701: A Triumph of Iroquois Diplomacy," *Ethnohistory* 43 (Spring 1996): 209–44. On the success of Iroquois neutrality, see Richard Aquila, *The Iroquois Restoration: Iroquois Diplomacy on the Colonial Frontier, 1701–1754* (1983; reprint, Lincoln: University of Nebraska Press, 1997).

8. See Richard R. Johnson, "The Search for a Usable Indian: An Aspect of the Defense of Colonial New England," *Journal of American History* 64 (Dec. 1977): 623–51.

9. For the Cherokee in Forbes' campaign, see Anderson, *Crucible of War*, 267–68; for the Iroquois in Amherst's campaign, see William N. Fenton, *The Great Law and the Longhouse: A Political History of the Iroquois Confederacy* (Norman: University of Oklahoma Press, 1998), 517–19, and *WJ Papers*, 13:224, 237.

10. For Shirley's efforts among the Iroquois, see Steele, *Betrayals*, 33–34, and *Claus' Narrative*, 9–12. For his previous success with the Louisbourg expedition, see John A. Schutz, *William Shirley: King's Governor of Massachusetts* (Chapel Hill: University of North Carolina Press, 1961), 80–103. For the recruitment and experience of Anglo-American soldiers in the Seven Years' War, see Fred Anderson, *A People's Army: Massachusetts Soldiers and Society in the Seven Years' War* (Chapel Hill: University of North Carolina Press, 1984).

11. See Timothy J. Shannon, *Indians and Colonists at the Crossroads of Empire: The Albany Congress of 1754* (Ithaca, NY: Cornell University Press, 2000), 52–54, 199–200.

12. [Thomas Pownall], *Proposals for Securing the Friendship of the Five Nations* (New York: J. Parker and W. Weyman, 1756), 7.

13. See Francis Jennings, *Empire of Fortune: Crowns, Colonies, and Tribes in the Seven Years War in America* (New York: W.W. Norton, 1988), 414–17.

14. For the negotiations between the French-allied and British-allied Iroquois, see Captain Pouchot's Journal of the Siege of Fort Niagara, NYCD, 10:981–90.

15. See *Claus' Narrative*, 13–14, and Steele, *Warpaths*, 48–50.

16. On the origins myth of the Iroquois League, see Richter, *Ordeal of the Longhouse*, 30–49; on the *pax Iroquoia*, see Anthony F.C. Wallace, *Death and Rebirth of the Seneca* (New York: Alfred A. Knopf, 1969), 39–48.

17. On British and French notions of nationhood during the Seven Years' War, see the essays by Paul Mapp and Jonathan Dull in this book, respectively.

18. On the emergence of the Ohio Indians as a powerful Indian group independent of the Iroquois, see Michael N. McConnell, A Country Between: The Upper Ohio Valley and its Peoples, 1724–1774 (Lincoln: University of Nebraska Press, 1992), 5–88; Eric Hinderaker, Elusive Empires: Constructing Colonialism in the Ohio Valley, 1673–1800 (Cambridge, UK: Cambridge University Press, 1997), 3–45; and Richard White, The Middle Ground: Indians, Empires, and Republics in the Great Lakes Region, 1650–1815 (Cambridge, UK: Cambridge University Press, 1991), 186–268.

19. Hugh Mercer to John Forbes, January 8, 1759, in Donald H. Kent, Louis M. Waddell, and Autumn L. Leonard, eds., The Papers of Henry Bouquet, 6 volumes (Harrisburg: Pennsylvania Historical and Museum Commission, 1972–1977), 3:25. See also Jennings, Empire of Fortune, 413–14.

20. See Jon W. Parmenter, "The Iroquois and the Native American Struggle for the Ohio Valley, 1754–1794," in The Sixty Years' War for the Great Lakes, 1754–1814, eds. David Curtis Skaggs and Larry L. Nelson (East Lansing: Michigan State University Press, 2001), 105–24.

21. Jennings briefly addresses the attacks on Kittanning, St. Francois, and Conestoga in Empire of Fortune, 200–202. For the devastation the Seven Years' War wrought on Indian communities in the Ohio Country, see Matthew C. Ward, Breaking the Backcountry: The Seven Years' War in Virginia and Pennsylvania. 1754–1765 (Pittsburgh: University of Pittsburgh Press, 2003), 100–107, 228–50.

22. Iroquois population estimates are always a tricky business, but the figures compiled by Parmenter indicate a healthy increase for the New York Iroquois between 1750 (4,680) and 1763 (6,900). See "At the Wood's Edge," Table 1, p. viii. (see Parmenter, n. 1).

23. For an assessment of Johnson's career as an Indian agent before the Seven Years' War, see Shannon, Indians and Colonists at the Crossroads of Empire, 30–45. For a recent biography of Johnson, see Fintan O'Toole, White Savage: William Johnson and the Invention of America (New York: Farrar, Straus, and Giroux, 2005).

24. See for example, the treaty conference Johnson convened at his home in June 1755, which was attended by approximately 1,100 Indians, NYCD, 96:964–89.

25. Shannon, Crossroads of Empire, 24–30.

26. On ginseng, see William M. Beauchamp, ed., Moravian Journals Relating to Central New York, 1745–1766 (1916; Bowie, MD: Heritage Books, 1999), 120–23.

27. Johnson detailed his disbursements in his accounts; see for example the detailed account for the period between November 1756 and March 1757 in WJ Papers, 9: 644–58, during which he spent £5,142 on his Indian agency.

28. On Johnson's Indian name, see Milton W. Hamilton, Sir William Johnson, Colonial American, 1715–1763 (Port Washington, NY: Kennikat Press, 1976), 45.

29. Johnson to Arthur Lee, February 28, 1771, in E. B. O'Callaghan, ed., Documentary History of the State of New-York, 4 volumes (Albany, NY: Weed, Parsons, and Company, 1849–51), 1:434.

30. See for example, references to Indian negotiations for blacksmiths at Shamokin, Onondaga, and other Iroquois villages in central New York and Pennsylvania in Beauchamp, ed., *Moravian Journals*, 8, 54–55, 96, 189, 204–5.

31. See Gregory Evans Dowd, *War Under Heaven: Pontiac, the Indian Nations, and the British Empire* (Baltimore, MD: Johns Hopkins University Press, 2002), 73–75, and Anderson, *Crucible of War*, 469–72.

32. Justin DiVirgilio, "Rum Punch and Cultural Revolution: The Impact of the Seven Years' War in Albany," *New York History* 86 (Fall 2005): 435–49.

33. Johnson to James Abercromby, May 17, 1758, in *WJ Papers*, 9:905.

34. See Peter Mancall, *Deadly Medicine: Indians and Alcohol in Early America* (Ithaca, NY: Cornell University Press, 1995), 162–64.

35. See Fenton, *Great Law and the Longhouse*, 396–97, 448–49, and Richter, *Ordeal of the Longhouse*, 21–22.

36. *WJ Papers*, 9:108–9.

37. Beauchamp, *Moravian Journals Relating to Central New York*, 237.

38. *WJ Papers*, 10:74–75.

39. *WJ Papers*, 12:390.

40. See Fenton, *Great Law and the Longhouse*, 535–40. Also see Peter Marshall, "Sir William Johnson and the Treaty of Fort Stanwix, 1768," *Journal of American Studies* 1 (August 1967): 149–79.

41. Addressing Iroquois participation in the American Revolution is beyond the scope of this essay, but the classic works on the topic remain authoritative: Barbara Graymont, *The Iroquois in the American Revolution* (Syracuse, NY: Syracuse University Press, 1972), and Wallace, *Death and Rebirth of the Seneca*. For the dispossession of the Iroquois in the Revolutionary Era, see Alan Taylor, *The Divided Ground: Indians, Settlers, and the Northern Borderland of the American Revolution* (New York: Alfred A. Knopf, 2006).

42. See Daniel K. Richter, *Facing East from Indian Country: A Native History of Early America* (Cambridge, MA: Harvard University Press, 2001), 191–201.

43. See Gregory Evans Dowd, *A Spirited Resistance: The North American Indian Struggle for Unity, 1745–1815* (Baltimore, MD: Johns Hopkins University Press, 1992), 27–35; Jane T. Merritt, *At the Crossroads: Indians and Empires on a Mid-Atlantic Frontier, 1700–1763* (Chapel Hill: University of North Carolina Press, 2003), 121–28; and Wallace, *Death and Rebirth of the Seneca*, 239–337.

44. Beauchamp, *Moravian Journals Relating to Central New York*, 200.

45. For the Mohawks, see Daniel K. Richter, "'Some of Them . . . Would Always Have a Minister with Them': Mohawk Protestantism, 1683–1719," *American Indian Quarterly* 16 (Fall 1992): 471–84; for the Oneidas, see Walter Pilkington, ed., *The Journals of Samuel Kirkland: Eighteenth-Century Missionary to the Iroquois, Government Agent, Father of Hamilton College* (Clinton, NY: Hamilton College, 1980), 1–90; for the Moravians among the Onondagas, see Beauchamp, *Moravian Journals Relating to Central New York*; and for the Onondagas at Oswegatchie, see Fenton, *Great Law and the Longhouse*, 472–80.

46. On the consumer revolution and its role in the coming of the American Revolution, see T. H. Breen, *The Marketplace of Revolution: How Consumer Politics Shaped American Independence* (New York: Oxford University Press, 2004). James Axtell applies the notion of a consumer revolution to the native peoples of eastern North America in his essay "The First Consumer Revolution" in *Beyond 1492: Encounters in Colonial North America* (New York: Oxford University Press, 1992), 125–51.

47. See Merritt, *At the Crossroads*, 89–159.

48. *WJ Papers*, 13:223–25.

~

CHAPTER FIVE

Declaring Independence: The Ohio Indians and the Seven Years' War

Eric Hinderaker

In early June 1747, the Provincial Council of Pennsylvania learned that George Croghan, an Indian trader active in the Ohio Valley, had just returned to Philadelphia with a letter from a group of Indians on the south shore of Lake Erie. Along with the letter, they sent a French scalp to demonstrate their commitment to a British alliance. In November, a delegation from the Ohio group arrived unannounced in Philadelphia and requested an audience with the Council. They introduced themselves as "Warriors, living at *Ohio*," apologized for their unexpected visit, and requested support for their efforts on Britain's behalf in the ongoing war against the French: the War of the Austrian Succession, known in Britain's American colonies as King George's War.[1]

This meeting marked the first appearance of a group identified as Ohio Indians in the records of Pennsylvania. It also presented the Pennsylvania Council with an awkward dilemma. The arrival of the Ohio Indians posed a challenge to the colony's prevailing practice of conducting its Indian relations through the Iroquois Confederacy and the so-called Covenant Chain that structured their contacts. The Ohio group linked themselves with the Iroquois—"We are of the *Six Nations*, who are your ancient friends," they noted, and they claimed to speak for themselves "and the rest of the Warriors of the *Six Nations*." Yet their message was, in part, an expression of frustration with confederacy leadership. The British had asked for Iroquois support in their war with the French; "the old men at Onondago however refus'd to do this" and the Iroquois warriors, both in Iroquoia and in the Ohio Valley, bided their time. "At last," however, "the young Indians, the Warriors, and Captains, consulted together, and resolved to take up the English Hatchet against the Will of their old People, and to lay their old People aside, as of no Use but in Time of Peace."[2]

This account of their actions must have given the Pennsylvania councilors pause. Before replying, they met privately with Conrad Weiser, an experienced observer of Indian affairs, to try to learn more about their visitors. Weiser explained that they represented a group of Iroquois who had moved to the Ohio Valley near the south shore of Lake Erie, that they consisted "principally of warriors," and that they were part of a large community of perhaps five hundred men—probably numbering two to three thousand in all—with "many allies more numerous than themselves." Weiser also noted that the Ohio Iroquois had decided to light a council fire of their own and invite all the Indians "at a considerable Distance around about" to convene there in the spring. This was a decisive political act: to light their own council fire meant, quite literally, to declare their independence from the council fire at Onondaga, at the heart of the Iroquois Confederacy. Their Philadelphia trip was an explicit declaration of alliance with Great Britain in the western theatre of King George's War and an urgent request for support. Weiser recommended that the colony affirm the alliance. In response, the Council gave the Ohio warriors cautious encouragement and promised them a present as a sign of friendship. The Indian spokesman "express'd high Satisfaction at what the Council had said," and the warriors set out for the Ohio Country.[3]

The contradictions of this scene are striking. Though the Ohio warriors professed to be Iroquois, everything about their actions reflected their independence from, even defiance of, Iroquois authority. It also marked the first appearance in the public record of a group identifying themselves as Ohio Indians. Yet in 1747 there was no coherent social group or political unit that could be called by that name. The Indian population of the Ohio Valley was still forming, as peoples from various points of origin and various cultural backgrounds moved into the region, made homes for themselves, and began to hammer out working relations with one another. The Ohio Indians need to be considered as central players in the Seven Years' War, but they must also be understood as a diverse, divided population that was trying to establish some basis for collective identity and action for the first time as the events of the war began to unfold.

The Ohio Indians' lack of unity and inexperienced leadership were crucial to the origins and progress of the Seven Years' War in North America.

They help to account for the erratic nature of the Ohio Indians' diplomacy in the years leading up to war, they are dramatically illustrated in the episode that triggered the conflict, and they intensified the brutality of the war on the Pennsylvania and Virginia frontiers. Wartime experience, and the pressures that followed, produced a clearer sense of cultural identity and common political cause than the Ohio Indians had ever previously known, but it can be argued that they came too late. At the outset, the actions of inexperienced leaders in the emerging Indian communities of the Ohio Valley shared little in common with the canny play-off strategies of more established Indian confederacies like the Iroquois and the Creeks.[4] While the Iroquois, as Timothy Shannon's essay in this volume shows, consistently acted to limit their military commitments during the Seven Years' War and thereby minimized the war's impact on their own communities, the Ohio Indians' choices helped to bring the force of two great European empires to bear on their home territory and accelerated their dispossession and displacement.

Origins: Migration, Hunting, and Trade

By the mid-eighteenth century, the Ohio Valley was home to a growing population of Indians. Thirty years earlier, the upper Ohio had been essentially vacant. Beginning in the 1720s, Shawnees and Delawares from Pennsylvania who had been using sites on the Allegheny River as hunting camps for many years began to relocate permanently to those sites. From there, they moved farther west into the Ohio Valley itself. In the early 1740s, a large number of Iroquois, mostly Senecas, followed their lead and likewise moved west into the valley, settling along the upper Allegheny and Beaver rivers. The Ohio Indians who visited Philadelphia in 1747 and introduced themselves as "Warriors, living at *Ohio*," represented these migrants.[5]

The Shawnees, Delawares, and Senecas who moved to the Ohio Valley all wanted to distance themselves from the pressures of the Anglo-Iroquois alliance. In Pennsylvania, the Iroquois Council had joined with the colony in demanding that Shawnee and Delaware communities accept the encroachment of colonial communities onto Indian land. In Seneca country, the founding of a French trading post at Niagara and its British counterpart at Oswego in the 1720s brought new economic opportunity but also a rising tide of liquor, violence, and disease, conditions for which many Senecas placed particular blame on the British traders at Oswego. By 1741, when a famine compounded these difficulties, the attractions of the Ohio Valley began to draw Senecas west in large numbers.[6]

Both Shawnees and Senecas initiated closer relations with New France as they moved into the Ohio Valley. Yet in neither case was the goal to exchange one imperial overlord for another. All the Indian groups migrating to the Ohio in this period wanted more autonomy, more control over their trading relationships and alliances, and more leverage in dealing with Europeans, French and British alike. In the case of the Shawnees and Delawares, and also to some extent in the case of the western Iroquois, the move to the Ohio was also undertaken to gain distance from the Iroquois Confederacy Council at Onondaga. The Shawnees were openly hostile to Iroquois leaders in this period, and all the Ohio Indians were unhappy about the confederacy's growing reliance on Britain. Distance from Britain meant, for all these groups, distance from the Iroquois Confederacy as well.[7]

But distance did not mean abandonment. On the contrary, from their new homes the Ohio Indians hoped they could maintain a better relationship with Britain's colonies than they had enjoyed before. During the 1740s, all the Indian communities on the upper Ohio developed an increasingly strong connection with the Pennsylvania traders who began to travel regularly to the valley, while their relations with New France steadily frayed. Indeed, it is striking how quickly the image and reputation of each European power was inverted. Now that Britain and its colonies stood at a distance from the Ohio communities, the threat they had earlier posed to the territorial claims of the Shawnees and Delawares in Pennsylvania seemed irrelevant. The French alliance, on the other hand, almost immediately became unsatisfactory. The governor of Canada pressured the Shawnees to abandon Pennsylvania entirely and move farther northwest, where they would fall under the sway of Detroit and be easier for the French to control. This threat to Shawnee independence was all too reminiscent of the Anglo-Iroquois Covenant Chain. Moreover, trade with the French grew steadily worse. Britain dominated the Atlantic theatre during King George's War, disrupting France's overseas trading connection, and when Louisbourg fell to New Englanders in 1745, it became impossible for French merchants to get any merchandise at all to the western posts.[8]

Into the void created by the collapse of New France's overseas trade stepped the Pennsylvania traders, who began traveling long circuits far into the Ohio Country. Shawnees and Delawares knew these traders well; they had long visited the Indian towns on the Allegheny River. As new Indian communities began to stretch downriver, they extended their trading routes until they were traveling hundreds of miles into the interior. They brought competitively priced merchandise to new Indian communities, but otherwise demanded little of them. The response was overwhelming. Logstown, founded by Shawnees in 1744 and soon home to a mixed population that included many Iroquois as well, quickly became a central entrepôt for the trade. At Detroit, a Wyandot leader named Orontony led a breakaway group to a new home on Sandusky Bay, where they would have easy access to the Pennsylvania traders. Farther downriver, a group of Miami Indians led by a headman named Memeskia left the French Fort Miamis on the Maumee River and migrated south to found the town of Pickawillany on the upper Miami. The Pennsylvania traders quickly added the town to their circuit. Throughout the Ohio Valley, formerly French-allied Indians voted with their feet and sought a trading connection with the British.[9]

These developments caused rapid shifts in the balance of power in the Ohio Country. Less than a year after the first visit of the Ohio Iroquois to Philadelphia, the Pennsylvania Council met with a much larger and more diverse group of Ohio Indians in Lancaster, Pennsylvania. Fifty-five Indians were present in all, including representatives of not only the Ohio Iroquois, the Shawnees, and the Delawares, but also the Miami Indians of Pickawillany. This conference symbolized with particular clarity the transformations taking place in the Ohio Country, and it is worth exploring its dynamics and implications in some detail.

Emergence: Diplomatic Encounters

Its participants gathered at the Lancaster courthouse beginning on a Tuesday in July. Though no one wanted to admit it, everything about this meeting was extraordinary. To begin with, a meeting in Lancaster, rather than Philadelphia, was unusual.[10] Because of its distance from Philadelphia, the Council sent four of its members to serve as commissioners. They told the Indians, "As the Government had shewn them great Indulgence in granting them a Council at Lancaster, so far from the usual Place of Business, and in so hot a Season, it was expected they wou'd not detain the Commiss[ione]rs, but deliver what they had to say tomorrow morning at ten o'Clock, and further to desire they wou'd use no manner of Reserve, but open their Hearts freely and fully." In this simple request, the commissioners swept away decades of tradition and dispensed with the formalities of the Covenant Chain's "At the Woods' Edge" ceremony that customarily opened such conferences. As they had done in the previous November, the commissioners in July continued to emphasize that they were dealing with their "Brethren of the Six Nations" on the Ohio, but the expediency of the Lancaster conversation only underscored the fact that this meeting fell outside the norms of Covenant Chain proceedings.[11]

Indeed, the most striking thing about the conference in retrospect is its inventiveness. Indian spokesmen and colonial commissioners alike were recasting diplomatic procedures and constructing a narrative of their relationship on the fly. Scarouady, an Oneida who had visited Philadelphia in the previous year, was supposed to be the Ohio Indians' spokesman, but they reported that he had fallen and was indisposed, so Andrew Montour (whose mother came from mixed French-Huron parentage, whose father was an Oneida warrior, and who had extensive experience as a translator and back-country go-between) spoke for them instead.[12] He introduced the Miamis and informed the commissioners that they had approached the Ohio Indians, through their nearest neighbors the Shawnees, to ask to "enter into the chain of Friendship with the English." With the approval of the Ohio Indians, the Miamis sent representatives to Lancaster with an interesting array of gifts. First, they carried two wampum strings, artifacts that would have been a foreign import for the Miami Indians. Originating on the Atlantic coast, the wampum presumably was carried to Pickawillany either by Pennsylvania traders or, more likely, by Ohio Indians who already had a relationship with Pennsylvania and the Iroquois. It was the Iroquois who had made wampum an indispensable artifact in diplomacy. They and their allies believed that wampum literally carried the speeches of those who used it and thereby conferred legitimacy on diplomatic proceedings. The Miamis knew about wampum—it had periodically appeared in their villages for half a century, both as an article of ornamentation and in the form of belts that arrived occasionally from either English traders or the Iroquois themselves—but the Miamis, like many of their Algonquian neighbors, were outsiders to the cultural system in which it was embedded.[13]

Along with the wampum, they presented the Pennsylvania commissioners with thirty beaver pelts. Again, this gift marked the Miamis as outsiders. While French traders had received beaver pelts from their Indian partners in the Great Lakes and Ohio Valley for many years, Pennsylvania's Ohio trade dealt almost exclusively in deerskins. (In fact, Pennsylvania's official record of the conference refers to the pelts as "skins.") Finally, the Miamis brought the Pennsylvania commissioners "a Calumet Pipe with a long stem curiously wrought, & wrapp'd round with Wampum of several Colours, & fill'd with Tobacco, which was smoked by the Commissioners & Indians according to Custom."[14] Just as the customs associated with wampum were relatively unfamiliar to the Miamis, the Pennsylvania commissioners had only limited experience with the calumet, which belonged to the world of the Great Lakes Indians and had been incorporated in only limited ways into the sphere of Iroquois influence.[15] By wrapping the calumet in wampum strings, the Mi-

This paired illustration juxtaposes wampum and calumet ceremonies. The caption says that the images "concern the diplomacy and trade of the Indians of North America." The upper scene shows "an Indian in council speaking through [par] his porcelain [or bead] collar." The lower image depicts "the calumet dance." On the mat in the center of the group is the "Manitou or spirit that is being honored in the dance," in this case "a serpent and weapons of war." Though comparable in function, wampum belts and calumets were embedded in distinct cultural contexts and practices. (Courtesy of the Library of Congress)

amis connected the central artifact of their diplomatic system with the one Pennsylvanians would have known best.

The Miami Indians also carried a second calumet pipe given to them by the residents of "twelve Towns or Nations" who were allies of the Miamis and who also hoped to be admitted into Pennsylvania's chain of friendship. They asked that the commissioners "speak to" the pipe "and return it with their answer." In imitation of the Miamis, the Pennsylvania commissioners returned the calumet wrapped in wampum and assured the Miamis that they were "always ready to receive" representatives from nations recommended to them by the Ohio Iroquois.[16] They did not know it yet, but in extending such an open-ended invitation to the French-allied Indians of the Ohio Valley, the Pennsylvania commissioners were getting in over their heads.

The Lancaster meeting was a landmark event in the creation of a collective identity for the principal Indian groups on the upper Ohio. By appearing together and affirming their ties to Pennsylvania, the Ohio Indians asserted their independence from the Covenant Chain and claimed to be free of the old system, according to which the Iroquois spoke and acted for them in public. The Pennsylvania commissioners did not want to acknowledge this shift openly and masked it by blurring the distinction between Iroquois leaders who spoke for Onondaga and the Iroquois from the Ohio, but the difference would have been clear to anyone who understood the dynamics of Indian relations and the structure of the Covenant Chain.

From Lancaster, the scene shifted west to Logstown, the recently founded trading village on the upper Ohio where, two months later in September 1748, the Ohio Indians officially gathered around their own council fire for the first time. Conrad Weiser attended on behalf of Pennsylvania, along with Andrew Montour and George Croghan. They met with representatives of each of the original Five Nations of the Iroquois, Shawnees, Delawares, Mahicans, and Wyandots. Like the Miamis at Lancaster, the Wyandots who had recently left the French post at Detroit received Weiser's particular attention. He assured them that they would be welcomed as "Brethren of the English." In contrast to the July meeting in Lancaster, this one followed the protocol of the "At the Woods' Edge" ceremony typical of Covenant Chain meetings. Thanayieson, a Seneca speaker, gave a string of wampum to clear the evil spirits from the travelers' eyes and minds and remove their bitterness, and then recounted the origins of the Covenant Chain.[17]

Despite borrowing the form of their proceedings from Iroquois practice, however, it was once again clear that this meeting deviated from Covenant Chain protocol. Simply by sending representatives to the Ohio, Pennsylvania acknowledged the Ohio Indians' independence. What this meant for Iroquois authority became clear when Weiser distributed gifts at the end of the conference. Had this been a typical Covenant Chain affair, the colony's gifts would have been given to representatives of the Iroquois, who would then have shared them out as they saw fit. Instead, Weiser's gift was divided into five shares and distributed in a way that reflected the balance of power on the upper Ohio. One share each went to the Ohio Senecas, Delawares, and Shawnees; a fourth share was divided among the four remaining Iroquois nations represented there; and a fifth share went to the Wyandots and Mahicans. This may seem like a small point, but it clarifies the extent to which Pennsylvania was ignoring its long-standing reliance on the Iroquois Council in managing its relations with other Indian groups. Weiser explained the colony's reasoning. The Ohio Indians had originally "settled the River of Ohio for the sake of Hunting," he noted, but "You are now become a People of Note, & are grown very numerous of late Years. . . . It therefore becomes you to Act the part of wise men, & for the future be more regular than You have been for some Years past, when only a few Young Hunters lived here."[18]

In Weiser's eyes, the Ohio Indians had come of age, but his admonition also suggests his uncertainty. And indeed, much remained uncertain. In only a few years, the Ohio had become a major crossroads in intercultural trade. Its Indian population was united by the shared cultural attributes of the region—above all, by the rise of Indian hunters eager for ties to the Pennsylvania traders. Various Indian groups who had been under the thumbs of more powerful neighbors experienced newfound independence and new forms of opportunity. Their new communities were especially fluid; chiefs were few and far between, and the towns were often led by coalitions of younger or less-established men. In Logstown and elsewhere, trading houses dominated the town center and British traders lived alongside diverse Indian populations. These communities were dynamic places in the late 1740s, filled with possibility.[19] They were also extraordinarily unstable, a quality that was clearly reflected in Conrad Weiser's plea to "Act the part of wise men, & for the future be more regular." Under the right conditions, his wish might have been fulfilled. Instead, events were about to overtake the Ohio Indians and sweep them toward war. The Ohio Indians were central players in the Seven Years' War, but they were disastrously unprepared for its effects. Not yet a sufficiently coherent social or cultural group to act in concert, they instead acted as a collection of independent communities and chose various paths. The war visited catastrophe on the Ohio Indians, and there was little they could do to control it.

Identities Forged in Violence

The Ohio Country was the focus of conflict between Britain and France in the late 1740s and early 1750s, and as conflict gave way to bloodshed, it became the pivot on which the fates of the British and French empires turned. The Ohio Indians were pawns in the conflict and worked desperately to turn the competition between empires to their advantage. As they did so, their independence from Onondaga was accentuated. The progress of events only confirmed, however, that despite their nominal independence from the Covenant Chain, the Ohio Indians remained profoundly dependent on the support of their colonial allies. When that support faltered, the Ohio Indians were exposed and vulnerable.

From 1749 until the outbreak of fighting in 1754, the Indian population of the Ohio Valley was caught between increasingly aggressive assertions of power by both France and Britain over their territory.[20] For the French, this came in the form of a terrifying attack on the town of Pickawillany, followed by a fort-building project that attempted to seal off the valley to Pennsylvania traders while it laid claim to the headwaters of the Ohio River. The British colonies behaved in these years with a disheartening combination of expediency and opportunism. Despite its professions of friendship, Pennsylvania supplied the Ohio Indians with only token gifts and ignored the Indians' request that they build a strong house that could help them defend the Pennsylvania traders against French raids. At the same time, the Ohio Company of Virginia was trying to secure a large area of land on the upper Ohio on which it hoped to plant a new settlement.[21] The Ohio Indians searched in vain for a way to exploit the interest of either Pennsylvania or Virginia for their benefit.[22]

Increasingly frustrated with the British colonies, one faction of the Ohio Indians led by the Seneca headman Tanaghrisson nevertheless twice offered aid to parties of Virginia militiamen under the command of George Washington, once in 1753 and again in the spring of 1754. Tanaghrisson had recently emerged as the principal spokesman for the Ohio Indians in their dealings with Pennsylvania and Virginia. Born a Catawba, Tanaghrisson and his mother were captured during an Iroquois raid when he was a boy and adopted by the Senecas. He had moved west to Logstown by 1747 and become village headman there. Representatives of the colonies called him an Iroquois "half-king" and, by virtue of that title, maintained that they were not violating their commitment to the Covenant Chain in dealing directly with the Ohio Indians.

Now, in the spring of 1754, Tanaghrisson persuaded a small party of Iroquois warriors to join him in scouting for Washington's men as they made their way toward the Ohio. What happened next is a familiar story. Washington, leading an advance group of Virginians and Iroquois, surprised a French reconnaissance party. Though Washington almost certainly intended only to confront them and demand that they withdraw, someone fired a shot and a battle ensued. Then Tanaghrisson jumped into the fray. Wielding a tomahawk, he crushed the skull of Joseph Coulon de Villiers de Jumonville, the commander of the French forces, plunged his hands into the open cavity, and washed them in the Frenchman's brains. His followers took their cue from Tanaghrisson and initiated a slaughter of the wounded. As Fred Anderson has convincingly demonstrated, Tanaghrisson hoped that his dramatic gesture would trigger a war and force the British colonies to make a stronger commitment to the defense of the Ohio Country. If those were his aims, he succeeded. He did trigger a war. He also forced a concerted British assault on the French in the region, though he did not live long enough observe the result, which turned out to be ruinous for the Ohio Indians.[23]

More immediately, Washington and his men left the scene of the slaughter in confusion. For a time they continued their advance on Fort Duquesne, but when reinforcements failed to arrive, Washington concluded that he was leading his men toward disaster. They retreated to a place called the Great Meadows and hastily threw up a log fort that came to be known as Fort Necessity. After a pitched battle on July 3, Washington agreed to terms of surrender, and on the morning of July 4, 1754, he led his defeated detachment back to Winchester.[24]

Tanaghrisson acted almost alone in supporting Washington's advance on the Ohio. The region's Shawnees, Delawares, and most of the Iroquois had grown so skeptical of the intentions of both Pennsylvania and Virginia that they refused to aid Washington's undermanned and apparently aimless expedition. Scarouady, the leading Oneida on the Ohio and a close associate of Tanaghrisson, burned and abandoned Logstown in late June of 1754—a dramatic gesture that affirmed the collapse of the British alliance.[25]

Scarouady, like Tanaghrisson, was identified as an Iroquois "half-king" on the Ohio. The label was conferred upon them at the time by representatives of Pennsylvania and Virginia and has been echoed by historians ever since. It is worth pausing for a moment to consider the meaning of this title. Clearly, the Onondaga Council and the British colonies recognized both men as legitimate leaders of the Ohio Indians. But scholars have sometimes implied that, in their capacity as half-kings, they were constrained to act in particular ways in accordance with the wishes of the Iroquois Council. This is an unfounded inference. On the contrary, Tanaghrisson and Scarouady acted out of their own concerns and interests; neither was following the lead of the Onondaga Council in 1754. As war approached, the Iroquois Council remained resolutely neutral, and with few exceptions maintained that stance throughout the war.[26] Tanaghrisson's flamboyant act of violence, arguably the trigger event of the Seven Years' War and a desperate attempt to redirect the course of events, would have appeared unconscionable from the perspective of Onondaga. The independence of his actions only underscores that the Ohio Indians had broken entirely with the expectations and dictates of Iroquois leadership.

This is not to say, however, that the Ohio Indians were united in their response to events. In the last half of 1754, as French and British forces moved toward war in the Ohio Valley, the Ohio Indians abandoned any pretense of collective action as each community made its own choices about what to do next. Tanaghrisson himself, bitter to the end about the failure of British power, died in the fall of 1754. In his absence, the Ohio Iroquois turned to Scarouady for guidance while the valley's other Indian populations did their best to adjust to the new realities of power in the region. The most senior Delaware leader on the Ohio at the beginning of the war was Shingas, who continued to hold out hope for reconciliation and aid from Pennsylvania. In the wake of Braddock's disastrous, failed campaign to capture Fort Duquesne, however, even Shingas threw in his lot with the French. In the fall of 1755, along with a Delaware war leader named Captain Jacobs, Shingas began to lead raiding parties in the Pennsylvania, Maryland, and Virginia backcountries.[27]

For nearly three years, these raids devastated the frontier settlements closest to the Ohio Country. They were an entirely new experience for the Delawares and Shawnees who participated. Though the men of both groups were seasoned hunters, and some had likely joined Iroquois war parties from time to time in their raids against southern Indians, neither had had a sustained involvement in war since the founding of Pennsylvania. These raids were conducted in the French style, with small, mobile forces made up of Indians and French soldiers. They combined the surprise, terror, and pursuit of plunder that were characteristic of Indian raids with a sustained and flexible strategy for pursuing key enemy targets. In many cases, raiders descended suddenly upon undefended farms and villages; at other times they attacked forts. The combination of French arms and the Delawares' and Shawnees' unerring knowledge of the landscape and population made these raids especially devastating. By the spring of 1756, the Virginia Regiment struggled to maintain communication with Fort Cumberland, and the residents of Virginia's frontier counties withdrew to safer ground. That summer Ohio Indians and their French allies struck closer and closer to the heart of Pennsylvania until in August they hit Lebanon, only seventy-five miles from Philadelphia, and burned it to the ground.[28]

In all, more than a thousand frontier residents were killed in these attacks, which were directed against communities that the Shawnee and Delaware raiders often knew intimately, located as they were on lands they once called their own. They victimized former friends and acquaintances and specifically targeted colonists who in Indian eyes had failed to live up to the terms of their former alliance. By the same token, they sometimes passed over households they held in high regard. They mutilated their victims' bodies in pointedly symbolic ways, removing or defacing sexual organs to emasculate their enemies. In one community after another, raiders brought terror and death to the colonies' exposed and largely undefended frontiers. They also took captives in large numbers. By war's end, as many as two thousand colonists had been incorporated into Indian communities on the Ohio and throughout the Great Lakes. Though some were subjected to mistreatment, many were adopted and came to view their captors as family. Mary Jemison, who was captured in western Pennsylvania in 1758, lived the rest of her life among the Senecas.[29]

For the Ohio Delawares and Shawnees, this kind of warfare was unprecedented. Even as it succeeded, it was also deeply troubling to them for several reasons. Their knowledge of the communities they were raiding was often all too intimate, and even at the height of the violence they looked forward to a day when they could live peacefully alongside their Anglo-American neighbors again.[30] Worse, their actions placed kinsmen who still lived within the colonies at risk. Substantial communities of both Delawares and Shawnees remained in the Susquehanna Valley of Pennsylvania, and their residents were subjected to growing pressure from Pennsylvania's government and civilian population alike. Finally, the seasons of raiding placed their communities on the Ohio in danger. It was always hard to sustain Indian economies in times of war, and these years were no different. Nor was hunger the only threat to which they were exposed. In August 1756, Colonel John Armstrong led a retaliatory raid against Kittanning, the Delaware town on the Allegheny River that was home to Shingas and Captain Jacobs. The Pennsylvanians set Kittanning's residents to flight, burned the town, and killed Captain Jacobs.[31]

Thus, even as they succeeded in their war aims, the Ohio Indians with closest ties to Pennsylvania had second thoughts about their actions. By

The German bleeds & bears y⁽Furs   Th⁽Hibernian frets with new Disaster   But help attend⁵ Paxtboes to hold down
Of Quaker Lords & Savage Ours   And kicks to fling his bread to ruin⁵ Master   Th⁽Hibernian⁵ Head for tumble all down.

The frontier violence of the Seven Years' War triggered hostility between Quakers sympathetic to Indian concerns, on the one hand, and backcountry German and Scots-Irish settlers, on the other. This cartoon portrays a Quaker and a Delaware Indian riding on the backs of two "Hibernian" colonists. (Historical Society of Pennsylvania, The German Bleeds & Bears ye Furs [Philadelphis, 1764])

1758, negotiations were underway with Pennsylvania that aimed to convince the Ohio Indians to lay down their arms and refuse support to the French while a British force under the command of General John Forbes marched on Fort Duquesne. The Ohio Indians finally agreed after they were assured that the lands on the Ohio would be their own and that they could enjoy a return to something like the *status quo ante bellum*. Without their continued support, the French army abandoned the site of Fort Duquesne without a fight.[32]

Very quickly, the Ohio Indians learned that the promises made to them during the negotiations in 1758 would not be honored. On the contrary: with alarming speed, British military personnel and private settlers descended on the region around the Forks of the Ohio while Britain's supreme commander in North America, Jeffery Amherst, imposed dramatic new limits on the Indian trade. The Ohio Indians were once again forced to reinvent themselves in order to oppose an imminent threat to their interests.

Prophecy, Culture, and Identity

War's end brought appalling conditions to the Ohio Country. Almost immediately, Fort Duquesne was replaced by Fort Pitt. More ominously, the fort was quickly surrounded by a rapidly growing civilian settlement. Frontier settlers with an eye for promising bottomland began to move into river valleys around the headwaters of the Ohio. The roads to the Ohio cut by the Braddock and Forbes expeditions became corridors of migration, and the speed with which opportunistic colonists took advantage of them was alarming to many of the Ohio Indians. Nor were colonial settlers alone in their interest in Ohio lands. In 1762 a detachment of soldiers from Fort Pitt traveled to Sandusky to build a blockhouse that would strengthen Britain's foothold in the region, while two Moravian missionaries, John Heckewelder and Christian Frederick Post, traveled to the Delaware community of Tuscawaras on the Muskingum River to seek converts. The locals doubted their motives. "Instead of instructing us or our children," they noted, "you are cutting down trees on our land! You have marked out a large spot of ground for a plantation, as the white people do everywhere; and bye and bye another, and another may come and do the same." Soon, "a fort will be built for the protection of these intruders, and thus our country will be claimed by the white people." This reaction aptly summarized a generation's bitter experience with British colonists.[33]

At the same time, Ohio Indian communities were in the throes of famine and sickness. The war brought food shortages to communities throughout the valley. In 1762 some towns were so decimated by disease that their residents were too feeble to plant or hunt. These problems were compounded by the sudden, dramatic restrictions that were imposed on diplomatic gifts and the Indian trade. The restrictions were the brainchild of General Jeffery Amherst, who believed it was time to get tough with the valley's Indian population. He thought Britain was spending too much on gifts to the Indians; he also believed that it would be good for them to have to earn every article of British merchandise they received. In 1761 he outlawed all gift-giving at the western posts. At the same time, fearful that the western Indians might plot against the British, Amherst imposed a tough system of oversight on the Indian trade. Indians now had to come to British posts to trade, instead of allowing traders to travel to their communities, while strict limits on gunpowder and lead made it increasingly difficult for Ohio hunters to ply their craft.[34]

To many Ohio Indians, these developments added up to a concerted conspiracy against them. The outcome of the war, about which many valley

Indians were cautiously optimistic in 1758, had turned out by 1763 to be cat-astrophic beyond their wildest imaginings. Having lost the "worldly war," the Ohio Indians, Gregory Evans Dowd has argued, embarked upon an "other-worldly war" against Great Britain. The most important visionary in this oth-erworldly war was a Delaware prophet named Neolin, who had a revelation in which he was instructed by the Master of Life. Based on his experience, he promoted a system of reform and renewal. Neolin taught that Indians and Europeans were created separately, and that the Master of Life was displeased with Indians for adopting European ways. He particularly disapproved of the use of guns by Indian hunters. With Neolin's urging, many Delawares adopted a new regimen of purification. For seven years, Delaware boys were to be trained with bows and arrows, eat nothing but dried meat, and period-ically purge themselves with a bitter black drink designed to flush out the evil influences of European contact. Finally, Neolin stressed the importance of keeping Europeans—especially the British—off Indian lands. Among other things, his gospel offered a powerful rationale for resisting the growth of British power in the Ohio Valley.[35]

From his home at Tuscawaras, Neolin's message made its way through the Ohio Valley and to Detroit and influenced warriors and community leaders from many backgrounds. Neolin fell into a prophetic tradition among the Delawares that was already decades old, and his message was adopted, ampli-fied, and subtly altered by those who took it up in the early 1760s. It is most famously associated with the uprisings named for Pontiac, an Ottawa leader at Detroit who was deeply influenced by Neolin's message and led a pro-longed siege of the fort there during the summer of 1763. Warriors through-out the region followed Pontiac's lead. By summer's end, every British fort in the West had been besieged and nine fell to their attackers.[36]

After the uprisings of 1763, it would take the British Army two full years to reclaim the West. For the Ohio Indians, the events of that summer con-stituted a fleeting but vividly meaningful episode in a long struggle to claim and defend their territory in the Ohio Valley. The prophetic tradition that preached the importance of radical separation of Indian and European worlds would persist in the Ohio Valley and Great Lakes and resurface again in the early nineteenth century. Then, as in 1763, it provided a powerful rationale for intertribal unity in a time of war. More than any other development that came to the region's Indian population in the last half of the eighteenth cen-tury, the idea of an intertribal, otherworldly war against British or American power expressed pressing concerns and a common goal that could establish the basis for shared identity and action among the Ohio Indians. In this re-spect, though the idea of an otherworldly war may seem chimerical today, it

B. West inv.   *Grignion sculp.*

The Indians giving a Talk to Colonel Bouquet in a Conference at a Council Fire, near his Camp on the Banks of Muskingum in North America, in Oct.ʳ 1764.

203

After the uprisings collectively known as Pontiac's War, it took the British army two years to reclaim the West. Here, Colonel Henry Bouquet and his aides listen as an Ohio Indian speaker presents a belt of wampum over a council fire. The first such fire in the Ohio Country was kindled at Logstown in 1748. (Special Collections Research Center, University of Chicago Library) was, at the time, the most powerful and effective tool the Ohio Indians had with which to face the challenges of the future.

Yet the Ohio Indians' otherworldly attack on European influence also reminds us that their political and cultural unity emerged too late to produce a sustained strategy in their worldly encounter with the French and British empires. Had the council fire at Logstown been in existence long enough to represent a genuine counterweight to Onondaga and a meaningful center of gravity in cross-cultural relations; had the various Indian communities of the Ohio Country responded in concert as pressure on their lands mounted in the 1750s; had Tanaghrisson acted with the patient restraint of a confederacy leader instead of the impetuous violence of a desperate warrior; had the Ohio Indians pursued a coordinated play-off strategy comparable to that employed by the Iroquois Confederacy—then events might have played out very differently in the Ohio Country. As it was, the actions of the Ohio Indians helped to precipitate a global war, intensify frontier violence, and hasten their dispossession from the headwaters of the Ohio, which would soon be known to a new generation of frontier settlers as their gateway to the continental interior.

Notes

1. Council minutes, June 8, 1747, in *Minutes of the Provincial Council of Pennsylvania, from the Organization to the Termination of the Proprietary Government*, 16 vols. (Harrisburg, PA: 1838–53) [hereafter *MPCP*], V: 72; the treaty between the president and Council of Pennsylvania and the Indians of Ohio held at Philadelphia, Nov. 13, 1747, appears in Julian P. Boyd, ed., *Indian Treaties Printed by Benjamin Franklin, 1736–1762* (Philadelphia: HSP, 1938), 103–8, quote: 103; it also appears in *MPCP*, V: 145–52.

2. Quotes: Boyd, ed., *Treaties*, 103–4.

3. Quotes: Boyd, ed., *Treaties*, 105, 108.

4. For a good overview of native strategies of diplomatic accommodation in this period, see Daniel K. Richter, "Native Peoples of North America and the Eighteenth-Century British Empire," in *The Oxford History of the British Empire*, ed. W. Roger Louis, vol. 2: *The Eighteenth Century*, ed. P. J. Marshall (Oxford: Oxford University Press, 1998), 347–71.

5. This migration is detailed in Michael N. McConnell, *A Country Between: The Upper Ohio Valley and its Peoples, 1724–1774* (Lincoln: University of Nebraska Press, 1992), esp. 5–15.

6. McConnell, *A Country Between*, 15–20.

7. McConnell, *A Country Between*, 17–20.

8. Eric Hinderaker, *Elusive Empires: Constructing Colonialism in the Ohio Valley, 1673–1800* (New York: Cambridge University Press, 1997), 30–32, 39–42.

9. McConnell, *A Country Between*, 47–60.

10. It was not, however, unheard of; four years earlier, another extraordinary gathering of colonists and Indians had occurred in Lancaster as well, this one involving representatives of the Iroquois Confederacy and the colonies of Pennsylvania, Maryland, and Virginia. This conference resulted in a land sale by the Iroquois to colonial representatives that Virginia's Ohio Company later used to justify their claims at the headwaters of the Ohio River. The conference proceedings are in *MPCP*, IV: 699–737; for context, see Francis Jennings, *The Ambiguous Iroquois Empire: The Covenant Chain Confederation of Indian Tribes with English Colonies from its beginnings to the Lancaster Treaty of 1744* (New York: W. W. Norton, 1984), 356–63 and ff.

11. The conference proceedings are in Boyd, ed., *Treaties*, 109–22, and *MPCP*, V: 307–19. Quotes: *MPCP*, V: 307, 312.

12. For Montour, see especially James H. Merrrell, "'The Cast of his Countenance': Reading Andrew Montour," in Ronald Hoffman, Mechal Sobel, and Fredrika J. Teute, eds., *Through a Glass Darkly: Reflections on Personal Identity in Early America* (Chapel Hill: University of North Carolina Press, 1997), 13–39; and, more generally, Merrell, *Into the American Woods: Negotiators on the Pennsylvania Frontier* (New York: W. W. Norton, 1999).

13. *MPCP*, V: 309.

14. *MPCP*, V: 309–10. For an account of the calumet's significance among Great Lakes Indians, see Richard White, *The Middle Ground: Indians, Empires, and Republics in the Great Lakes Region, 1650–1815* (New York: Cambridge University Press, 1991), 20–23. Nancy Shoemaker discusses the movement of such objects across the boundaries of culture regions in *A Strange Likeness: Becoming Red and White in Eighteenth-Century North America* (New York: Oxford University Press, 2004), 67–68.

15. Both Pennsylvania officials and Iroquois leaders had some familiarity with calumet diplomacy. A calumet was smoked, and a calumet dance performed, at the Montreal treaty council of 1701, to which Iroquois representatives were a party. According to William Fenton, the Fox Indians introduced the Iroquois to the calumet in the 1720s; the Iroquois then adapted it to their own uses, and it made occasional appearances in Iroquois diplomacy thereafter. See William Fenton, *The Great Law and the Longhouse: A Political History of the Iroquois Confederacy* (Norman: University of Oklahoma Press, 1998), 210, 347–48, 403–4. In 1707, when Governor John Evans traveled to Susquehanna to investigate charges that French traders were stirring up anti-English sentiment among the colony's allies, he smoked "a large pipe with Tobacco" with representatives of Shawnee, Seneca, Conoy, and Nanticoke Indians; see *MPCP* II: 385–91, quote: 386. Five years later, a delegation of Delawares met with Pennsylvania officials before traveling to Iroquoia to pay tribute to the Five Nations. Along with thirty-two wampum belts that contained messages for the Iroquois, the Delawares also carried "a long Indian pipe called the Calumet, with a stone head, a wooden or cane shaft & feathers fixt to it like wings, with other ornaments." They explained that the Iroquois had given them the pipe many years earlier, so "that at all times thereafter, upon shewing this pipe where they Came they

might be known to be the friends & subjects of the five Nations, and be received by them when they Came amongst them." This episode is hard to square with Fenton's chronology, but it highlights the extent to which Indian groups inventively worked new artifacts and practices into their own activities when the opportunity arose. See the record of the council at White Marsh, May 19, 1712, in *MPCP*, II: 546–49. On the history of the pipe tomahawk, which was adapted from the calumet, see Timothy J. Shannon, "Queequeg's Tomahawk: A Cultural Biography, 1750–1900," *Ethnohistory* 52 (2005), 589–633.

16. *MPCP*, V: 310, 314; see also the exchange with the Miamis about their allies on 315. These would have included Piankashaw, Ouiatenon, and perhaps Illinois Indians.

17. The Journal of Conrad Weiser Esqr., Indian Interpreter to Ohio, *MPCP*, V: 348–58; quote: 351; Thanayieson's speech, 352–53.

18. *MPCP*, V: 356–58.

19. Hinderaker, *Elusive Empires*, 46–77; McConnell, *A Country Between*, 21–46.

20. The essays by Jonathan Dull and Paul Mapp in this book trace these changes in French and British policy to the competitive logic of the European state system, which produced an exaggerated fear on the part of each nation toward its chief rival. For the French, this fear was behind an uncharacteristically assertive defense of territory in the Ohio Valley; for the British, it encouraged a shift from a mercantile to a territorial empire. These are complementary perspectives and together help to explain the ways in which the diplomatic ground was shifting beneath the Ohio Indians' feet.

21. For the attack on Pickawillany, French strategy, and Pennsylvania's neglect of the Ohio Indians, see White, *Middle Ground*, 223–40. Documents relating to the Ohio Company's efforts are collected in Lois Mulkearn, ed., *George Mercer Papers: Relating to the Ohio Company of Virginia* (Pittsburgh: University of Pittsburgh Press, 1954).

22. McConnell, *A Country Between*, 82–105.

23. Fred Anderson, *Crucible of War: The Seven Years' War and the Fate of Empire in British North America, 1754–1766* (New York: Knopf, 2000), 5–7, 42–59.

24. Anderson, *Crucible of War*, 59–65.

25. McConnell, *A Country Between*, 110.

26. As Timothy J. Shannon's essay in this book makes clear, the Iroquois Confederacy pursued a very different course in the Seven Years' War than the Ohio Indians. This has less to do with the war's impact on their interests and territory—Iroquoia, like the Ohio Country, was directly in harm's way—than it does with the long experience of Iroquois diplomats, who had learned to deflect European wars as much as possible to limit the damage they could do to their lives, property, and interests.

27. Anderson, *Crucible of War*, 94–107; McConnell, *A Country Between*, 115–24.

28. Matthew C. Ward, *Breaking the Backcountry: The Seven Years' War in Virginia and Pennsylvania, 1754–1765* (Pittsburgh: University of Pittsburgh Press, 2003), 59–70; Anderson, *Crucible of War*, 158–65; Hinderaker, *Elusive Empires*, 140–43.

29. Jane T. Merritt, *At the Crossroads: Indians and Empires on a Mid-Atlantic Frontier, 1700–1763* (Chapel Hill: University of North Carolina Press, 2003), 176–87;

Ward, *Breaking the Backcountry*, 70, 49–57. For Jemison's story, see James E. Seaver, ed., *A Narrative of the Life of Mrs. Mary Jemison* (Norman: University of Oklahoma Press, 1995).

30. See, for example, the remarks attributed to Shingas in "The Captivity of Charles Stuart, 1755–1757," Beverley W. Bond, Jr., ed., *Mississippi Valley Historical Review*, 13 (June 1926), 64–65.

31. McConnell, *A Country Between*, 121–26.

32. Anderson, *Crucible of War*, 267–85.

33. "List of Houses and Inhabitants at Fort Pitt," 14 Apr. 1761, in S. K. Stevens, et al., eds., *The Papers of Henry Bouquet*, 5 vols. (Harrisburg, PA: 1972–1984), V: 407–21; "The Journal of James Kenny, 1761–1763," John W. Jordan, ed., *Pennsylvania Magazine of History and Biography*, 37 (Jan. 1913), 6, 14, 27–29, 152, 39–40; John Heckewelder, *A Narrative of the Mission of the United Brethren Among the Delaware and Mohegan Indians, from Its Commencement, in the Year 1741, to the Close of the Year 1808* (Phila., 1820 [repr. NY: Arno Press, 1971]), 59–64; quotes: 61–62.

34. Hinderaker, *Elusive Empires*, 146–49; for the larger context of Amherst's policies, see especially Gregory Evans Dowd, *War Under Heaven: Pontiac, the Indian Nations, and the British Empire* (Baltimore, MD: Johns Hopkins University Press, 2002), 54–89.

35. Dowd, *War Under Heaven*, 90–104.

36. Gregory Evans Dowd, *A Spirited Resistance: The North American Indian Struggle for Unity, 1745–1815* (Baltimore, MD: Johns Hopkins University Press, 1992), 1–46; Dowd, *War Under Heaven*, 114–47.

CHAPTER SIX

~

How the Seven Years' War Turned Americans into (British) Patriots

Woody Holton

One of the few scholarly hypotheses that has escaped oedipal challenges from subsequent generations is the notion that the Seven Years' War was a crucial stepping-stone to the American Revolution. Historians differ about just how the Great War for Empire, which ended in 1763, fueled the imperial conflict that began that same year—but not about whether it did.

One link between the two conflicts comes down to us from the 1760s. Imperial officials and the home-grown opponents of the American Revolution, the Loyalists, often contended that at the conclusion of the Seven Years' War, many British colonists in North America simply cast up accounts. The one major benefit they had derived from the British Empire—protection from France—had just been eliminated, so they were no longer willing to shoulder their share of the costs. In 1954, that partisan theory acquired powerful academic backing, as the respected scholar Lawrence Henry Gipson contended that American independence became inevitable the moment British Americans escaped the so-called Gallic Peril.[1]

Later generations of historians discovered additional links between the Seven Years' War and the American Revolution. Even as "the French war" alerted British imperial officials to American disloyalty, it also gave them a chance to do something about it. Having sent tens of thousands of soldiers to America to fight the French and Indians, the British decided to leave ten thousand of them there, partly to keep an eye on their own colonists. Driving the French out of North America also allowed Britain to crack down on its own colonists without fear of offending essential allies in the epic struggle against Albion's archenemy.[2] Moreover, many of the reforms the imperial government tried to adopt in the 1760s were designed to solve problems that had emerged early in the struggle against France.[3]

Scholars have also drawn other connections between the two conflicts—more, in fact, than can be briefly itemized here. Most of them are plausible enough. And yet I am not sure the Seven Years' War really did increase the likelihood that the thirteen colonies extending from Georgia to New Hampshire would rebel against Britain. Indeed, the case can be made that the first conflict actually made the second one less likely.

The bulk of this essay lists ways in which the war that concluded in 1763 slowed the growth of anti-imperial sentiment. Historians have always been somewhat mystified by the rapid spread of revolutionary ideas among colonists who were arguably the freest and wealthiest people in the world, and the more we learn about the impact of the Seven Years' War on free British colonists, the more mysterious the Revolution becomes. The essay concludes with two possible solutions to the mystery, one unabashedly political and the other borrowing from the cultural approach this volume is intended to promote.

～

Some of the obstacles the Seven Years' War placed in the path of a colonial revolt are impossible to measure, yet still significant. Among them were gratitude and imperial pride. The pamphlets and sermons that poured from American presses in the wake of James Wolfe's posthumous victory on the Plains of Abraham brimmed with British patriotism. In the first flush of victory, free British Americans exuded undisguised gratitude for the imperial troops and bullion that had defeated the French and their Indian allies. Colonists who remained loyal to Britain during the subsequent imperial conflict tried to reawaken that sense of gratitude. In 1774, a year before George Washington took command of the Continental Army, Rev. Jonathan Boucher, who had been Washington's step-son's teacher, published a pamphlet recalling that Britain had expended "much Blood, and Treasure" in rescuing free Americans "from Enemies, who threatned us with Slavery, and Destruction."[4]

Sentiment was not the only thread attaching free colonists to the empire, for cold, hard, political calculation also reinforced their loyalty. British Americans were fond of using the lamp of experience to illuminate their possible futures, and modern scholarship depicts them ransacking Greek and Roman history for edifying lessons.[5] Yet the colonists did not neglect their own recent past, either, and the Seven Years' War supplied them with numerous useful precepts.

Loyalists and other cautious Americans would not let anyone forget what earlier conflicts had taught them about how a war with the mother country might go. Britain would encounter little difficulty in enforcing its decrees in America, Martin Howard affirmed in a 1765 pamphlet. Had the mother country not, by the end of the Seven Years' War, "arrived to the highest pitch of glory and power"?[6]

In a pamphlet published in Virginia in the summer of 1774, John Randolph, that province's attorney general, cautioned his countrymen not to challenge the British military establishment that had proven so effective in crushing their enemies. "The People of *England* are brave, and powerful," he wrote. Indeed, the colonists had been able to form their own direct impressions of British soldiers and sailors, since "Their Strength has been frequently exerted in our Protection" (there was the gratitude card again).[7] The colonists, on the other hand, were, as Thomas Chandler warned in a 1775 pamphlet, "without fortresses, without discipline, without military stores, without money."[8]

In *Common Sense*, which appeared in January 1776, Thomas Paine urged his fellow Americans not to be intimidated by British military might. James Chalmers replied several months later in an anonymous pamphlet entitled *Plain Truth*. Free colonists were fooling themselves if they believed it was their militias that had defeated the French and their Spanish and Indian allies. The British Empire had already established its dominance before the Seven Years' War, Chalmers wrote, and during that conflict, "her glory was, if possible, more eminently exalted; in every quarter of the globe did victory hover round her armies and navies, and her fame re-echoed from pole to pole."[9] In response to Paine's claim that Americans could easily build, equip, and man enough ships to drive the imperial navy from their shores, Chalmers reminded his readers that the British sailors whom Paine deprecated "constantly drub the French ships."[10]

Loyalists never failed to emphasize that the British Navy could not only be a daunting potential enemy but a steadfast and valuable friend. "Past experience"—not only in the Seven Years' War but in earlier conflicts—"shews that Britain is able to defend our commerce, and our coasts," another of Paine's critics, Charles Inglis, wrote, "and we have no reason to doubt of her being able to do so for the future."[11] Chalmers went further. With France out of North America, and with George III (who reportedly lacked his forbears' determination to defend their German homeland) on the British throne, he claimed, the United Kingdom's future wars would be fought at sea. For Americans, that not only meant less property destruction and fewer civilian casualties but also enormous economic opportunity. While ships based in British ports were busy fighting the French, American merchants would be able to take over their trade routes. "Nor is the object of captures inconsiderable," Chalmers wrote. He was talking about the tremendous profits American merchants had made, especially during the Seven Years' War, as "privateers" (government-sanctioned pirates preying upon enemy merchant ships), and he was suggesting that additional windfalls beckoned.[12]

If things went the other way, however, Britain possessed not only the power to crush a colonial revolt but the will to do so, Loyalist writers argued. "Depend upon it," Howard declared in his 1765 pamphlet, "a nation who, for the defence and safety of *America* only, staked their all in the late war . . . will not patiently be dictated to by those whom they have ever considered as dependant upon them."[13] Does anyone really believe, Chalmers asked, that the mother country, "who but yesterday made such prodigious efforts to save us from France, will not exert herself as powerfully to preserve us from our frantic schemes of independency[?]"[14]

In the mid-1770s, as hostilities threatened and then finally erupted, Patriots assured each other that they would be able to count on French aid. Surely France, smarting from its humiliation in 1763, would jump at the chance for a rematch.[15] We should not let hindsight—our knowledge that Louis XVI did indeed end up playing a decisive role in the War of Independence—blind us to the fact that at the time, many greeted the assurance of French aid with skepticism. "France is now at peace with Great-Britain," Inglis wrote in his reply to *Common Sense*, "and is it probable that France would interrupt that peace, and hazard a war with the power which lately reduced her so low, from a *disinterested* motive of aiding and protecting these Colonies?"[16]

The colonists also knew that if they rebelled, Britain would not be the only enemy they faced. Gipson argued that the British colonists did not dare resist the British yoke until the British Army had freed them from their fear of a French empire "having at its command thousands of ferocious redskins."[17] Today, as Eric Hinderaker and Timothy Shannon demonstrate elsewhere in this book, hardly anyone thinks the Indians were their European allies' bloodthirsty puppets. And yet the battles that raged between 1754 and 1764 did show that Native American warriors equipped with French supplies could be formidable. The British Americans knew they had even more to fear from an alliance linking Indians to their own imperial government, since English and Scottish merchants could offer the Indians better and cheaper manufactured goods than France ever had. In addition, the supply lines along which that merchandise would travel from the British to the Indians were generally much shorter. Moreover, in the hands of skillful Indian recruiters, a little European backing could go a long way. Even a false rumor of renewed French support served as a crucial adhesive for the far-flung Indian coalition that attacked the British colonies in 1763 in what became known as Pontiac's War.[18]

Loyalists and moderates tried to use the specter of renewed Indian attacks to scare their fellow free colonists into standing down. Years later, in his *History of Virginia*, Edmund Randolph recalled that Patriots in the Old Dominion challenged the British despite their "conviction that the merciless tomahawk would be uplifted against her" if the imperial conflict turned deadly.[19]

Nor were death and destruction the only evils free British colonists would be courting if they rebelled. In the half century since the bicentennial of the Seven Years' War in 1954, students of the war have documented that it subjected British Americans to shortages, massive currency inflation, trade restrictions, massive tax increases (threefold in the case of Massachusetts), a monumental loss of work time, and a postwar recession. Collectively these side effects inflicted more damage on the North American economy than did all the various nations' warriors. Of course in 1763 none of the British North Americans could know, as we do now, that their subsequent conflict against their own mother country would cost them even more. Yet people still recovering from one war could hardly have deluded themselves into thinking they could come through another one unscathed.[20]

During the 1760s, as colonists simultaneously looked back upon the French war and forward toward a possible conflict against the imperial government, one thing was especially clear. As recent scholarship has emphasized, both the French in the 1750s and the rebel colonists in the 1770s had to contend with British naval blockades. During the Seven Years' War, the United Kingdom's victories at sea starved French garrisons in the American interior of vital supplies. The severing of supply lines played a crucial role in French decisions to abandon forts like Duquesne, Frédéric, and Carillon without a fight.[21]

The British imperial navy came very close to playing the same role in the American War of Independence.[22] Although by no means impermeable, the British blockade was a primary reason the rebelling colonies suffered crippling shortages. The naval cordon also kept American farmers and fishermen from selling their produce, impoverishing not only individuals but also the state and federal governments. Thus the blockade can in large measure be

blamed for the war's infamous financial disasters, especially the runaway inflation that gave birth to the expression "not worth a Continental." The
British North Americans did not need a crystal ball to predict these possible
consequences of challenging the imperial government because Loyalist writers continually harped on that theme.[23]

As worrying as the prospect of another round of death, destruction, shortages, inflation, and poverty must have been, these horrors were expected to
produce a secondary effect that was probably even more daunting. Although
the war against France and its Indian allies had sometimes united British
Americans, it had just as often divided them. The colonists had continued to
battle each other even after defeating the French, and Loyalists predicted
that these intestine broils would intensify if they declared independence.

Of all the forms of internal discord the Seven Years' War had produced,
none perhaps was more ominous than class conflict. Even as the war impoverished many Americans, it gave some of their countrymen the opportunity
to become fabulously wealthy. Some supplied the army at prices only a Hal-
liburton executive could love. Others struck it rich as privateers. As one historian describes it, "the parallel emergence of the fabulously wealthy and the
desperately poor" during the Seven Years' War led to an upsurge in "the language of class consciousness." "Is it equitable," one postwar writer demanded,
"that 99, rather 999, should suffer for the Extravagance or Grandeur of one?
Especially when it is considered that Men frequently owe their Wealth to the
impoverishment of their Neighbors?"[24] Social conflict continued during the
1760s, and the colonists had every reason to believe another war would also
demand unequal sacrifices from Americans and thereby fan the flames. As in
fact the War of Independence did.[25]

Perhaps the most severe class conflicts ushered in by both wars were over
military service. Whether the enemy was the French and Indians or the
British, military burdens nearly always fell disproportionately on the least
powerful colonists, and anger at this inequity fueled draft resistance and
mutiny.[26] In particular, in both the 1750s and the 1770s, western settlers re-
sented being sent far from home to accomplish some general's dubious objectives while leaving their own families vulnerable to attack by Indians
and their European allies.[27] Early in the Seven Years' War, Virginia lieutenant governor Robert Dinwiddie despairingly reported the "Dissatisfact'n,
Discontent and Clamours of All ranks" in his colony.[28] In Massachusetts,
British officers accustomed to treating their men as slaves provoked stiff resistance from Massachusetts militiamen demanding respect.[29] Although the
cultural gap that would later separate American soldiers from their Continental officers was not nearly so great, it was still wide enough to create

conflict—as numerous scholars have shown.[30] Loyalists had predicted this manpower crisis. Patriot soldiers, Thomas Chandler wrote, would "soon grow tired of the service," "learn to be jealous of their own rights and liberties," and "become mutinous."[31]

Nor were these the only wounds that opened during "the French war" and remained tender afterwards. New Englanders, Pennsylvanians, and Virginians all quarreled among themselves—and all over different issues. In Pennsylvania, rioters targeted pacifists and the conflicts were generally ethnic. More than a decade after the end of the war, Chalmers pointed out in his reply to *Common Sense* that any census of Pennsylvania's fighting men would have to "deduct the people called Quakers, Anabaptists, and other religionists averse to arms."[32]

Both wars also exposed tensions among the British colonies and the independent states that replaced them.[33] Not one of them approved the Plan of Union proposed by the Albany Congress in 1754, and the war that began later that year revealed additional faultlines.[34] Indeed, the inability of the British provinces to coordinate their activities during the Seven Years' War seems to have given the British imperial administration the impression it could encroach on their ancient privileges without incurring concerted resistance. Indeed, Benjamin Franklin assured imperial officials that the colonies' "jealousy of each other was so great" that they would never be "able to effect . . . an union among themselves" that could be "*dangerous*" to Britain.[35]

One historian contends that British officials were emboldened by the belief that they could reform fiscal and commercial arrangements without uniting the North American provinces in opposition. He describes this imperial confidence, which of course turned out to have been misplaced, as one more link between the Seven Years' War and the Revolutionary War.[36] Fair enough. Yet the breakdown of intercolonial cooperation during the French war was just as obvious to the colonists themselves, and their anxiety about a recurrence of this failure must be ranked as yet another lesson from the Seven Years' War that acted as a brake on colonial resistance. Loyalists asserted that even an American victory over the mother country, unlikely as that seemed, would be disastrous, since it was only British supervision that kept the various colonies from attacking their neighbors, especially over disputed borders.[37]

Any list of British subjects whose conflicts with their fellow colonists intensified during both the Seven Years' War and the Revolutionary War must include those whom the others had enslaved. Today it is widely known that thousands of enslaved Americans took advantage of the chaos of the

Revolutionary War to run away and that some even launched rebellions.[38] Many escaped to the British lines, served for the duration, and received their freedom. Historians have begun to show that numerous African Americans had sought liberation during the wars for empire as well. In July 1755, Charles Carter reported to Robert Dinwiddie, the lieutenant governor of Virginia, that enslaved workers had gathered near his son's home, possibly with a view to allying with the Native American and French warriors who had just defeated Edward Braddock's army near Fort Duquesne.

Dinwiddie replied on July 18. "The Villany of the Negroes on any Emergency of Gov't is w't I always fear'd," the governor told Carter, "I greatly approve of Y'r send'g the Sheriffs with proper Strength to take up those th[a]t apear'd in a Body at Y'r Son's House." If the slaves were "found guilty of the Expressions mention'd," Dinwiddie said, "an Example of one or two at first may prevent those Creatures enter'g into Combinat's and wicked Designs."[39] Later in the war, Richard Henry Lee warned the House of Burgesses that slaves, "from the nature of their situation, can never feel an interest in our cause, because they . . . observe their masters possessed of liberty which is denied to them."[40]

As it would during the American Revolution, the black presence interfered with southern legislators' attempts to prosecute the Seven Years' War. When the Virginia House of Burgesses adopted its 1756 appropriation, it earmarked only 45 percent of the money for the regiment it had created to fight the French and Indians—and 55 percent for the militia, which was in charge of internal security, including the prevention of slave revolt.[41] The following year, Lord Loudoun peeled off two hundred of Colonel George Washington's soldiers to garrison Charleston, South Carolina, where what officials apparently feared was not a French naval attack but a slave insurrection. White Charlestonians would once again fear slave revolt in 1760 during the Cherokee War.[42]

Free British colonists, especially in Virginia, became especially alarmed about their slaves during Pontiac's War. For the first time in recent memory, the Indian raiders spared the lives of blacks at the settlements they attacked; freemen wondered why. "As the Indians are saving & Carressing all the Negroes they take," Staunton, Virginia, physician William Fleming told Governor Fauquier in July 1763, "should it be productive of an Insurrection it may be attended with the most serious Consequences."[43] The following month, a Virginia clergyman reported that the rebel Indians had "carried a great number of women and children, as well as some men, and (for the first time too) a good many negroes, into captivity."[44]

As it would be in the Revolutionary War, the existence of a large enslaved population during the war against the French was not only a grave threat in itself but a source of tension among freemen. Samuel Davies, one of the leading Presbyterian ministers in the British colonies, thought he was helping slaveholders when he published *The Duty of Christians to Propagate Their Religion Among Heathens, Earnestly Recommended to the Masters of Negroe Slaves in Virginia* in 1758—at the height of the war. He argued, as many of his clerical colleagues had and would, that Christianizing the growing enslaved population would make them more obedient. Davies ought to have known better, because slaveholders were touchy people. One Virginian, Colonel Edwin Conway, charged that Davies had "much Reproached Virginia" in his pamphlet. Conway pointed out that Davies had "inform[ed] the Negroes they are Stronger than the Whites being Equal in Number then, and having an Annual addition of thousands." "I Can't See any Advantage to the Country to give this account to the Negroes," he wrote.[45]

Free British colonists were well aware that a new military conflict would provide renewed opportunities to the people they claimed to own. "Our most fertile provinces" are "filled with unnumbered domestic enemies, slaves," Chalmers reminded his fellow freemen. The southern colonies were also "intersected by navigable rivers, every where accessible to the fleets and armies of Britain." If imperial troops landed, he predicted, free southern whites could "make no defence."[46] Long after independence, Edmund Randolph recalled that white Virginians were fully aware that if they challenged British officials, their slaves "might butcher their masters and their families, instigated by promises of emancipation."[47]

It seems clear that the clash between the two empires taught British colonists a wealth of cautionary tales they could not afford to ignore as they began to contemplate secession. Which raises an obvious question: How do we account for the fact that the British colonists did in fact rebel?

One way to answer that question is to recall that the British Americans who best understood the lessons of the Seven Years' War were not necessarily those who started the Revolutionary War. There is also an important sense in which the War for Independence was not started by anyone. Historians of the Revolution are increasingly convinced that the British colonists were backed into it. The imperial government in London wanted to reform the three "T"s of its relationship with the colonies—taxation, territory, and trade. The colonists protested those reforms. Yet right up until the morning of April 19, 1775, when British troops were supposed to march past, not toward, the minutemen on Lexington Green, who were not blocking their way, neither side wanted war. When the colonists reluctantly chose independence more than a year later, the majority of the twenty-eight grievances they listed in their Declaration of Independence had nothing to do with the original disputes over the three Ts. Most of the Declaration actually focused on the violent measures the British had taken to punish the colonists for protesting the original grievances.

Thus the Seven Years' War may have fueled the Revolutionary War without directly persuading a single American to take up arms against the Crown. Simply by emboldening the colonists to launch nonlethal protests, the 1763 victory may have set in motion a chain of events that led—imperceptibly, even accidentally, and yet almost inevitably—to independence.

Another approach that may help explain the mystery of the American Revolution is the one this volume advocates: moving beyond politics to culture. One way in which the Seven Years' War emboldened free Americans to challenge the imperial government was by strengthening intercolonial ties. At same time, the battle against the French and Indians may have helped widen the cultural breach between the colonies and the mother country.

It is well known that the Continental Congress hoped to draw Quebec into the Patriot coalition. Although of course that effort failed, the delegates' confidence in their ability to recruit the French Canadians was a crucial element in their larger optimism about their prospects for victory without violence. Why did the rebels expect the Quebeckers to join them? One possible explanation is based on the numerous personal links the inhabitants of the older British colonies had forged with the Quebeckers even as they slugged it out between 1754 and 1763.

Scholars have emphasized that many French-allied Indians who attacked British settlements chose neither to kill their captives nor to adopt them but to turn them over to the French in Quebec. Some Anglo-American prisoners spent years in Quebec, with their status varying from diverse forms of servitude all the way up to the freedom of the town. Many became unofficial members of French colonial families, and we know that some captives kept in touch long after being redeemed. A few even chose to stay on with the French and Indians even when they had a chance to go home, two of the most famous of these being Eunice Williams, captured during the 1704 raid on Deerfield, Massachusetts, and Mary Jemison, a captive who was adopted by the Senecas near the end of the Seven Years' War. Perhaps the complex web linking former captives to their former captors created a bond that bolstered the rebelling colonists' confidence that they could persuade the Canadians to support the common cause.[48]

The Seven Years' War also instilled in many British Americans an even more potent form of self-confidence. Both the dark early days of the conflict and the ultimate victory over the French increased the colonists' conviction that they were God's chosen people. Along with a series of midcentury earthquakes, the war also strengthened numerous Americans' belief in the imminence of the second coming of Jesus Christ. Many would define the struggle against Britain in millennial terms, and David will not shrink from taking on Goliath if he believes he is on a mission from God.[49]

Yet another recently discovered link between the Seven Years' War and the Revolution is a by-product of the blossoming scholarship on the eighteenth-century "consumer revolution." During the 1760s, numerous North Americans fretted that the lavish hospitality they had shown British Army officers who crossed the Atlantic to fight the French and Indians was now coming back to haunt them. As the colonists saw it, the officers returned to Britain filled with tales of the fabulous wealth abounding in America—and of the colonists' consequent ability to tolerate heavy imperial taxes.[50] As Rev. Ebenezer Baldwin put it in a 1774 sermon, "The luxury and superfluities in which even the lower ranks of people here indulge themselves being reported in England by the officers and soldiers upon their return, excited in the people there a very exalted idea of the riches of this country, and the abilities of the inhabitants to bear taxes."[51] Here, then, was yet another way in which the battle against the French and Indians helped pave the way for the War of Independence. At least in the free colonists' eyes, the first war led to the second by teaching British officers lessons that would prove as fateful as they were inaccurate.

One factor that historians of political culture have always considered important is emotion, and here, too, the links between the two conflicts were numerous and powerful. I noted above that one way in which the Seven Years' War slowed the growth of anti-imperial sentiment in North America was by instilling in the free colonists a tremendous sense of gratitude toward their red-coated rescuers. Yet gratitude was seldom a simple matter. Loyalists and politically minded inhabitants of the mother country believed British men and material had produced a grand triumph from which free Americans would surely reap the greatest benefit. The colonists ought to be grateful. The problem was that many British Americans came away from the epic victory over the French convinced that it would primarily benefit the mother country. It was Britons back home who owed colonial militiamen gratitude for what John Dickinson called "the hearty assistance they gave to *Great-Britain* in the late war."[52]

This mutual expectation of gratitude of course went unfulfilled. If, as numerous contemporaries insisted, America was Britain's child, it was, in imperial eyes, a spoiled child that needed a lesson in gratitude. Benjamin Franklin was one American who understood that many Britons considered their colonial cousins "ungreatful, and unreasonable, and unjust" for having put the mother country "to immense expence for their defence, and refusing to bear any part of that expence."[53] For their part, free colonists believed that, having "been lavish of their blood and treasure in the late war" (as Oxenbridge Thacher put it in a 1764 pamphlet), they deserved at least a few years to nurse their wounds before having to make additional sacrifices. "Blood and treasure" were (as Jonathan Boucher would point out a decade later) the very elements the mother country had expended so lavishly in rescuing the British colonists from the clutches of the French and Indians, giving the United Kingdom, Loyalists and imperial officials believed, full title to the colonists' eternal gratitude.[54] Each side's anger at the other's seeming ingratitude left a residue of bitterness that would stiffen its resolve in the impending trans-Atlantic conflict and make reconciliation that much harder.

By stirring British Americans' imperial pride and their gratitude to their saviors, and even more by educating them about what they could expect if they ever tried to secede, the battle against the French and Indians made free colonists less likely to make a conscious choice in favor of independence. At the same time, however, the war strengthened the religious bonds and fictive family ties that united the colonists, emboldening them to resist any sort of imperial encroachment in less lethal ways. The problem was that the success of British arms in North America also emboldened imperial officials to demand concessions from their own colonists—especially in the areas of taxation, territory, and trade. Self-assured British ministers adopted measures that provoked protests from equally confident colonists, and these demonstrations in turn led to British punitive measures. It was these punishments, not the original imperial innovations, that drove the Americans to declare independence. It was only in this very indirect way that the Seven Years' War led to the American Revolution.

I think this explanation of the link between the two wars is more satisfactory than any of those that describe independence as a conscious choice. Like other interpretations, however, this one benefits immensely from our knowledge that a revolution was in fact on the way. If we did not know that, even the cultural connections I have drawn between the two wars might be viewed not as bridges to a movement of colonial resistance but as barriers.

While temporary, forced adoption gave some former British captives pen pals in Quebec, it caused a host of others to loathe their northern neighbors.

Or take the issue of consumerism. Americans feared British army veterans had, in conversations with members of Parliament, exaggerated the colonists' ability to pay imperial taxes. Yet it is also possible that the officers' reports only confirmed what the Customs books already showed: that the colonies were an insatiable market for British manufactures—a golden goose that should be coddled, not cooked.

Religion cut both ways, too. During the 1760s and 1770s, the defeat of the French Papists was generally seen as a divine blessing not on British North Americans but on the United Kingdom of which the colonies formed only one part. In 1776, Charles Inglis reminded his fellow subjects that Britons on opposite sides of the Atlantic were "connected by the endearing ties of religion," and it seems likely that the epic victory of 1763 had strengthened British Americans' sense that they were part of a transoceanic Protestant community.[55]

All of which is simply to underscore an old maxim: that hindsight makes the historian's job far too easy. The difference between us and (say) economists and meteorologists is that the events we predict have already happened.

Notes

1. Lawrence Henry Gipson, *The Coming of the Revolution, 1763–1775* (New York: Harper & Row, 1954); Gipson, "The American Revolution as an Aftermath of the Great War for the Empire, 1754–1763," *Political Science Quarterly* 65 (March 1950), 86–104.

2. Jack P. Greene, "The Seven Years' War and the American Revolution: The Causal Relationship Reconsidered," *Journal of Imperial and Commonwealth History* 8 (March 1980), 93–94.

3. John M. Murrin, "The French and Indian War, the American Revolution, and the Counterfactual Hypothesis: Reflections on Lawrence Henry Gipson and John Shy," *Reviews in American History* 2 (Sept. 1973), 307–18.

4. [Jonathan Boucher], *A Letter from a Virginian to the Members of the Congress to be Held at Philadelphia on the First of September, 1774* (n.p.: n.p., 1774), 26.

5. Trevor Colbourn, *The Lamp of Experience: Whig History and the Intellectual Origins of the American Revolution* (orig. pub. 1965; Indianapolis, IN: Liberty Fund, 1998).

6. [Martin Howard], *A Letter from a Gentleman at Halifax to his Friend in Rhode-Island, Containing Remarks Upon a Pamphlet, Entitled, The Rights of Colonies Examined* (Newport, RI: S. Hall, 1765), 5–6.

7. [John Randolph], *Considerations on the Present State of Virginia* ([Williamsburg, Va.]: n.p., 1774), 9; "A.W. Farmer" [Samuel Seabury], *The Congress Canvassed, or, An Examination into the Conduct of the Delegates at their Grand Convention . . .* ([New York]: [James Rivington], 1774), 27.

8. [Thomas Chandler], *What Think Ye of the Congress Now? or, An Enquiry How Far the Americans are Bound to Abide by, and Execute the Decisions of the Late Congress?* (New York: James Rivington, 1775), 25–26; Edmund Randolph, *History of Virginia* (Charlottesville: University Press of Virginia, 1970), 195.

9. "Candidus" [James Chalmers], *Plain Truth: Addressed to the Inhabitants of America, Containing, Remarks on a Late Pamphlet, Entitled Common Sense* (Philadelphia: R. Bell, 1776), 31.

10. [Chalmers], *Plain Truth*, 35.

11. "An American" [Charles Inglis], *The True Interest of America Impartially Stated, in Certain Strictures on a Pamphlet Intitled Common Sense* (Philadelphia: James Humphreys, 1776), 48–49; [Boucher], *Letter from a Virginian to the Members of the Congress*, 26.

12. [Chalmers], *Plain Truth*, 51.

13. [Howard], *Letter from a Gentleman at Halifax*, 5–6.

14. [Chalmers], *Plain Truth*, 36; [Chandler] *What Think Ye of the Congress Now?*, 40–41; [Boucher], *Letter from a Virginian to the Members of the Congress*, 23.

15. "Extract of a Letter Which May Be Depended on, Dated Sept. 8, 1775," *New Hampshire Gazette*, Dec. 5, 1775; "An American," *Virginia Gazette* (Purdie), March 29, 1776. See Jonathan Dull's essay in this book.

16. [Inglis], *True Interest of America*, 63–64; [Chalmers], *Plain Truth*, 29–30.

17. Gipson, "American Revolution as Aftermath," 103; Colbourn, *Lamp of Experience*.

18. Gregory Evans Dowd, *War Under Heaven: Pontiac, the Indian Nations, & the British Empire* (Baltimore, MD: Johns Hopkins University Press, 2002).

19. Randolph, *History of Virginia*, 195; [Boucher], *Letter from a Virginian to the Members of the Congress*, 29.

20. Gary B. Nash, *The Urban Crucible: The Northern Seaports and the Origins of the American Revolution* (abridged ed.; Cambridge, MA: Harvard University Press, 1986), 155, 158.

21. Gipson, "American Revolution as Aftermath," 87–88; Fred Anderson, *Crucible of War: The Seven Years' War and the Fate of Empire in British North America, 1754–1766* (New York: Knopf, 2000), 381–83, 395, 412, 453–54.

22. Richard Buel Jr., *In Irons: Britain's Naval Supremacy and the American Revolutionary Economy* (New Haven, CT: Yale University Press, 1998).

23. [Inglis], *True Interest of America*, 51, 59–60; [Chandler] *What Think Ye of the Congress Now?*, 40–41.

24. Nash, *Urban Crucible*, 162, 166; Gregory H. Nobles, *Divisions Throughout the Whole: Politics and Society in Hampshire County, Massachusetts, 1740–1775* (Cambridge: Cambridge University Press, 1983), 127; Matthew C. Ward, *Breaking the Backcountry: The Seven Years' War in Virginia and Pennsylvania, 1754–1765* (Pittsburgh: University of Pittsburgh Press, 2003), 77–90, 260–61.

25. On social conflict during the interwar years, see Marvin L. Michael Kay, "The North Carolina Regulation, 1766–1776: A Class Conflict," in Alfred F. Young, ed.,

The American Revolution: Explorations in the History of American Radicalism (Dekalb: Northern Illinois University Press, 1976), 71–123; Rhys Isaac, "Evangelical Revolt: The Nature of the Baptists' Challenge to the Traditional Order in Virginia, 1765–1775," *William and Mary Quarterly*, 3rd ser., 31 (July 1974), 345–68; Brendan McConville, *These Daring Disturbers of the Public Peace: The Struggle for Property and Power in Early New Jersey* (Ithaca, NY: Cornell University Press, 1999); Marjoleine Kars, *Breaking Loose Together: The Regulator Rebellion in Pre-Revolutionary North Carolina* (Chapel Hill: University of North Carolina Press, 2002); Thomas J. Humphrey, *Land and Liberty: Hudson Valley Riots in the Age of Revolution* (DeKalb: Northern Illinois University Press, 2004). On class conflict during the Revolutionary War, see Humphrey, *Land and Liberty*; Michael A. McDonnell, "Class War? Class Struggles During the American Revolution in Virginia," *William and Mary Quarterly*, 3rd ser., 63 (April 2006), 305–44; McDonnell, *The Politics of War: Race, Class, and Conflict in Revolutionary Virginia* (Chapel Hill: University of North Carolina Press, 2007).

26. James Titus, *The Old Dominion at War: Society, Politics, and Warfare in Late Colonial Virginia* (Columbia: University of South Carolina Press, 1991).

27. Nobles, *Divisions Throughout the Whole*, 128; Ward, *Breaking the Backcountry*, ch. 3 (refusal to march out of the county is at 61); Albert H. Tillson Jr., *Gentry and Common Folk: Political Culture on a Virginia Frontier, 1740–1789* (Lexington: University Press of Kentucky, 1991).

28. Dinwiddie, quoted in Ward, *Breaking the Backcountry*, 60.

29. Fred Anderson, *A People's Army: Massachusetts Soldiers and Society in the Seven Years' War* (Chapel Hill: University of North Carolina Press, 1984). While not denying the harshness of the British army's disciplinary regime, Stephen Brumwell argues that the contrast between the fractious colonial militiaman and the blindly obedient British regular has been overdrawn. *Redcoats: The British Soldier and War in the Americas, 1755–1763* (Cambridge: Cambridge University Press, 2002).

30. Ward, *Breaking the Backcountry*, ch. 3; Mary A. Y. Gallagher, "Reinterpreting the 'Very Trifling Mutiny' at Philadelphia in June 1783," *Pennsylvania Magazine of History and Biography*, 119 (Jan.–April 1995), 3–35; Michael A. McDonnell, "Popular Mobilization and Political Culture in Revolutionary Virginia: The Failure of the Minutemen and the Revolution from Below," *Journal of American History*, 85 (Dec. 1998), 946–81.

31. [Chandler], *What Think Ye of the Congress Now?*, 26.

32. [Chalmers], *Plain Truth*, 26; Ward, *Breaking the Backcountry*, 60, 65.

33. David C. Hendrickson, *Peace Pact: The Lost World of the American Founding* (Lawrence: University of Kansas Press, 2003).

34. Timothy J. Shannon, *Indians and Colonists at the Crossroads of Empire: The Albany Congress of 1754* (Ithaca, NY: Cornell University Press, 2000), 220.

35. Franklin, quoted in Greene, "Causal Relationship Reconsidered," 94.

36. Greene, "Causal Relationship Reconsidered," 94.

37. [Randolph], *Considerations on the Present State of Virginia*, 11; [Seabury], *Congress Canvassed*, 25, 27; [Chandler], *What Think Ye of the Congress Now?*, 25.

38. Benjamin Quarles, *The Negro in the American Revolution* (Chapel Hill: University of North Carolina Press, 1961); Sylvia R. Frey, "Between Slavery and Freedom: Virginia Blacks in the American Revolution," *Journal of Southern History* 49 (Aug. 1983), 375–98, and *Water From the Rock: Black Resistance in a Revolutionary Age* (Princeton, NJ: Princeton University Press, 1991); Peter H. Wood, "'The Dream Deferred': Black Freedom Struggles on the Eve of White Independence," in Gary Y. Okihiro, ed., *In Resistance: Studies in African, Caribbean, and Afro-American History* (Amherst: University of Massachusetts Press, 1986), 166–87; Wood, "'Liberty Is Sweet': African-American Freedom Struggles in the Years before White Independence," in Alfred F. Young, ed., *Beyond the American Revolution: Explorations in the History of American Radicalism* (DeKalb: Northern Illinois University Press, 1993), 149–84; Robert A. Olwell, "'Domestick Enemies': Slavery and Political Independence in South Carolina, May 1775–March 1776," *Journal of Southern History* 55 (Feb. 1989), 21–48; Olwell, *Masters, Slaves, & Subjects: The Culture of Power in the South Carolina Low Country, 1740–1790* (Ithaca, NY: Cornell University Press, 1998), 225–43; Woody Holton, *Forced Founders: Indians, Debtors, Slaves, and the Making of the American Revolution in Virginia* (Chapel Hill: University of North Carolina Press, 1999), 133–63; Rhys Isaac, *Landon Carter's Uneasy Kingdom: Revolution and Rebellion on a Virginia Plantation* (New York: Oxford University Press, 2004); Simon Schama, *Rough Crossings: Britain, the Slaves and the American Revolution* (London: BBC Books, 2005); Gary B. Nash, *The Forgotten Fifth: African Americans in the Age of Revolution* (Cambridge, MA: Harvard University Press, 2006); Cassandra Pybus, *Epic Journeys of Freedom: Runaway Slaves of the American Revolution and Their Global Quest for Liberty* (Boston: Beacon Press, 2006).

39. Dinwiddie to Carter, July 18, 1755, in R. A. Brock, ed., *The Official Records of Robert Dinwiddie . . .* (2 vols.; Richmond: Virginia Historical Society, 1883–1884), II, 102; Philip J. Schwarz, *Twice Condemned: Slaves and the Criminal Laws of Virginia, 1705–1865* (Baton Rouge: Louisiana University Press, 1988), 171, 174–76; Mark J. Stegmaier, "Maryland's Fear of Insurrection at the Time of Braddock's Defeat," *Maryland Historical Magazine* 71 (Winter 1976), 467–83; Wood, "Liberty is Sweet," 154–56.

40. Undated speech, in Richard Henry Lee, ed., *Memoir of the Life of Richard H. Lee, and His Correspondence With the Most Distinguished Men in America and Europe . . .* (2 vols.; Philadelphia: H. C. Carey and I. Lea, 1825), I, 18.

41. Anderson, *Crucible of War*, 159–60.

42. Anderson, *Crucible of War*, 204, 461.

43. William Fleming to Francis Fauquier, July 26, 1763, in George Reese, ed., *The Official Papers of Francis Fauquier, Lieutenant Governor of Virginia, 1758–1768* (3 vols.; Charlottesville: University Press of Virginia, 1980–1983), II, 998. In January 1764, at the height of the Indian war, a Southampton County official billed the court for "whipping 11 Negroes by Order of a justice on Suspicion of an insurrection" and for maintaining twenty-five blacks in the county jail on the same charge. Southampton County court, minute book, Jan. 13, 1764, cited in Thomas C. Parramore, *Southampton County, Virginia* (Charlottesville: University Press of Virginia, 1978), 30.

44. Peter Fontaine to Moses and John Fontaine and Daniel Torin, August 7, 1763, in Ann Maury, ed., *Memoirs of a Huguenot Family* (New York: G. P. Putnam's Sons, 1852), 372; Benjamin Johnston, advertisement, *Virginia Gazette*, December 16, 1773 (Rind). For a March 1755 effort by the South Carolina legislature to promote enmity between Indians and slaves, see Wood, "Liberty is Sweet," 154.

45. Conway, quoted in Wesley M. Gewehr, *The Great Awakening in Virginia, 1740–1790* (Durham, NC: Duke University Press, 1930), 96, 96n.

46. [Chalmers], *Plain Truth*, 26.

47. Randolph, *History of Virginia*, 195; [Boucher], *Letter from a Virginian to the Members of the Congress*, 29.

48. On the variety of relationships among French-allied Indians, their British captives, and the French Canadians to whom the captives were often turned over, see Ian K. Steele, *Betrayals: Fort William Henry and the "Massacre"* (New York: Oxford University Press, 1990); John Demos, *The Unredeemed Captive: A Family Story from Early America* (New York: Knopf, 1994); Evan Haefeli and Kevin Sweeney, *Captors and Captives: The 1704 French and Indian Raid on Deerfield* (Amherst: University of Massachusetts Press, 2003); William Henry Foster, *The Captors' Narrative: Catholic Women and Their Puritan Men on the Early American Frontier* (Ithaca, NY: Cornell University Press, 2003).

49. Ruth H. Bloch, *Visionary Republic: Millennial Themes in American Thought, 1756–1800* (Cambridge: Cambridge University Press, 1985), especially 36–42, 57; Kerry A. Trask, *In the Pursuit of Shadows: Massachusetts Millenialism and the Seven Years' War* (New York: Garland Press, 1989); Anderson, *Crucible of War*, 373–76; David McCullough, *1776* (New York: Simon & Schuster, 2005).

50. T. H. Breen labels this American explanation for British taxation the "Tale of the Hospitable Consumer." Breen, *The Marketplace of Revolution: How Consumer Politics Shaped American Independence* (New York: Oxford University Press, 2004), 10–17; Greene, "Causal Relationship Reconsidered," 95.

51. Baldwin, quoted in Breen, *Marketplace of Revolution*, 15.

52. [Dickinson], *Letters from a Farmer in Pennsylvania to the Inhabitants of the British Colonies* (Philadelphia: David Hall and William Sellers, 1768), 40.

53. *The Examination of Doctor Benjamin Franklin, Before an August Assembly, Relating to the Repeal of the Stamp-Act, &c.* ([Boston]: n.p., [1766]), 16, 18; [Howard], *Letter from a Gentleman at Halifax*, 5; [Martin Howard], *A Defence of the Letter from a Gentleman at Halifax, To his Friend in Rhode-Island* (Newport, RI: Samuel Hall, 1765), 3; "A Pennsylvanian" [Jabez Fisher], *Americanus Examined, And his Principles Compared with those of the Approved Advocates for America* (Philadelphia: n.p., 1774), 6-8, 12.

54. [Oxenbridge Thacher], *The Sentiments of a British American* (Boston: Edes and Gill, 1764), 3, 6.

55. [Inglis], *True Interest of America*, 48.

~

CHAPTER SEVEN

The Seven Years' War in Canadian History and Memory

Catherine Desbarats and Allan Greer

All wars involve some degree of cultural conflict, writes Jonathan Dull.[1] So, one might add, does writing the history of war. Material hardship, violent death, invasion, conquest, and deportation leave scars that not only last but continue to evolve long after the final volleys have been fired. The Seven Years' War in Canada, as lived, and then later as written, is no exception. Above all, Canadian memories and histories of this complex series of international events have registered the central fact of its dramatic local outcome: conquest. The incorporation after 1763 of a defeated, mainly Catholic, French-speaking population, into a self-confident, Protestant British Empire unleashed sometimes traumatic reconfigurations of power, wealth, and identity. These subsequent struggles have made it surprisingly hard to recover firsthand French colonial experiences of the Seven Years' War, including those that relate to culture.

In practice, the fact of conquest narrowed the range of plotlines and the kinds of events recounted in both popular memory and history. Among the myriad stories that might have been told about a period of unprecedented mobilization of men, crops, and animals, about epidemics or acutely disrupted grain markets, about the emergence of new state practices, not to mention the destruction of hundreds of peasant farms, and even spiritual certainties, it is largely battles that have been narrated: battles deemed somehow pivotal, or thought to reveal a "world that might have been," battles, in short, that might somehow shed light on who was responsible for the troublesome conquest of Canada, and on whether it might have been avoided. The cast of characters found in these portraits of Canadian combat has been similarly simplified. Instead of reflecting the very real fault lines dividing this prenational, early French colonial society, they have tended anachronistically to personify the homogeneous national identities of later political discourse.

There is, in short, a story that needs to be told about how the Seven Year's War in Canada has been emplotted in both popular memories and professional histories. We tell some of it here, for its own sake, since it takes us to the heart of the cultural conflicts that have accompanied the writing of this consequential chapter of Canada's past. But we do so also with the view to getting closer, in the end, to a broader understanding of firsthand French colonial experiences, including some of the cultural conflicts long erased in the national narratives produced from the early nineteenth century onward. This has only recently become possible as a major new work on war in New France by the late Louise Dechêne emerges into print, though only in the French language in the first instance.[2] One of our objects in this article is thus more particularly to summarize for the benefit of American readers some of Dechêne's findings as they relate to the cultural history of the Seven Years' War.

∼

Perhaps the first thing that can be said about the Seven Years' War in Canada is that it is far from forgotten. While American historians search for ways to situate the "French and Indian War" within the metanarratives of United States history, while they hitch its star to seemingly more important events, such as the Revolution, and while they lament the absence of commemorative monuments in the nation's capital,[3] Canadian historians grapple with a problem of a very different sort. Here, memory threatens to overwhelm history. For French-speaking Canadians especially, though for English Canadians as well, the events of 1755 and 1759 retain the power to evoke strong passions. Like other historical mythologies, they are called upon to illuminate current national issues and to explain who we are and who we are not; and, of course, in a binational country, that "we" is dual, even multiple, and so popular historical memories can diverge and collide. The Seven Years' War, or the "War of the Conquest" as it is usually denominated here, is history fully loaded and ready to explode.

Only with great difficulty can most Acadians of the Maritime Provinces contemplate the "grand dérangement," when their ancestors were brutally torn from their settlements and deported to distant coasts, as a neutral historical fact. It lives on as a central theme of their oral culture, in folk songs and stories.[4] "Nonetheless," writes the poet Clive Doucet, "1755 forever divides Acadie into two places: the Acadie before 1755 and the one that came after. . . . Two hundred and fifty years later, the scars of poverty and dispersal remain."[5] Before the deportation, Acadian settlers occupied the best agricultural lands in the region; when some exiles straggled back a decade and more later, they found their farms occupied by Yankee newcomers, and they had to settle for marginal lands on the periphery. Right down to the present day, Acadians tend to have a lower standard of living than English-speaking Maritimers: thus do the effects of an ancient tragedy seem still to structure and limit personal possibilities.[6]

Similarly, French-speaking Quebeckers tend to associate the war and the climactic battle on the Plains of Abraham with a humiliating defeat that led to lasting subjugation. In a 1996 film, *Le sort de l'Amérique* ("*The Fate of America*"), a playful treatment of the Battle of Quebec that combines documentary and fictional techniques, director Jacques Godbout quotes his own father: "Don't forget, Jacques, the English burned our farms and our homes."[7] Expressed in such direct terms, this is a sentiment characteristic of an older generation and Godbout hastens to add that his children, preoccupied for the most part with computer games, have very little sense of the past at all. Yet, of course, everyone—even digitally distracted teenagers—carries around in their brain some sort of narrative of earlier ages.

Jocelyn Létourneau and Sabrina Moisan conducted investigations designed to probe the raw historical consciousness of French-Canadian young people. They asked students, aged between fifteen and twenty-five and unprepared for this exercise, simply to write down the history of Quebec as they understood it. Here is the story, in broad outline and as distilled by the researchers from hundreds of responses:

In the beginning, there were people who had come from France. They lived a fairly rudimentary, but peaceful, life, in a world they were building together in French. . . . They suffered few internal conflicts, continued to be dominated by French interests [i.e. those of the European metropole], but did not have to fight to preserve their rights or their language.

Then came the Great Upheaval, touched off by the 1759 Conquest of New France by the British. Thus began the francophones' history of unending struggle to emancipate and liberate themselves from continual attempts at assimilation, whether warlike or underhanded, inflicted on them by the anglophones.

Statistically, Létourneau and Moisan found that the Conquest of 1759 was by far the most frequently cited event in the version of history that lay embedded in the minds of the students they surveyed.[8]

Equally noteworthy in the young people's sense of their past is the notion of "unending struggle" pitting an ever-beleaguered French Canada/Quebec against an always threatening anglophone antagonist. It is as though "the English" formed an undifferentiated whole, stretching across the centuries and uniting General James Wolfe leading his troops in 1759, Prime Minister John A. Macdonald ordering the hanging of *métis* leader Louis Riel in 1885, the National Hockey League suspending Montreal *Canadiens* star Maurice Richard in 1955, and Clyde Wells, the Newfoundland premier who galvanized opposition to constitutional adjustments that would have recognized the unique culture of Quebec in 1990. This is certainly not a view that students would have imbibed from their French-language history textbooks. Nor would modern historians of Quebec nationalist sympathies support such unhistorical interpretations.[9] However, there does seem to be an inchoate sense of injury in many Québécois minds, a buried narrative line prior to reflection and study that links the military dénouement of the Seven Years' War with current sources of tension and grievance in the never-ending negotiation of French-English relations within the Canadian federation. To this day, memories of military defeat tend to come to the fore whenever Quebec's autonomy, culture, and language appear to be under threat. This was the case in the 1980s and 1990s when the Canadian constitution was first repatriated in defiance of the will of the government of Quebec and when two attempts to negotiate an arrangement agreeable to Quebec were defeated by English-Canadian opposition.

In English Canada, by contrast (and with the possible exceptions of founding myths surrounding the Loyalists or the War of 1812), popular historical consciousness tends to fade to the vanishing point somewhere around the turn of the last century. The Seven Years' War seems very remote, and few feel any connection between themselves and Wolfe's conquering armies. Even so, there are still moments of tension in the ongoing debates over Quebec's place in confederation when the exasperated cry goes up: "Who won on the Plains of Abraham anyway!" Shortly after the referendum of 1995 when Quebec voters rejected a proposal to secede from Canada by the thinnest of margins (50.6 percent to 49.4), one journalist replied to separatist claims that the result was a virtual dead heat with this sarcastic observation: "When Wolfe climbed the cliffs to the Plains of Abraham and beat Montcalm, the French thought it was a tie."[10] English-Canadians, it seems, can harbor nasty historical sentiments of their own.

It is perhaps not surprising that an episode that continues to surface in Canada's fragmented popular historical consciousness should also have figured prominently in canonical national histories. From the very first efforts to emplot it, the eighteenth-century conflict has proven a touchy subject. For successive generations of historians, the contemporary implications have seemed almost too close for comfort. How could one construct a peaceable, integrated, national community from the painful shards of conquest and defeat, not to mention differences of language and mutually hostile faiths? What narrative alchemy could transform such an inauspicious episode into a past useable for nation-building? Was it even possible? For nearly two centuries after the capitulation of Montreal, historians' hopes and fears on this score have inflected their recreations of the Seven Years' War.

"Foreign domination is the greatest affliction a country can suffer," wrote the original "national" historian, François-Xavier Garneau (1809–1866) at a time of heightened metropolitan-colonial political conflict.[11] A nineteenth-century contemporary of Bancroft, whiggish in his faith that history represents the progressive advance of human liberty and nationalist in his desire to give (French) Canada the honor it deserved, Garneau published his three-volume *Histoire du Canada depuis la découverte* in 1845–1848. It is a patriotic work that highlights the heroic deeds of the explorers and frontier fighters of New France.[12] War naturally features prominently in the central part of the work, which covers the period 1683–1776, and the author adopts a flagrantly partisan stance, missing no opportunity to glorify the successes of French-Canadian arms and to excoriate the evil Anglo-American enemy and the ineffectual French ally alike.

The 1759 siege and battle of Quebec present Garneau with a basic dilemma: on the one hand, this dramatic event is French Canada's moment of international fame, an occasion when the spotlight of history comes to focus on the affairs of an otherwise obscure colony; on the other hand, the dénouement brings anything but glory for Canadian and French arms. One part of his solution is to lay the blame for the defeat on the Plains of Abraham on the tactical errors of General Montcalm, France's commanding officer in Canada. When the French troops broke and ran, he notes, the colonial militia held their ground.[13] Playing up Canadian courage, Garneau just as consistently deflects responsibility for defeat onto the mother country. In one overwrought passage, he imagines the impact on the French people, unaware that their government had more or less abandoned to its fate the country's "oldest and finest overseas colony."

> Shame flushed their faces, chagrin gnawed their hearts, on learning the subjugation of 60,000 of their fellow-subjects,—a race speaking the same language, living under the same laws as they; and who had in vain made every sacrifice, during seven years of trials and suffering, to escape a fate which a good government would have found means to save them from.[14]

Garneau's other device for dealing with the humiliation of the Battle of Quebec is to drown that defeat in a flurry of chapters dedicated to French-Canadian victories in the Seven Years' War. His account of the defeat on the Plains of Abraham shares a chapter with the earlier triumph at Montmorency; moreover, that chapter is sandwiched between chapters devoted to the victories at Oswego (1756), William Henry (1757), Carillon (1758), and the Second Battle of the Plains of Abraham (1760). Readers of the *History of Canada* might well gain the impression that the Seven Years' War was a series of successes for French-Canadian arms interrupted only by one (admittedly consequential) setback! In this and in other respects, Garneau's work is shot through with fantasies of inversion and revenge. Any sense of a national emasculation in 1759–1760 is displaced by historic visions of power and ferocity directed against the conquerors. He dwells, for example, on the successful frontier raids mounted against Schenectady, Salmon Falls, and Casco in 1690, early instances of what would become known as a favorite "Canadian" method of waging war. The native warriors who made up the bulk of the fighters get short shrift in Garneau's account and so does the suffering of the civilian victims of these terrible incursions. The tone, echoing that of the earliest dispatches, is exultant.

> These intrepid bands did not merely ravage the open country, as they were directed: they attacked fortified posts also. Heedless of distances, winter rigors, fatigues, and perils of every kind, they made the English colonist practically cognizant of the fact that a superior genius guided the destinies of New France, and that her military prospects were in the ascendant. In truth, these excursions had the effect of keeping our enemies within their own lines. . . .[15]

To head off any moral objections that might intrude in his heroic narrative, the historian inserts a heart-rending description of the earlier massacre of French-Canadian civilians at Lachine at the hands of Iroquois encouraged—instigated, he insists—by the English of New York. With ethical concerns disposed of in advance, Garneau is able to sustain a constant flow of heroic exploits featuring a series of named leaders such as Hertel de Rouville and Le Moyne d'Iberville, as well as a more vaguely delineated collective actor, the *canadiens*. The impression is created of a small but powerful nation-in-arms ultimately betrayed by an indifferent France.

⌣

Long after Garneau's death, an Ontarian with the appropriately Loyalist-sounding name of William Kingsford produced an exhaustive ten-volume *History of Canada*; the Seven Years' War occupied a central position as the exclusive subject of one entire volume plus part of another.[16] Writing during the late nineteenth-century peak of imperial sentiment, Kingsford approached his subject as an overseas Briton inclined to identify both with Canada and with the empire of which his country formed an integral part.[17] This complicated sense of national identity ensured that his interpretation of the war would not be as exuberantly nationalist as that of Garneau, a tendency that was only reinforced by the anti-Romantic pretensions to objectivity then prevailing in historical circles. Accordingly, Kingsford's tone remains relentlessly (and boringly) factual and dispassionate. Even so, and notwithstanding his research in French sources, his treatment of the duel for North America has a definite point of view and that point of view is British. Less flagrantly partisan than his French-Canadian predecessor in claiming a monopoly of virtue for one side of the conflict, he does tend to see events mainly in terms of British aims, strategies, setbacks, and successes.[18]

If any French-Canadian nationalists read Kingsford's account, they would likely have objected not so much to what he wrote about the war but to what he left out, most notably the heroic role of the *canadiens* and the tragic consequences of the conquest. Like many American historians, he generally refers to "the French" without differentiating colonials and Europeans. Furthermore, his observations on the Canadian militia are, from a Garneau perspective, infuriatingly clinical and slighting:

> The force was admirably fitted for scouting and fighting in the woods; the species of war in accordance with Canadian traditions. These expeditions had been remarkable for endurance, patience, and courage, which had been shewn. But the Canadian militia could not be relied upon for movement in the field, when perfect and firm discipline ensure the unshrinking steadiness by which so many fields have been won. The number appeared large upon paper, but the *habitants* could not in numbers be called away from their farms, without causing

distress by the non-production of food. They were therefore not present in the field in great force, except when called out, owing to some emergency.[19]

Kingsford drops the detached tone only at the end of his volume on the war when he confronts the outrageous claim, advanced by some French-Canadian writers, that the military government established in the wake of the British conquest was despotic and oppressive. What a shocking way to characterize liberators! It was under French rule, Kingsford insists, that the *canadiens* were kept in ignorance and poverty by the combined misgovernment of church and state.

> The *habitant* was held to till the soil, to pay his *cens et rentes* and to be simply counted among the number of men capable of bearing arms. . . . It was British rule which first awoke the French Canadian rural population to the duties, the obligations and independence of manhood.[20]

The reference to "manhood" echoes Francis Parkman's emasculating treatment of the French-Canadians: tough and hardy they may have been when it came to wilderness warfare, but they lacked the steady purpose and political independence of the masculine Anglo-American race. Kingsford continues in this vein: "It is impossible not to contrast the benefits which Canada has enjoyed from the date of the conquest, with the hard, stern, depressing rule which weighed them down under the French government."[21]

Kingsford's condescending attitude toward French Canada exemplifies a long tradition of Orientalism in English-Canadian scholarship on French-Canadian history. The articles of faith of this outlook included several interlocking notions: (1) that French Canadians past and present shared an essential character that was traditionalist, unenterprising, and unsuited to self-government; (2) that this character had been formed under the French régime through the combined influence of a despotic government and an obscurantist Catholic Church; (3) that the Conquest, by instituting British law and parliamentary government, offered the possibility of liberation and progress; (4) that French-Canadian nationalist resistance to Anglo-Saxon influence has been and remains the main impediment to progress. These propositions, rarely spelled out but frequently taken for granted in English-Canadian, as well as British and American,[22] writings on the topic, had the predictable effect of inflaming nationalist reactions among French-Canadian historians. One reaction, increasingly discernible in the late nineteenth century and through the first half of the twentieth, was to portray New France as a lost golden age and the Seven Years' War as a disaster of colossal proportions. Lionel Groulx articulated a version of that nationalist view that resonated strongly with French Canadians' sense of themselves through the first half of the twentieth century.

⁓

For a century following Garneau's death in 1866, French-Canadian historiography was dominated by historian-priests and lay colleagues who shared a conservative Catholic vision of the past: nationalist certainly, but purged of the liberal and secular spirit that animated Garneau. Abbé Lionel Groulx (1878–1967), author of a two-volume "History of French Canada," was a particularly influential representative of this outlook in its late phase (his work dates mainly from the 1930s to the 1950s).[23] As with Garneau, the central character of Groulx's early volumes is "le Canada," meaning the French settler society of the St. Lawrence Valley prior to the Conquest. Small, beleaguered, threatened by Iroquois "savages" and then increasingly by the growing menace of British power and the overwhelmingly numerous colonial Americans, Canada was never adequately supported by France and therefore had to depend on its own resources of courage, toughened by long experience of adversity and reinforced by a shared Catholic faith.

Confronting the history of frontier raids against Anglo-American settlements, Groulx resorts to the kind of special pleading favored by those who defend the tactics of terror: attacks against civilians are an unfortunate necessity for the weaker party in a heavily uneven armed struggle. He describes the 1690 raids on Schenectady, Salmon Falls, and Casco as "expeditions of superhuman audacity, undertaken through the midst of winter snows and giving proof of the extraordinary vigor of the leaders and of their men." These operations were indeed accompanied by "cruelty" and "massacres," he admits (while studiously avoiding any and all particulars), and they have been severely condemned by American historians. However, "The weakness of New France, the extent of the field of battle and the shortage of men forced them to fight as best they could; guerilla took the place of regular warfare, a style of fighting that was, in any case, characteristic of the savages and the *canadiens*." Besides, he adds, the Anglo-Americans employed similar tactics whenever they could secure Indian allies.[24]

Groulx pays tribute to the various heroes of the struggles of the late seventeenth and early eighteenth century, but his warmest praise goes to the "forgotten hero" who contributed the most to the defense of New France, "the Canadian militiaman." "Even more than at the time of the first Iroquois War, the sons of the seigneurs and the sons of the habitants proved they were skilled in Indian tactics: able to fight like an Indian behind the cover of trees, the Indian's equal in wilderness travel, as good as the Indian at clever ambushes and hand-to-hand combat."[25] In Groulx's nationalist vision, class divisions melt away and the unnamed warrior-citizen comes to the fore as the personification of the nation: not savage himself, but just as capable as the "savages" in the ways of irregular warfare.

Groulx's treatment of the Seven Years' War is actually quite brief and schematic. The tone is sombre and tragic, and the interpretation insists on the inevitability of defeat: for too many years, Canada had carried the burden of France's overweening imperial ambitions with grossly inadequate support from the mother country. Through its negligence, France had lost a golden opportunity to possess and develop a continent,[26] but it left "un petit peuple" deeply rooted on the banks of the St. Lawrence. "This emergent people, homogeneous in its faith and its ethnic origin, was in possession of the religious, political, juridical, social, and intellectual institutions of an adult nation. . . . A vibrant Catholicism, nourished from the best sources, an original culture adapted from that of France of the time, produced a race of men with inner strength and admirable vitality."[27] Now disarmed and under British rule, this "people" would continue under peacetime conditions the stubborn struggle to preserve its unique identity.

Though the Conquest was a tragedy for Groulx, brutally terminating as it did the dream of a French and Catholic empire stretching across North America, the underlying themes of French-Canadian history continued after 1760. Pure in its blood and its values, favored by Providence, the small nation would continue its battle for survival on a different front and using different weapons, now within the British Empire and then the Canadian confederation. Cultural and political struggle would henceforth take the place of armed conflict, though the enemy remained essentially the same, which is to say English in language and Protestant in religion.

Guy Frégault (1918–1977) represents a later generation of French-Canadian nationalist historians who emerged in the 1960s in the atmosphere of the "Quiet Revolution," a period of rapid secularization and liberalization that transformed Quebec society from top to bottom. Initially a disciple of Groulx, Frégault eventually distanced himself from the master's clerical outlook. He was one of the first Quebec historians to boast a PhD, and his more rigorous, professional approach to the past represents a late transition from the gentleman-scholar-ideologue historian, more associated in the English-speaking world with the nineteenth century, to the modern academic style. By 1955 when he wrote *La Guerre de la Conquête*, Frégault had renounced the notion that French Canada embodied a spiritual essence and was destined by Providence to struggle against the malignant materialism of Protestant Anglo-America.

> Canadians fought, not in order to be or to remain different from Anglo-Americans, but because they were resolved to be masters in their own country, masters of their economy, their political organization, their society; not in order to avoid becoming American (they were, though in their own way, just as American as their British neighbours), but in order to prevent the dismemberment of their economy, their political organization, their society. . . . They were fighting for existence.[28]

The phrase "masters in their own country" foreshadows the slogan of the Quiet Revolution, "maîtres chez nous" ("masters of our own house/homeland"), a call to strengthen Quebec and to affirm its autonomy (and eventually its independence) as the political embodiment of French Canada. Similarly, Frégault set the tone for later nationalist historians by emphasizing the modern and "American" nature of New France. Accordingly, the war was not a "clash of civilizations," but rather a struggle between essentially similar empires and colonial societies.

For this modernizing nationalist, any feudal, Catholic, agrarian, obscurantist tendencies within French Canada were not the *cause* of conflict with the British Empire, they were the *result* of defeat. A particular view of New France as a lost golden age of liberty and dynamic enterprise lies buried in this formulation. The consequences of defeat were above all social, economic, and cultural; it permitted anglophones to take over the levers of political and economic power, depriving the *canadiens* of secular leaders and leaving them dominated by a conservative Catholic hierarchy. More so than with Groulx, the conquest appears in Frégault's account as a devastating event of profound and lasting consequences; the conclusion of his book puts the point in these ominous terms:

> As we complete our study of a troubled period in Canada's history, it would be an error to suppose that at the end of the chapter we can simply turn the page and go on with the story. With the end of the War of the Conquest a book is closed. The story does not continue: a new one begins. An evolution is halted, to resume, with a change of direction, as a different evolution.[29]

Frégault saw his interpretation as "pessimistic," a hard-headed response to providentialist fantasies of moral superiority, and though his work draws no explicit conclusions as to how the damage of the conquest might be reversed, others soon took that step. If the conquest had brought about the political and economic subjugation of French Canada, many in the sixties and seventies reasoned, then the solution to the problem of poverty and backwardness lay in the independence of Quebec so that French Canadians could be once more "masters in their own country."[30]

Although Guy Frégault's work was, in many respects, a bold departure from the interpretive traditions of Garneau and Groulx, it also represents continuity at many levels. The framing of the narrative—the very title of the book—remains resolutely national. A characteristic sentence sums up the situation at the end of 1757: "Although England and her colonies had repeatedly suffered defeat at the hands of Canada, Canada herself was on the brink of disaster. If her enemies could once reorganize their forces they would destroy her."[31] Frégault's book tells the story of a *Canadian* war with other dimensions of the Seven Years' War appearing as background to the real plot. Far from the partisan flag-waving of a Garneau, Frégault is at pains to maintain an objective tone and to avoid demonizing the enemy; he conducted extensive research in British and American sources and did his best to understand British perceptions, aims, and strategies. And yet, French Canada is the central character in his drama, its tragic fate the dominant theme. Much as he might ridicule the notion, dear to many of his predecessors, of a Laurentian colony embodying superior moral and religious qualities and charged with a special mission in the world, he did still see French Canada as a fully integrated entity.

Like any nationalist, Frégault enunciated a vision structured around an "imagined community" with clear-cut boundaries and a single, enduring identity. Officers in the colonial marine forces, habitant militiamen, merchants, clerics, and all others of Canadian birth or longtime residence in the colony form part of the [French]-Canadian proto-nation. Indians might be important auxiliary fighters, but they are not really part of this collectivity. The French of France are not merely external to it, they are the ultimate Other, the counter-identity which provides definition-through-opposition to Frégault's protagonist group. Like Garneau and Groulx, he dwells upon the theme of abandonment and betrayal on the part of the metropole, but Frégault's refusal to demonize the British and Anglo-Americans for simply pursuing their competitive interests vigorously and successfully meant that the only real villain in his account is France. Some of the most dramatic passages in *La Guerre de la Conquête* are those dedicated to the conflict between the aggressive governor Vaudreuil and the defense-minded, even defeatist, general Montcalm. Since the former was Canadian-born and the latter was an officer in the regular French army, their duel seems to personify the conflict of colonial and French interests and outlooks.

For English-Canadian historians of a nationalist bent, the problem with the Seven Years' War has been the choice of an object upon which to lavish sympathy. The imperial patriot Kingsford sided with the "British" as against "the French," but more recent writers, less British in their sense of identity and allegiance, were more likely to side with what they saw as a "Canadian" protagonist. W. J. Eccles, whose most important works appeared in the 1960s and 1970s, is the prime exemplar of this non-imperial, pan-Canadian approach to the topic.[32] His interpretive stance seems in many respects a throwback to that of François-Xavier Garneau, except that Eccles regards the conquered of 1759 as his compatriots, national, rather than lineal, ancestors. At a time of rising separatist sentiment in Quebec, when many Canadians anticipated the breakup of their country, Eccles sought to erase distinctions between English and French, exactly the division that Kingsford emphasized. In his work, the internal Canadian conflicts that Kingsford, Garneau, and Groulx read backwards into the period of the Seven Years' War are instead displaced outward and directed against an external antagonist. That hostile other is neither Britain nor France; for Eccles the enemy is American.

In his studies of New France, Eccles always notes, with a certain approval, the military complexion of the colony, stressing especially the role of the militia as the expression of a tough and manly Canadian character. He treats the Deerfield raid of 1704 not as an atrocity but as a Canadian victory, and he makes sure his readers know who the losers were: "In this type of guerrilla warfare the New England militia proved no match for the Canadians and the Indians."[33] Elsewhere, he writes in a similar vein, slighting the native warriors, who actually did most of the fighting, as well as the Americans: "The Canadian frontier experience garnered in the western fur trade was the best training imaginable for this type of warfare. The Anglo-American frontiersman, more familiar with the axe and the plow, than with the musket and canoe paddle . . . was no match for the Canadians and their allies."[34] The French marine forces also receive the occasional slagging (They stayed at home and worked the farms while colonial militiamen were off raiding the American frontier.),[35] but the Americans remain Eccles's prime target.[36]

When Eccles's account arrives at the final battles that decided the fate of New France, it is clear that the wilderness *petite guerre* is no longer a factor and the register changes to adapt to a more conventional story of siege and pitched battle. And yet the embattled patriot-historian cannot resist a parting shot in the form of a rather bizarre counter-factual speculation. "Canada had finally been conquered," he writes. "Yet that conquest had, by no means, been inevitable. Had no regular troops been involved on either side it is highly unlikely that the Anglo-Americans could have conquered New France."[37] Had it been Canadian versus American, in other words, we know who would have prevailed!

Fantasy operates at more than one level in the histories of W. J. Eccles. His studies of the French regime represent, first of all, an appropriation of French-Canadian nationalist historical fables of a lost golden age of ethnic purity and religious unanimity, only now the mythic past is no longer characterized as French and Catholic; it is simply *Canadian*. Moreover, New France was a time of unity and strength of a particularly masculine variety. It was indeed defeated, but only by a combination of treachery, bad luck, and impossible odds. The second part of the fantasy concerns relations between Canada and the United States, conceived at a time when one country was beset by grave internal divisions that seemed to threaten its very survival and the other country had consolidated its position as an unstoppable world superpower. Under these circumstances, the appeal of stories of a nation in arms and capable of whipping American "frontiersmen" from Schenectady to Deerfield was nearly irresistible.

While nationalist narratives of French-Canadian or Canadian heroism, betrayal, defeat, and revenge long dominated the historiography in both the French and the English languages, a more emotionally detached military literature on the Seven Years' War also developed. The prime exemplar of this more focused, specialized approach is C. P. Stacey's *Quebec, 1759: The Siege and the Battle*, published on the two-hundredth anniversary of the fall of Quebec.[38] Head of the Canadian army's history directorate during the Second World War, Colonel Stacey undertook a rigorously technical analysis of the contest for the capital of New France, deliberately isolating his subject from nationalist interpretive currents. Quite properly, given the parameters of his topic, Stacey emphasized the role of European forces and conventional European tactics; this phase of the war was hardly a Canadian national struggle and in Stacey's account, the militia played a modest part in the drama. G. F. G. Stanley, a contemporary of Stacey's and therefore a member of the World-War-Two generation, when Canadian society was more thoroughly militarized than at any other time in its modern history, also wrote about the Seven Years' War from a soldier's perspective. Stanley's *New France, the Last Phase* encompasses the period from 1744 to 1760 and largely avoids patriotic effusions.[39]

From the 1970s until the end of the century (and with the vitally important exception of work such as that of Ian Steele's, which broke with patterns of national historical writing by paying close attention to native perspectives on war[40]) academic research in early Canadian history turned decisively away from military topics as *Annales*-inspired economic and social studies dominated the field. To some degree, social historians were following up on an agenda set by Guy Frégault and other interpreters of the Conquest. Had New France, they asked, really been engaged in a "normal" pattern of development and advancing in the direction of prosperity and independence before the war?[41] Did the imposition of British rule truly sideline the French-Canadian social and business elite and reduce the *canadiens* to the status of hewers of wood and drawers of water? Or was the putative backwardness and poverty of the post-Conquest era simply a continuation of tendencies begun under French rule?[42] Exploring these issues and debating their controversial and politically charged implications involved the establishment of long-term price series, the analysis of demographic data, and the investigation of habitant material culture over the course of the eighteenth and the early nineteenth centuries, and though the transfer of Canada from the French to the British Empire was a crucial issue in this social history literature, the war that precipitated that cession was nowhere to be found.

Though the influential social historian Louise Dechêne had deliberately tried to free the study of everyday life in New France from teleological debates over the Conquest and its effects, she came, in time, to think of the absence of war as a widely shared blind spot. How on earth could it be, she wondered, that the Seven Years' War, indeed all wars, should be so absent from the portraits of everyday colonial life produced by a generation of scholars?[43] Multiple quantitative studies of death, birth, and marriage rates, of wealth distribution and land ownership seemed indeed to imply that very little had changed in the St. Lawrence Valley after 1760 and seemed also to pre-empt the need for further enquiry.[44] After all, both before and after the Seven Years' War, the St. Lawrence Valley retained its enduring traits as a predominantly rural society of peasant household producers. Prevailing conceptions about the primacy of "structures" over "events" helped eclipse the Seven Years' War and resulting Conquest, though these perhaps still lay buried somewhere in the memories of even professional historians. Demographers, noted Louise Dechêne, so vigilant elsewhere, never bothered to estimate war-related mortality, or to assess the importance of underreporting of male deaths, perhaps unconsciously led astray themselves by popular stereotypes about the protective powers of skilled militiamen.[45] The fact that habitual economic measurements were so seldom attempted for the interval 1756–1763, moreover, due to the relative dearth of the standard underlying sources such as estate inventories, was hardly ever probed for its significance. In retrospect, it appears as a first, negative clue that war did not hum in some distant background but now occupied the center stage of everyday life.

Telling that story, without the further benefit of the military rolls, combatant letters, or diaries so crucial to Fred Anderson's study of Massachusetts would pose special challenges to the researcher.

Louise Dechêne followed through on her sense that something important was missing. The resulting posthumous work is the most ambitious recent effort to come to grips with French colonial experiences of war.[46] It focuses unapologetically on the people of European origin living in the St. Lawrence Valley, taking a richly contextualized story of the militia from its antecedents in the first decades of the seventeenth century to 1760, the year Canada capitulated before its British invaders. If this is a "provincial perspective," to echo Fred Anderson's rueful characterization of his own writing, it resembles that of A People's Army, rather than that of The Crucible of War.[47] Louise Dechêne was convinced that far from being parochial, her intense, local focus was the only one apposite to her subject, and the only one with the power to rattle the larger-scale narratives that troubled her. It also afforded her the luxury of persuasively covering such a long time span. Spread over the last four of twelve chapters, her treatment of the Seven Years' War is all the more potent because it builds upon systematic discussions of earlier conflicts. A sense of "what came before" the late 1750s and early 1760s enriched her treatment of the surviving records and rendered all the more conspicuous the utter disruption of lives, property, and work visiting the St. Lawrence Valley during the years of total war and their immediate aftermath.

Her aim was not, in the first instance, to provide an explicit "cultural" interpretation of war in Canada. In practice, however, she took issue with the cultural and social reductionism operating in many national histories. Above all, she objected to the romantic erasure of social conflicts and power that occurred whenever early modern colonists were cast as mouthpieces for homogeneous nations identifiable through a discrete set of stable, shared traits. Like so much of Louise Dechêne's writing, beginning with her now classic Habitants et marchands de Montréal au XVIIe siècle, her final book thus draws narrative force from its clinical yet passionate stance as myth deconstruction.[48] "Stereotypes abolish time and social cleavages" wrote Dechêne in an opening passage that bears traces of her position as reluctant ironist, "attributing to an entire population behavior, qualities, or flaws that are in fact unevenly distributed and represented from one period to another."[49] The historical corpus on New France, she felt, was riddled with infuriating characterizations that betrayed both past and present: the courageous proto-national militiaman, the libertine coureur de bois, the lazy, alternatively jolly or crushed habitant, to name only those with the widest currency. Whether recycled with gentlemanly intention in the service of Canadian (even sometimes American) Orientalism or with utopian flourish in the name of a nation construed as a homogeneous, claustrophobic family-writ-large, such stereotypes offended her, one sensed, not just as historian, but as engaged female francophone citizen.[50] Paternalistic English-language history that shored up popular images of an anti-modern French-Canadian "folk society" was hardly neutral in the endlessly fraught arena of Canadian constitutional politics. Nor was monolithic French-language nationalist history that seemed to hand to English Canadians on a silver platter reasons for denying legitimate cultural and political aspirations. But worse, perhaps, both kinds of history betrayed New France's peasants, merchants, artisans, or soldiers by reducing their lives either to the fantasies of historians or to what anxious social superiors—priests, governors, and military officers—said of them at the time.

Accordingly, Dechêne approached her topic like a meticulous archeologist, sorting the jumbled accretion of historical discourse surrounding the hardy, bellicose, Canadian forest warrior into temporally and socially stratified layers, digging for plural experiences of war, attentive, always, to what may have been irretrievably lost or destroyed.[51] A primordial task, it turned out, was to recover the language of contemporaries. With what words did they speak, in New France, of compulsory, mainly unpaid, working and fighting in the cause of state-sanctioned violence at a time when such practices had all but vanished in France?[52] Terms like "guerrilla warfare," or even "*milice*" itself (and all the more so the English "militia") stamped out much of the mental and social worlds in the colony with their ulterior semantic freight. As a result, counting men and sorting out the evolving nature of what they did would be anything but simple. The historian had to negotiate shifting congeries of terms like "*Français,*" "*Canadiens,*" "*guerriers,*" "*soldats,*" or "*volontaires,*" each of which could connote just the opposite of what a hasty modern reader might expect. In the articles of the 1629 capitulation of Quebec to Kirke, Dechêne notes, "*soldats*" marked a social rank rather than a distinction relative to a "civilian" population. Unlike their armed social superiors, or "*gens de qualité,*" the *soldats* had to relinquish their weapons under the new rulers.[53] And later when the mystic nun Marie de l'Incarnation lauded "toute cette sainte milice," she was in fact referring both to colonists and to the recently arrived Carignan Salières Regiment, a group of paid soldiers from France's standing army (the *troupes de terre*), sent over to exterminate the Iroquois for once and for all.[54] In doing so, Marie neatly conflated contemporary uses of the term: the celestial armies of ecclesiastical Latin, and the more widespread meaning, extant since the sixteenth century, that referred without specificity to men in arms. Both meanings bore the inscription of what Dechêne portrays as Canada's baroque military culture: a New Jerusalem in which all men knew how to bear arms and occasionally did, in which distinctions between civilian and military were not clear cut, in which enrollments were episodic, brief, and mainly private, and in which hierarchies and channels of command were fluid and imprecise. By the Seven Years' War, however, this world had long since vanished.[55] As for the golden age of Canada's "militia," lamented by disappointed officers fresh from France during the 1750s, it was, literally, a pious fiction, kept alive in writings such as those of the Jesuit Pierre-François-Xavier de Charlevoix, which many read in preparation for service overseas.[56]

Whatever the language contemporaries used to designate them, early seventeenth-century men with arms in Canada seldom ventured into the forests beyond their communities.[57] The "Canadian militiaman" as "natural forest warrior" proved to be just as elusive a historical figure in later periods and as such was one of the major casualties of Dechêne's enquiry.

To begin with, a militia in the sense of unpaid, conscripted troops acting as subordinates to a professional army really enters the historical stage only in the 1680s, in the midst of renewed conflicts with the Iroquois, and at roughly the same time as naval troops (*troupes de la marine*) were sent from France. In the minds of Louis XIV and the successive naval secretaries who oversaw the colony, these regular soldiers were dispatched only on a temporary, emergency basis.[58] In the long run, colonists were expected to defend the king's overseas territories on their own and for free, though not since the sixteenth century had France's monarchs expected as much of subjects living on French soil. This wish was never realized, but neither did it quite die altogether. Enduring mercantilist parsimony ensured both that there would be no money to train or equip colonists and that Canada's standing army would remain modest in size.

Regardless of what was expected from them, as Louise Dechêne shows from the 1680s onward, militiamen did not look much like talented forest warriors. Prior to 1715, they tended to join large-scale expeditions that seldom faced actual military engagement. These time-consuming nonencounters were hardly glorious occasions for exhibiting skills of any sort.[59] As for the small raids thought to be so typically "Canadian," they drew on a very narrow subset of the population rather than on conscripted militiamen: officers from the *troupes de la marine*, as well as paid volunteers of elite status aspiring to the ranks of their professional companions, to whom they were often related.[60] From 1745 onward, militia service would become much more widespread. Still, the men recruited did not get much closer to, or fonder of, "the forest." Like the overall population of the St. Lawrence

Valley, recruits to unpaid military service during the "long hard war" (1744–1760) beginning with the War of the Austrian Succession, were mainly peasant farmers.[61] Nothing in their working lives particularly cultivated in them either the taste or the skill for fighting. Nor, for that matter, once again, were they particularly called upon to fight much "in the forest." Some two thousand men would be summoned annually between 1744 and 1748. Apart from a laborious expedition to Acadia, militia recruits spent much time in the town of Quebec waiting for a naval invasion that never materialized, or guarding, and maintaining fortified places, such as Fort St. Frédéric (Crown Point). They balked at escorting fur traders to the Great Lakes to shore up alliances damaged by the war-induced dearth of trade goods.[62] They were virtually absent from the total of eighty-two documented frontier raids during 1746 and the thirteen known to have occurred in 1747, and even then, apart from the officers and cadets from the *troupes de la marine*, the hundred or so colonists found in the records for these two years appear to have acted as paid volunteers rather than as unpaid conscripts. Though French sources tended to gloss over their participation, it is clear that native men predominated in all these expeditions.[63]

The pattern of service looked quite similar during the years leading up to the Seven Years' War. Far from letting up after the Treaty of Aix-la-Chapelle, the numbers of militiamen called up for active service doubled by 1753, then tripled by 1755. By the time the British invaded, most able-bodied men had been called upon to serve and had acquired useful military experience, which at the beginning of the war they had lacked utterly. Militiamen once again provided garrisons for far-flung posts, often camping outside their walls under dismal conditions, again making up for the endemically small size of Canada's professional army; again, they provided much of the manpower for the building of new forts or the repairs of existing ones; they built boats, transported all manner of material and artillery. Like the colony's professional soldiers, they seem to have received modest payment for work that did not directly involve combat or garrison duty. From September to June 1759, more than six thousand militiamen were assembled far closer to home, in farmers' fields on the outskirts of Quebec. Without tents (mainly reserved for regular soldiers), without the skills for pooling and cooking rations in an orderly fashion, and with inadequate clothing brought from home, militiamen everywhere succumbed to illness in greater numbers than did their fellow soldiers from the *troupes de la marine*, amongst whom they were intermingled under the command of naval officers.[64]

The notion that the fur trade somehow formed a breeding ground for "guerilla warriors," given its most recent lease on life in Eccles' work, was in fact suspect to Dechêne even before she began her systematic enquiries into who was called up for what kind of military service. It bore a family resemblance to another enduring cultural archetype, that of the *coureur de bois*, who continues to this day to crop up even in professional histories as all-purpose fur trader. Less frequently, he survives as the authority-defying pillar of a Canadian economy thought to rest almost exclusively on fur, or as the libertine forest-loving saboteur of Canadian agriculture once so deplored by clerical nationalists.[65] As with related colonial archetypes, mythification begins in the writings of contemporaries, giving expression to relations of rank and power in a profoundly hierarchical "old regime" setting that subsequent historians repeatedly mistook for transparent description.[66]

Over thirty years ago, in *Habitants et marchands de Montréal*, Louise Dechêne had argued that the young men who traveled to the Great Lakes in search of pelts during the mid- to late seventeenth century without sanction by the state were far fewer in number than frantic official reports seemed to imply.[67] As Thomas Wien has more recently argued, the term *coureur de bois* rapidly became a monolithic label nervously applied by state officials and clerics to a heterogeneous body of men at a time of geographic and regulatory readjustment in the fur trade roughly confined to the years 1665–1715.[68] Indeed after the destruction of Huron villages at midcentury, French traders no longer waited for native partners to bring furs to the neighborhood of established settlements like Montreal but began to venture to distant places where previously only missionaries had traveled. Beyond the purview of state and church authorities, these individuals seemed to pose a threat to the colony's social order. As the fur trade took more definitive, regulated shape, subject to the gaze of military commanders in the so-called *pays d'en haut*, the phrase *coureur de bois* faded from colonial use. It retained pejorative currency in overseas eighteenth-century texts, in which it expressed metropolitan ideas about colonial degeneracy. Like the related terms *coureur de côtes*, which contemptuously connoted "peddlers" of a different sort, and like the more general notion of *course* (as in "*guerre de course*") *coureur de bois* also betrayed classic early-modern state fears about mobility.[69]

The men who eventually traveled legally to the Great Lakes as hired fur-trade labour (*engagés*) or as independent traders (*voyageurs*) linked to Montreal merchants, were by and large not the same, argues Dechêne, as the men conscripted into active militia service in Canada. If anything, fur traders, like sailors and some traveling merchants, were more likely than peasants to escape service altogether by virtue of their absence during recruitment campaigns.[70] Apart from interruptions during the trade blockade of 1746–1747, points out Dechêne, the number of notarized fur trade contracts seems to have been largely unaffected by war during the last twenty years of French rule, or until 1758.[71] Neither *engagés* nor *voyageurs*, nor indeed the merchants who backed or paid them, showed particular enthusiasm for risking lives, incomes, or capital in ventures that had little to do with collecting furs. Skill at paddling a canoe or traveling well-known routes did not translate necessarily or easily into those required for the tedium of fort-building, or for mounting guard in a fortified post in the Richelieu or Ohio valleys, let alone in a farmer's field. In the eyes of military officers in the *troupes de la marine*, moreover, such men provided a vital service of a different sort: by ensuring the flow of goods to the Great Lakes, they helped maintain the native alliances without which Canada lost its most important fighting power. The War of the Austrian Succession had shown how such alliances could crumble when goods were scarce and just how dangerous such episodes could be, threatening lives, and jeopardizing the recruitment both of native and colonial fighters.[72]

Perhaps not surprisingly, romantic notions of Franco-Indian cultural complicity in war take a collateral beating in this book. Alternately frightened or over-confident, awkwardly lugging their noisy pots and pans, dressed mainly in personal garb brought from their homes, Dechêne's poorly trained farmer militiamen of the 1740s and early 1750s were hardly to be confused with the colony's native allies. By 1759 and 1760, by virtue of their ability to march together and keep rank if not by virtue of their tired homespun dress, they looked if anything like their fellow soldiers in the *troupes de la marine*. Kept in separate military encampments, blessed and accompanied by Recollect chaplains rather than by Jesuit missionaries, absent from the preparatory feasts of native warriors, terrified by the sight of European scalps, and perhaps by the sound of languages they did not understand, in hierarchical rather than allied relation with officers from the *troupes de la marine*, Canada's militiamen lived war in a parallel social universe from even the colony's baptized native allies. If anything, Dechêne seems to suggest, propinquity within limits may simply have given concrete, newly precise cause for continued mutual wariness, not to mention resentment.

If something resembling a military middle ground of French-native cultural accommodation existed, it did so perhaps in the mixed, smaller-scale expeditions referred to in the sources as "*partis,*" and with which New Englanders and New Yorkers were all too familiar. The militia, as we have noted, were largely absent from these forays. The latter were, however, by far the most frequent type of military outing. When all kinds of mobilization efforts are counted, whether for defensive purposes or for large and small expeditions beyond the colony's settled areas, and insofar as both British and

French sources allow, it is clear that frontier raids involving fewer than one hundred men predominated. And though colonial accounts lavish detail on the slightest action involving men of noble extraction and tend to gloss over native involvement in generic terms (". . . our Indians have continued to ravage settlements . . ."),[73] it is clear enough that most *partisans* were native and that in practice, and regardless of their own understanding of their actions, native men long formed the backbone of Canada's defense. Occasionally, they were accompanied rather than led by the men alluded to earlier: officers from Canada's increasingly top-heavy *troupes de la marine* and young paid volunteers hoping to gain experience that might lead to a military commission.[74] These men, relatively few in number and with few exceptions from Canada's social elite, had the most intimate acquaintance with native military cultures. Even here, however, Dechêne is cautious. French-speaking officers and volunteers might well have fought side-by-side with native warriors and shared some tactics, including surprise, and shared intelligence, but they too lived by rules that remained to a great degree socially incommensurable with those of their native partners. They could certainly not be conflated into the "French and Indian" composite that so horrified British colonists. The young men who volunteered for small campaigns against their "British" neighbors may have been unusually adventurous, but this did not mean jettisoning French social or military norms altogether.

Once again, Dechêne draws our attention to the language used by those who reported on war and in particular to its insistence on "order," which the anachronistic terms "guerrilla" or even "petite guerre" gloss over. Indeed, even *"petite guerre,"* which historians sometimes project back to the entire French regime, really only appears in records dating from the 1750s onward. And ironically, it was a term first used by Europeans to describe new European forms of warfare. In the aftermath of the War of the Austrian Succession" military strategists had coopted the phrase *"petite guerre"* to capture the small mobile units flanking armies for purposes of reconnaissance, diversion, or other risky enterprises, and which had gained recent respectability. Direct knowledge and experience of such practices would migrate to North America during the Seven Years' War through the likes of Montcalm and Levis, who had served in the rugged mountains of Piedmont, or the Baron Dieskau who as the Maréchal de Saxe's aide de camp served in Bohemia against Marie Thérèse's Hussars.[75] Prior to the 1750s, the term *"petite guerre"* had connoted undisciplined marauding. Not surprisingly, it is not found in earlier accounts of colonial war. In the writing of late seventeenth- and eighteenth-century colonial military officers, invariably addressed to their superiors, and thus concerned about their reputations as commanders, *partis* were precisely the opposite of *petite guerre*. As Dechêne points out further, Furetière's dictionary neatly if implicitly captures this contrast between legitimate and illicit modes of fighting: "le parti est une petite formation militaire offensive qui agit selon les ordres, ce qui le distingue d'une troupe de brigands."[76]

Patriarchal, royal, military, not to mention spiritual lines of authority did not dissolve in North American forests, or so the colony's officers were often at pains to convince the overseas correspondents who evaluated their military conduct. Embarrassing disasters such as transpired at Fort William Henry in 1757, involving the killing of prisoners, women, and children, would ultimately be blamed on savagery and its contempt for "les règles." Meanwhile, they exposed the cultural chasm which persisted around ideas of acceptable violence and the nature of authority.

Dechêne eschews the romance of homogenizing identities as much as the romance of war. "Toutes les guerres sont atroces," she writes, dryly noting the tendency of both French sources and Canada's historians to gloss over the violence dealt to the colony's civilian enemies. To seek consolation for conquest and its long legacy of emasculating humiliation by conjuring up the virile militiaman fighting against punishing odds for his newly hatched *canadien* identity was to compound anachronism with blindness to *ancien régime* social tensions, not to mention to the fate of war's victims. From Garneau to Frégault, as we have seen, the Seven Years' War was indeed seen as a stage that revealed and intensified a new, separate and spirited Canadian community of belonging. The notorious conflicts between New France's Canadian-born governor general Philippe Rigaud de Vaudreuil and the newly arrived French general, the Marquis de Montcalm, were often made to personify such a putative, gutsy-colonial/metropolitan split. "Canadians," it went almost without saying, lined up behind their beloved governor general and a handful of heroic Canadian-born military officers, making clear also their contempt for the French-born *intendant* François Bigot, deemed to be as corrupt as his "*bande*" [gang] of venal acolytes.[77]

The question of how an "imagined" political community might find expression and what forms it might take within early modern France, and more broadly within the French Empire, has just recently begun to preoccupy historians on either side of the Atlantic. They remain tricky to grapple with in an absolutist political system.[78] It does seem, however, that the Seven Year's War occasioned important and still poorly understood shifts in metropolitan political culture. At one level, historian David Bell reminds us, *nation* did not yet mean the kind of community that rulers saw as amenable to the influence of political will. Nations were God-given entities, part of the natural order, sharing traits such as language. The official, absolutist discourse of France's ruling Bourbon dynasty, moreover, did not yet acknowledge the political (even ontological . . .) existence of any collectivity outside the body of the king. Authority flowed downward from God, rather than upward from any people whose consent was required. The lawyers of France's eighteenth-century *parlements* busily disputed these claims, however, in a series of spectacular confrontations with Louis XV over religious and fiscal matters. The print currency of the term "nation" itself seems moreover to have increased exponentially during the Seven Years' War in France. It did so in dialogue with British propaganda, as the monarchy's own publicists covertly engaged in unprecedented attempts to legitimate France's protracted involvement in a costly war in the eyes of a "public" confined to a literate elite.[79]

The embryonic state of thinking about early modern French national sentiment did not much hamper Dechêne. Above all, four decades of familiarity with virtually the entire body of known extant records from Canada cautioned her against viewing "canadien" and "français" as markers for essentialized national identities. As she notes, their meanings were highly contextualized, and conveyed no stable emotional, political, or even geographic content. More to the point, they hardly ever encompassed multiple groups in this society based on rank and privilege and certainly not a shared "Canadian" identity that might transcend social distinctions and cleavages. A Canadian-born noble officer like Vaudreuil might clash with a French-born Montcalm, but at the end of the day, the governor general's place of birth hardly trumped his aspirations to promotion within the French naval hierarchy and the sense of belonging to an ancient French lineage. He knew full well that the value of his social capital was mainly determined in France, not Canada. Merchants were just as locked into transatlantic networks that fanned out from France. As for militiamen of modest status, Dechêne might perhaps have added that their intensive military experience during the last two decades of French rule hardly conspired to build a sense of camaraderie that might ultimately give rise to a shared sense of being "Canadian" rather than "French." Though on paper, the militia sprang from tightly-knit parish units, in practice, when it came time to serve or fight, they did not do so as men from the same locality following the orders of those whom they knew well, and with whom they had long trained. Instead, they were scattered as poorly trained individuals among companies of regular soldiers, fighting under commanders whom they hardly knew, at least until the very last year of war.[80] By the time the British fleet sailed up the St. Lawrence, militiamen were recruited, commanded, and moved about in company units, with their own commanding officers. If they developed new affinities with anybody at this time, it may well have been with the soldiers of France's *troupes de terre*, fresh off the boat from France, and beside whom they served.

Insofar as colonists of different social origin shared an overarching sense of belonging, Dechêne hints, it was to the French king, on the one hand, and perhaps more importantly, to the God who watched over his own "most Christian King" as well as his subjects. There is little reason to believe that distance was a greater barrier to such bonds in the colony than they would have been in the metropolitan provinces. Why would collective prebattle chants of "Vive le Roi" be any less moving or persuasive than the empty seat that incarnated the king's indivisible power in royal councils in France? Symbols of benevolence and paternalism traveled overseas easily enough, and Canadian rulers carefully nurtured them in rituals and monuments. The annual arrival of the king's vessel was a case in point, and so were the far more frequent reminders of royal events contained in regular pastoral exhortations from priests and bishops.

Beyond the king was God. This was indeed the vital message preached to Canada's militiamen from the very beginning, according to Dechêne, and it served a dual purpose. It invested state recruitment efforts with spiritual authority: to shirk an order for service was cast by those in positions of power as an act of religious defiance. More positively, Canada's priests and nuns helped reassure militiamen not only that their combats were holy but that they enjoyed the protective mantle of Providence. There were plenty of signs to cling to: Iroquois villages empty but for mounds of harvested crops, foiled invasions, like those of Phips and Walker in 1690 and 1711 respectively, or even the chants of returning native parties, from which all had learned to decode (with mixed feelings perhaps) the exact numbers of scalps and prisoners. In the town of Quebec, parishioners celebrated mass in a church consecrated *Notre Dame des victoires* (Our Lady of the Victories): the name captured a mix of vulnerability and hubris that seems to have endured right up to Wolfe's 1759 invasion. That the latter apparently took so many by surprise is further testimony, according to Dechêne, that a sense of being shielded by a protective divinity was a vital ingredient of social identity in this early modern colony.

It is admittedly difficult to discern a mainly unlettered population's views of God and king. Though a cautious historian, Dechêne nonetheless ventures some of her bolder conclusions in this regard. There is little reason to believe that in spiritual matters at least, colonists did not respect and internalize the prescriptions of their clergy, including those related to war. By and large, they did not marry or conceive during the holy seasons when abstinence was required; they did not miss sacraments for frivolous reasons; and though there are hints that they occasionally grumbled, men from the "vilest ranks" of society seem seldom to have shirked militia duty though the opportunity costs to their families mounted sharply from the 1740s onward. Perhaps, at some level, they accepted the hierarchy of intentions sketched out by the bishop in the midst of the War of the Austrian Succession: to bear arms to protect one's home and property was a natural enough inclination. To fight for one's king was an inexorable act of duty. But to fight for God, and to do so against heretics who threatened the holy sacraments, was to enlist the aid of a force more potent than any earthly one.[81] And in the end, suggests Dechêne, as this frightened population contemplated not just invasion and the bombardment of their capital, but starvation, the virtual extinction of local herds of cattle, and then the meticulously executed burning of hundreds of farms on (both shores) of the St. Lawrence, they perhaps experienced also a deep sense of abandonment. Not by a fickle France, as suggested anachronistically by so many historians, but, suggests Dechêne, by God himself.[82] This was indeed the conclusion preached cruelly by the colony's bishop, months before his death in 1760. Colonists had, in the end, abused God's benevolence, and reaped the harvest of their sins. Heretic rulers, hostile to the sacraments, would be the instrument of God's own punishment, and regardless of what the colony's military officers might still think, there was no further point resisting divinely ordained fate, no matter how ghastly.

As Dechêne's musings on the enduring religious significance of war suggests, it would be highly unfair to reduce her book to an exercise in nationalist myth-bashing, or in dismantling cultural stereotypes, however fertile her impatience with her fellow historians. Her larger aim was to analyze the relationship between subjects and state in an *ancien régime* colonial society and to recognize the ways in which war shaped power relations both on the battlefield and beyond. Militia service, in fact, was only one of the theoretically universal personal obligations exacted in kind from colonists and examined in this work. There were others, such as the need to billet ("fournir le feu, la paille et la marmite") troops, or provide labor for building fortifications surrounding Montreal and the town of Quebec. Canada's *intendant* also requisitioned grain and livestock for the sake of feeding the troops. In each case what is striking is how increasingly burdensome such exactions became, not just for the last seven years of French rule, but for the last two decades. From the perspective of the inhabitants of the St. Lawrence Valley, this was not so much a "Seven Years" war as "a long hard war" beginning in 1744 or so, and lasting at least until the capitulation of 1760. What also strikes Dechêne is how little overt resistance accompanied these different exactions, which fell disproportionately on those living at the modest end of the social hierarchy. By and large, militiamen marched, peasants yielded their grain and when also necessary, provided space in their houses. Far from attributing such systematic compliance to any cultural affinity for war, Dechêne sees rather the workings of a complex system of deference to heavy-handed authorities who enjoyed few obstacles to the exercise of power, not to mention, as we have seen, the active ideological support of the church.

We have lingered disproportionately over Dechêne, her findings and her historical voice, perhaps because they speak to us more effectively now than do her predecessors. Like the Bavarian-born writer W. G. Sebald, whose genre-confounding books *Austerlitz* and *On the Natural History of Destruction* have done so much to prod us into thinking in new ways about twentieth-century wars, Dechêne found a potent if somewhat surprising mode of writing about a war that occupies an awkward space in Canadian memories.[83] For Sebald, the clinical notes of a doctor were among the bits of writing that came closest to historical or moral truth amid the fairly scant but overwrought prose on Germany's experience of allied bombing. The Seven Years' War, needless to say, sprang from a vastly different world and is far more remote from us now. Still, as we have seen, in Canada at least, the memories it generated continue to blend in with those of more recent conflicts. And beginning in the bewildering eighteenth-century aftermath of Canada's defeat by conquerors casting themselves as liberators, the erasure of firsthand experiences was just as quick and complete. Under the circumstances, Dechêne's own doggedly clinical descriptions, her attention to easily overlooked fragments, to the records left by all sides, her attention also to the range of work disrupted by military service and to the households left behind, to forests filled not with stereotypes, but, in 1759 at least, with exhausted hungry refugee mothers, grandfathers, and children, surviving "who knew how," seem at last to give genuine substance to lives long flattened in narratives bounded mainly by profoundly gendered national imaginations.

Notes

1. See Jonathan Dull's contribution to this collection.
2. Louise Dechêne died in 2000, leaving an unfinished manuscript that she had been working on for well over a decade. An edited version, prepared by Hélène Paré, Sylvie Dépatie, Catherine Desbarats, and Thomas Wien, will be published by Les

Éditions du Boréal in Montreal, under the title, *Le peuple, l'État et la guerre au Canada sous le régime français*. All references herein will be to the 719-page manuscript now in the hands of the publisher.

3. See Fred Anderson's contribution to this collection.

4. Such an organic, living sense of the past constitutes, for Pierre Nora, the essence of collective memory, as opposed to history, an external and intellectualized approach to earlier ages. Pierre Nora, "General Introduction: Between Memory and History," in P. Nora, ed., *Realms of Memory: Rethinking the French Past*, trans. A. Goldhammer, 3 vols. (New York: Columbia University Press, 1996), 1: 1–20.

5. Clive Doucet, *Lost and Found in Acadie* (Halifax: Nimbus, 2004), 44–45.

6. Maurice Beaudin, René Boudreau, and George De Benedetti, *The Socioeconomic Vitality of Official Language Communities* (Ottawa: Department of Canadian Heritage, 1999).

7. Jacques Godbout, *Le Sort de l'Amérique* (Montreal: National Film Board of Canada, 1996), quoted in Jocelyn Létourneau, *A History for the Future: Rewriting Memory and Identity in Quebec*, trans. P. Aronoff and H. Scott (Montreal and Kingston: McGill-Queen's University Press, 2004), 9.

8. Jocelyn Létourneau and Sabrina Moisan, "Mémoire et récit de l'aventure historique du Québec chez les jeunes Québécois d'héritage canadien-français: coup de sonde, amorce d'analyse des résultats, questionnements," *Canadian Historical Review* 84 (June 2004): 325–56; Jocelyn Létourneau and Sabrina Moisan, "Young People's Assimilation of a Collective Historical Memory: A Case Study of Quebeckers of French-Canadian Heritage," in *Theorizing Historical Consciousness*, ed. Peter Seixas (Toronto: University of Toronto Press, 2004): 109–28 (quotation on p. 109).

9. See, for example, the sophisticated nationalist positions of Gérard Bouchard: "La réécriture de l'histoire nationale au Québec. Quelle histoire, quelle nation?," in *À propos de l'histoire nationale*, ed. Robert Comeau and Bernard Dionne (Sillery, QC, Canada: Septentrion, 1999), 115–41. On the other hand, paranoid anglophobia is not utterly absent from the public discourse of Quebec. Witness Normand Lester's diatribe on the misdeeds of "les anglais" from the Hundred Years' War down to the Quebec referendum of 1995. Normand Lester, *The Black Book of English Canada*, trans. Ray Conlogue (Toronto: McClelland and Stewart, 2002).

10. Allan Fotheringham, "An Epic Struggle that will Never End," *MacLean's*, November 6, 1995.

11. Quoted in Serge Gagnon, *Quebec and its Historians 1840–1920* (Montreal: Harvest House, 1982), 33.

12. François-Xavier Garneau, *Histoire du Canada depuis la découverte jusqu'à nos jours*, 4 vols. (Quebec: Napoléon Aubin, 1845–1848). Garneau's *Histoire* went through several editions, over the course of which his interpretation changed somewhat to accommodate the more conservative and Catholic mood of Quebec in the second half of the nineteenth century. An English translation of the third edition was published in 1862 and is the source of the quotations presented in this text. F-X. Garneau, *History of Canada from the Time of its Discovery till the Union Year 1840–41*, 2

vols., trans. Andrew Bell (Montreal: Lovell, 1862). On Garneau, see J. S. Pritchard, "Some Aspects of the Thought of F. X. Garneau," *Canadian Historical Review* 51 (Sept. 1970): 276–91; Serge Gagnon, *Quebec and its Historians 1840 to 1920* (Montreal: Harvest House, 1982), 9–43.

13. Garneau, *History*, 2:40.

14. Garneau, *History*, 2:73.

15. Garneau, *History*, 1:325. Garneau scarcely mentions the Deerfield attack of 1704.

16. William Kingsford, *The History of Canada*, 10 vols. (Toronto: Rowsell & Hutchison, 1887–1898).

17. On Kingsford, see Carl Berger, *The Writing of Canadian History: Aspects of English-Canadian Historical Writing since 1900*, rev. ed. (Toronto: University of Toronto Press, 1986), 2–3. See also Carl Berger, *The Sense of Power: Studies in the Ideas of Canadian Imperialism: 1867–1914* (Toronto: University of Toronto Press, 1970) on English-Canadian imperial sentiment of the period.

18. In this respect, Kingsford's interpretation resembles that of most American historians down to the present day.

19. Kingsford, *History*, 3:554–55.

20. Kingsford, *History*, 4:451.

21. Kingsford, *History*, 4:503.

22. Works by Lord Durham and Francis Parkman strongly reinforced Orientalist tendencies in English-Canadian intellectual circles of the nineteenth century.

23. Lionel Groulx, *Histoire du Canada français depuis la découverte*, 4th ed., 2 vols. (Montreal: Fides, 1960). On Groulx, see Ronald Rudin *Making History in Twentieth-Century Quebec* (Toronto: University of Toronto Press, 1997), 48–128, and Michel Bock, *Quand la nation débordait les frontières. Les minorités françaises dans la pensée de Lionel Groulx* (Montréal: Éditions Hurtubise HMH, 2004).

24. Groulx, *Histoire du Canada français*, 1: 142. ". . . Expéditions d'une audace surhumaine, menées en plein hiver à travers les neiges, et qui font voir la vitalité extraordinaire de ces chefs de bandes et de leurs hommes." "La faiblesse de la Nouvelle-France, l'étendue du champ de bataille, la disette d'hommes font que l'on se bat comme l'on peut et qu'à la guerre on substitue la guérilla, façon de se battre propre d'ailleurs aux sauvages et aux Canadiens."

25. Groulx, *Histoire du Canada français*, I: 146. "Plus encore que dans la première guerre iroquoise, fils de seigneurs et fils d'habitants se sont montrés rompus à la tactique de l'Indien, capables de se battre comme lui d'arbre en arbre, de l'égaler dans la course à travers bois, capables aussi, autant que lui, de ruse dans les embûches, de force et d'adresse dans les corps à corps."

26. Counterfactual fantasies of a lasting New France stretching to the Gulf of Mexico and the Pacific crop up from time to time. See, for example, Lionel Groulx's later work, *Notre grande aventure: l'empire français en Amérique du nord (1535–1760)* (Montreal: Fides, 1958), a stirring chronicle of exploration and "civilizing mission" to the indigenous nations, containing no mention of the Seven Years' War or the conquest of Canada.

27. Groulx, *Histoire du Canada français*, 2: 273. "Ce peuple naissant, homogène par la foi et l'origine ethnique, possède les institutions religieuses, politiques, juridiques, sociales, intellectuelles, des nations adultes . . . Son catholicisme vivant, jailli des meilleures sources, sa culture originelle, celle de la France de son temps, convenablement assimilée, assurent à cette race d'hommes un robuste équilibre intérieur, lui promettent d'admirables lignes de force."

28. Guy Frégault, *Canada: the War of the Conquest*, trans. Margaret M. Cameron (Toronto: Oxford University Press, 1969) [original: Guy Frégault, *La Guerre de la conquête* (Montreal: Fides, 1955)], 9

29. Frégault, *Canada*, 236.

30. See Maurice Séguin, "The Conquest and French-Canadian Economic Life," in *Society and Conquest: the Debate on the Bourgeoisie and Social Change in French Canada, 1700–1850*, ed. Dale Miquelon (Vancouver: Copp Clark, 1977), 67–79; Michel Brunet, "The British Conquest and the Decline of the French-Canadian Bourgeoisie," in *Society and Conquest*, 143–61.

31. Frégault, *Canada*, 162.

32. See two very similar books bearing different titles: *The Canadian Frontier 1534–1760* (New York: Holt, Rinehart and Winston, 1969); *The French in North America 1500–1783*, rev. ed. (Markham, ON, Canada: Fitzhenry & Whiteside, 1998) [original edition *France in America* (1972)]. See also W. J. Eccles, "The Social, Economic, and Political Significance of the Military Establishment in New France," *Canadian Historical Review* 52 (March 1971): 1–22.

33. Eccles, *French in North America*, 118.

34. Eccles, *The Canadian Frontier*, 173.

35. Eccles, *French in North America*, 108.

36. In a revised edition of *The French in North America*, Eccles added a new chapter advancing the narrative forward to the end of the American Revolution. His central purpose appears to have been to argue that it was only through the assistance of France that the inept Americans managed to secure their independence.

37. Eccles, *French in North America*, 233–34.

38. C. P. Stacey, *Quebec, 1759: the Siege and the Battle* (Toronto: Macmillan, 1959).

39. G. F. G. Stanley, *New France, the Last Phase, 1644–1760* (Toronto: McClelland and Stewart, 1968). There are nevertheless points in the narrative when Stanley indulges in nationalistic observations as in this reflection on the role of the French-Canadian militia in the Battle of the Plains of Abraham (p. 232): "What honour belongs to the defenders of Canada on that fatal September 13, 1759 must go to the men who, fighting for their native land in their traditional way, made it possible for the regulars of France to make good their escape across the St Charles to the temporary safety of their camp at Beauport."

40. Ian K. Steele, *Betrayals: Fort William Henry and the "Massacre"* (New York: Oxford University Press, 1990) and *Warpaths. Invasions of North America* (New York: Oxford University Press, 1994). See also, D. Peter MacLeod, *The Canadian Iroquois*

and the Seven Years' War (Ottawa and Toronto: The Canadian War Museum and Dundurn Press, 1996).

41. See, Guy Frégault, *Canadian Society in the French Régime*, CHA booklet (Ottawa: Canadian Historical Association, 1971); Jean Hamelin, *Economie et société en Nouvelle-France* (Quebec: Presses de l'Université Laval, 1960).

42. See, Fernand Ouellet, *Economic and Social History of Quebec, 1760–1850: Structures and Conjonctures* (Toronto: Gage, 1980) [*Histoire économique et sociale du Québec, 1760–1850* (Montreal: Fides, 1966)]; Maurice Séguin, "The Conquest and French-Canadian Economic Life," in Miquelon ed., *Society and Conquest*, 67–80.

43. The "state" was likewise sidelined in such studies, and Dechêne wanted to bring both back into her vision of colonial society. She began to do so in her study of grain regulation, *Le partage des subsistances au Canada sous le régime français* (Montreal: Les Éditions du Boréal, 1994). See also, Catherine Desbarats, "La question de l'État en Nouvelle-France," in Philippe Joutard and Thomas Wien, *Mémoires de Nouvelle-France. De France en Nouvelle-France* (Rennes, France: Presses universitaires de Rennes, 2005), 187–98.

44. Catherine Desbarats, "Agriculture within the Seigneurial Régime of Eighteenth-Century Canada: Some Thoughts on the Recent Literature, *Canadian Historical Review* 73 (March 1992): 1–29. See also Allan Greer, *The People of New France* (Toronto: University of Toronto Press, 1997) for a synthesis of the findings of social history that largely avoids the topic of war and makes the case for little social change after the conquest.

45. Louise Dechêne, *Le peuple, l'État et la guerre au Canada sous le régime français* (Montreal: Les Éditions du Boréal, forthcoming), chap. 10.

46. Louise Dechêne, *Le peuple, l'État et la guerre au Canada sous le régime français*, chap. 10, 548–52 and notes.

47. Fred Anderson, *A People's Army: Massachusetts Soldiers and Society in the Seven Years' War* (Chapel Hill: University of North Carolina Press, 1984). Dechêne became acquainted with *A Crucible of War* (New York: Alfred A. Knopf, 2000) far too late into her illness to frame a response.

48. Louise Dechêne, *Habitants et marchands de Montréal au XVIIe siècle* (Paris: Plon, 1974). The book was only translated into English in 1992, as *Habitants and Merchants of Seventeenth-Century Montreal*, trans. Liana Vardi (Montreal and Kingston: McGill-Queen's Press, 1992). For a sense of this book's major impact on the field of early Canadian social history, see Sylvie Dépatie et al., *Vingt ans après, "Habitants and merchants." Lectures de l'histoire des XVIIe et XVIIIe siècles canadiens* (Montreal and Kingston: McGill-Queen's University Press, 1998), and especially, the introduction by Thomas Wien.

49. "Le propre du stereotype est d'abolir le temps et les clivages sociaux, d'attribuer à toute une population des comportements, des qualités ou des défauts qui sont en fait très inégalement distribués et représentés d'une période à l'autres." Dechêne, *Le peuple, l'État et la guerre au Canada sous le régime français*, introduction.

50. The first chapter of Peter Moogk's *La Nouvelle France: The Making of French Canada—A Cultural History* (East Lansing: Michigan State University Press, 2003) entitled "My Discovery of French Canada" is a striking recent example of such Orientalism.

51. The myth persists in books and films that Louise Dechêne was unacquainted with by the time of her death in 2000. The cinematic flop *La Nouvelle-France* regurgitates many of its ingredients.

52. By the late seventeenth century, according to Dechêne, there were three distinct remaining forms of compulsory "free" service, all limited in scope.

53. Dechêne, chap. 2. See Peter Pope, *Fish Into Wine: The Newfoundland Plantation in the Seventeenth Century* (Chapel Hill: University of North Carolina Press, 2004) for the best description of this "first" conquest.

54. Chap. 2. Jack Verney, *The Good Regiment: The Carignan-Salières Regiment in Canada 1665–1667* (Montreal and Kingston: McGill-Queen's University Press, 1991). On Marie de l'Incarnation, see Natalie Zemon Davis, *Women on the Margins: Three Seventeenth-Century Lives* (Cambridge, MA: Harvard University Press, 1995).

55. Dechêne's notion of baroque military practices is inspired partly from André Corvisier's work.

56. Dechêne, *Le peuple, l'État et la guerre au Canada sous le régime français*, chap. 8. Dechêne argues that the Jesuit Pierre-François-Xavier de Charlevoix's *Histoire et description générale de la Nouvelle-France* (Paris: Rollin fils, 1744) was an important source of information for French officers—a veritable *vade mecum*.

57. Dechêne, *Le peuple, l'État et la guerre au Canada sous le régime français*, chap. 2.

58. "un corps de réserve subordonné à l'armée," as defined by Dechêne.

59. A 1687 expedition against the Senecas offers a particularly well-documented illustration of the great distance separating this "foule de paysans excités" from "une armée disciplinée." Dechêne, *Le peuple, l'État et la guerre au Canada sous le régime français*, chap. 3.

60. Dechêne, *Le peuple, l'État et la guerre au Canada sous le régime français*, chap. 3.

61. "Une guerre de seize ans (1744–1760)" is the title of Dechêne's eighth chapter.

62. Dechêne, *Le peuple, l'État et la guerre au Canada sous le régime français*, chap. 8.

63. Dechêne, *Le peuple, l'État et la guerre au Canada sous le régime français*, chap. 8.

64. The milita captain is a famously misunderstood figure in Canadian history. Louise Dechêne points out here that in general, these militia officers filled administrative functions in the colony's parishes. In times of war, they either fought as plain militiamen under the command of officers from the *troupes de la marine* or stayed home and continued to help with administrative tasks such as recruitment.

65. Thomas Wien, "Vie et transformation du coureur de bois," in Philippe Joutard and Thomas Wien, *Mémoires de la Nouvelle-France* (Rennes, France: Presses universitaires de Rennes, 2005), 179–86. Wien points out that the myth lives on in works such as Philippe Jacquin, *Les Indiens blancs: français et indiens en Amérique du Nord, XVIe-XVIIIe siècles* (Paris: Payot, 1987).

66. See, for example, the fate of the term *habitant* in Sylvie Dépatie, "¿El ser más independiente del mundo? La construcción del arquetipo del *habitant* canadiense," in Catherine Poupeney Hart and A. Chacón Guitiérrez, *El discorso colonial: construcción de una diferencia Americana* (Heredia, Costa Rica: EUNA, 2002), 189–221.

67. Dechêne, *Habitants and Merchants*, 92–93.

68. Dechêne sees the term used for the first time in 1672.

69. James Scott's *Seeing Like a State: How Certain Schemes To Improve the Human Condition Have Failed* (New Haven, CT: Yale University Press, 1998) makes the original point about states' preferences for fixity—whether of place or identity. Christophe Horguelin pointed out to us the relevance of Scott's work to thinking about the "course de bois."

70. Dechêne, *Le peuple, l'État et la guerre au Canada sous le régime français*, chap. 9.

71. Dechêne, *Le peuple, l'État et la guerre au Canada sous le régime français*, chap. 9.

72. Richard White, *The Middle Ground: Indians, Empires, and Republics in the Great Lakes Region, 1650–1815* (Cambridge: Cambridge University Press, 1991). See also D. Peter MacLeod, "The Exercise of Power by the Amerindians of the Great Lakes during the War of the Austrian Succession, 1744–1748." (PhD thesis, University of Ottawa, 1991) on the reduced recruitment of native warriors during the War of the Austrian Succession.

73. "Nos Sauvages ont continué de harceler les côtes" in Dechêne, *Le peuple, l'État et la guerre au Canada sous le régime français*, chap. 4.

74. Canada's standing army was indeed quite officer heavy. If one includes *cadets*, the ratio drops from 1 for 13 at the time of the definitive arrival of the troupes de la marine in the colony in the 1680s, to 1 in 5, or even less during the second half of the eighteenth century. Dechêne, *Le peuple, l'État et la guerre au Canada sous le régime français*, chap. 3.

75. On Jean-Armand Dieskau, see *Online Dictionary of Canadian Biography*, www.biographi.ca/EN, article by J. R. Turnbull.

76. A. Furetière, *Dictionaire Universel, Contenant generalement tous les Mots François tant vieux que modernes, & les Termes de toutes les Sciences & des Arts [. . .] Recueilli & compilé par feu Messire Antoine Furetière, Abbé de Chalivoy, de l'Académie Françoise* (The Hague and Rotterdam: Arnout & Reinier Leers, 1690). Dechêne, *Le peuple, l'État et la guerre au Canada sous le régime français*.

77. On Bigot, see Guy Frégault, *François Bigot, administrateur français*, 2 vols. (Montreal: Imprimerie Saint-Joseph, 1948) and J. F. Bosher and J. C. Dubés's entry on Bigot in the *Online Dictionary of Canadian Biography*, www.biographi.ca/EN.

78. As David Bell has argued, France has not yet received the treatment that Britain received in Linda Colley's work and in subsequent commentary. David Bell, "Recent Works on Early Modern French National Identity," *Journal of Modern History* 58, no. 1 (March 1996): 84–113.

79. Edmond Dziembowski, *Un nouveau patriotisme français, 1750–1770: La France face à la puissance anglaise à l'époque de la guerre de Sept Ans* (Oxford: The Voltaire

Foundation, 1998). David A. Bell, *The Cult of Nation in France: Inventing National-ism, 1680–1800* (Cambridge, MA: Harvard University Press, 2001).

80. Dechêne, *Le peuple, l'État et la guerre au Canada sous le régime français*, chap. 10.

81. Bishop Henri-Marie Dubreuil de Pontbriand, "Mandement sur les prières publiques, 20 juin 1745," in H. Têtu and C. O. Gagnon, *Mandements, lettres pastorales et circulaires des Évêques de Québec*, 6 vols. (Quebec: Imprimerie générale A. Coté et cie, 1888–1890, 2:44.) Chapter 12 of Dechêne's book discusses the question of why militiamen fought, and the conclusion returns to this question.

82. Jonathan Dull has argued persuasively against the view that France somehow "abandoned" New France both in this volume and in his larger magisterial study of the French Navy in the Seven Years' War. Jonathan R. Dull, *The French Navy and the Seven Years' War* (Lincoln: University of Nebraska Press, 2005).

83. W. G. Sebald, *Austerlitz*, trans. Anthea Bell (New York: Random House, 2001), and *On the Natural History of Destruction*, trans. Anthea Bell (New York: Random House, 2004, [org.ed.1999]).

~

Index

Note: Page numbers in *italics* indicate figures.

~

About the Contributors

Fred Anderson received his BA from Colorado State University in 1971 and his PhD from Harvard in 1981. He has taught at Harvard and at the University of Colorado, Boulder, where he is currently professor of history. His publications include *Crucible of War: The Seven Years' War and the Fate of Empire in British North America, 1754–1766* and, with Andrew Cayton, *The Dominion of War: Empire and Liberty in North America, 1500–2000*.

Catherine Desbarats is associate professor in the Department of History at McGill University in Montreal and specializes in the history of New France. She is editor of *Lettres édifiantes et curieuses écrites par des missionnaires jésuites*. Her essays on colonial finances and on the writing of history have appeared in journals, such as the *Canadian Historical Review, French History,* and the *William and Mary Quarterly*. Most recently she helped edit Louise Dechêne's *Le peuple, l'Etat et la guerre au Canada sous le régime français* for posthumous publication.

Jonathan R. Dull is the senior associate editor of the Papers of Benjamin Franklin. He is the author of four books, including *The French Navy and American Independence: A Study of Arms and Diplomacy, 1774–1787* and *A Diplomatic History of the American Revolution*. His most recent book, *The*

French Navy and the Seven Years' War was awarded the 2005 Prix Littéraire of the Association France-Amériques.

Allan Greer is professor of history at the University of Toronto specializing in Canadian and comparative colonial history. His books include *Mohawk Saint: Catherine Tekakwitha and the Jesuits; The People of New France; Peasant, Lord, and Merchant: Rural Society in Three Quebec Parishes, 1740–1840;* and *The Jesuit Relations: Natives and Missionaries in Seventeenth-Century North America.* These works have merited several prizes, including the John A. Macdonald Prize, the Gilbert Chinard Prize, the Allan Sharlin Prize, and the Prix Lionel-Groulx.

Eric Hinderaker is professor and chair of the Department of History at the University of Utah. He is the author of *Elusive Empires: Constructing Colonialism in the Ohio Valley, 1673–1800* and, with Peter C. Mancall, coauthor of *At the Edge of Empire: The Backcountry in British North America.*

Warren R. Hofstra is Stewart Bell Professor of History at Shenandoah University in Winchester, Virginia, where he also directs the Community History Project of the university. He has written or edited five books, including *The Planting of New Virginia: Settlement and Landscape in the Shenandoah Valley; A Separate Place: The Formation of Clarke County, Virginia; George Washington and the Virginia Backcountry; After the Backcountry: Rural Life in the Great Valley of Virginia, 1800–1900;* and *Virginia Reconsidered: New Histories of the Old Dominion.*

Woody Holton received his PhD from Duke in 1990 and has taught Early American history at George Mason University, Randolph-Macon Woman's College, Bloomsburg University, and the University of Richmond, where he is an associate professor. In 2000 the Organization of American Historians awarded his first book, *Forced Founders: Indians, Debtors, Slaves and the Making of the American Revolution in Virginia,* its prestigious Merle Curti Social History award.

Paul Mapp is assistant professor in the Department of History at the College of William and Mary. He is currently working on a book about "European Geographic Uncertainty and North American Imperial Rivalry: The Role of the Uncharted American West in International Affairs, 1713–1763."

Timothy J. Shannon teaches Early American and Native American history at Gettysburg College in Gettysburg, Pennsylvania. He is the author of *Indians and Colonists at the Crossroads of Empire: The Albany Congress of 1754*, and his articles on Native American diplomacy have appeared in the *William and Mary Quarterly* and *Ethnohistory*. He is currently working on a book about the Iroquois in eighteenth-century North America.